WAYS THROUGH THE WALL

APPROACHES TO CITIZENSHIP IN AN INTERCONNECTING WORLD

Edited by

John Drew and
David Lorimer

Michael Wilson
with best wishes

John Drew

March 2006

First Stone Publishing

© Copyright First Stone Publishing 2005 and the Authors

First published in 2005 by
First Stone Publishing
PO Box 8, Lydney, Gloucestershire, GL15 6YD, UK.

British Library Cataloguing in Publication Data
A CIP record for this book is available from the British Library

ISBN 1 904439-54-3

Printed and bound in Great Britain
by Bell & Bain Ltd., Glasgow

CONTENTS

The Transpersonal as a Framework for Dialogue

Experiential Approaches to Consciousness

Consciousness and Healing: Therapeutic Applications

INTRODUCTION

John Drew and David Lorimer

The last thirty years have seen the emergence of a new way of thinking about the world. Not only have our communications systems been revolutionised to provide instant access to information and to each other, but new patterns and metaphors have come to the fore in the sciences pointing towards the unity and interconnectedness of life and consciousness. The most prevalent metaphor is that of the web: the web of life, as well as the world-wide web. Another major (and similar) metaphor is the network, which consists of three main elements: nodes, ties and flows. Nodes are distinct points of connection, while flows pass between nodes through ties. These flows may consist of energy, thoughts, information, feelings, and, at the highest level, love. Another social phenomenon has been the grassroots spirituality revolution where people have sought meaning beyond the ideological limitations of both traditional religions and scientific materialism.

Hence many people from different backgrounds, cultures and spiritual traditions across the world are beginning to review their concepts of consciousness and spirituality. Some come through a scientific approach – beyond the brain, consciousness, awareness. Others take a religious, mystical or spiritual approach – the meaning of life, the big unanswered questions of where we came from and where, if anywhere, we are going.

More sense has to be made of this complex and interconnecting world society into which we find ourselves travelling at a pace of change more rapid than ever in the history of the planet. Many are beginning to understand the concepts of transpersonal psychology[1] which has developed over the past 100 years, even if they would not necessarily subscribe in any detail to this approach developed by William James, Abraham Maslow, Carl Jung and others.

In London in 2004, some two hundred thoughtful people from many different backgrounds and from over twenty different countries came together to reflect on what might be called broadly transpersonal aspects of society. Transpersonal psychology has a role to play as an interpretive approach to some of these issues, but it is neither elitist, comprehensive nor in any way threatening to established ways of living, thinking or reflecting. It does, however, offer an understanding of consciousness and spirituality that can inform the new thinking required about citizenship in an actively interconnecting world.

Ways through the Wall takes some of the concepts of transpersonal psychology and shows how they are contributing in a practical way to our thinking about the complex and interrelated issues of our fast changing society. Effective frameworks for reflection and action need to be developed – ones to which citizens from different cultures, religions, nations and economic and social backgrounds can relate.

This short book of essays is an introduction to practical issues raised about Citizenship in an Interconnected World. It does not cover the subject in detail, nor does it attempt to define the transpersonal in any particular way. It represents the thoughts and experience of twenty-nine people who raised the issues of citizenship at the EUROTAS London conference in their own different ways and all of whom took part in the Conference.[2]

What are the rights and duties of citizens of an interconnected world? What are the paths that individuals can follow to make sense of their fast changing and interacting environments? How can the different approaches of states, religions, movements and organisations be blended or accorded their appropriate roles, granted that some of their aims and ideals are different and sometimes even opposed?

This volume, like the Conference itself, aims to raise the questions and issues and to further the discussion. It does not provide definitive answers, but looks at different paths towards an interconnected world and draws on the wide experience of its contributors and their own approaches to this important subject. The tone of the book is deliberately diverse. Some essays lean towards the scientific and academic approach, while others are written as reflections on the author's own experience. We believe that this adds to the richness of the volume, which seeks to interest and inform a general audience linking the concept of the transpersonal to everyday life.

This Sixth European Transpersonal Conference was organised in the United Kingdom by the Centre for Transpersonal Psychology (C.T.P.) exactly 10 years after Ian Gordon-Brown and C.T.P. led the inspirational Third European Transpersonal Conference in London in 1994. The sponsors of the Conference and the book are The European Transpersonal Association (EUROTAS), with its member associations from 16 European Countries, and the Centre for Transpersonal Psychology in the United Kingdom.

Professor David Fontana gave a Celebratory Lecture: "Psychology, Religion and Spirituality" at the London Conference (reproduced as Chapter 10) to commemorate Ian and to honour the debt which so many of us owe to both him and Barbara Somers who were among the pioneers in the United Kingdom of transpersonal psychology. Sadly Ian died in 1994, before he could see the full fruits of his work. His seminal contribution "Transpersonal Psychology" is reproduced as Chapter 9.

The chapters of the volume cover transpersonal aspects of Health, Education, Society and Consciousness. It is divided into five related sections: *Consciousness, Ethics and Society*; *Consciousness, Spirituality and Growth*; *The Transpersonal as a Framework for Dialogue*; *Experiential Approaches to Consciousness* and finally *Consciousness and Healing: Therapeutic Applications*. Each chapter contains a summary and a short biography of the author. Subsumed in these are sections on transpersonal connections with the environment, the faith traditions, management and spiritual emergency. Many of the chapters illustrate how the concepts of transpersonal psychology are applied to daily life while others balance the practice with the theory underlying the work. Chapters 15-17 are written by those coming from the Faith Traditions and show how the connections between these traditional paths and the newer approaches of transpersonal psychology are not incompatible.

Transpersonal psychology is a rapidly developing innovative field with a fast growing research sector. This work is represented here although a further book in this series will be published after the Seventh EUROTAS Conference in 2005 in Moscow and will be a more comprehensive survey of transpersonal research in Europe.

The aim of EUROTAS is to facilitate communication between national transpersonal associations and groups and to promote joint activities in the transpersonal field. You can find more about EUROTAS online by visiting www.eurotas.org. If you'd like to find out more about CTP please visit www.transpersonalcentre.co.uk. The EUROTAS Conference website is www.citizen shipconference.com. Most European countries have transpersonal associations and participants gather annually in Europe to meet friends from all over the world.

The London Conference was a celebration of transpersonal psychology in the wider world and appealed to all those looking to refresh themselves in the company of like-minded people from many different cultures, backgrounds and disciplines. It is hoped by the editors, and in particular by the authors of this book who have given their time and work so generously, that *Ways through the Wall* will be a small contribution to 'seeing with new eyes' and to understanding the paths towards a more harmonious and interconnecting world.

The words of T.S. Eliot were a theme of the Conference, also reflected in this volume:

"We shall not cease from exploration
And the end of all our exploring
Will be to arrive where we started
And know the place for the first time."

NOTES

1. The term "transpersonal" refers to that spiritual dimension of being that transcends the everyday ego and points us towards the realm of the 'soul' and of the 'archetypes'. Transpersonal studies range over our understanding of the self and consciousness in ways that inspire a fresh look at the limits of human potential, different from that promulgated by physicalist and reductionist science. No one tradition has a monopoly on the understanding of our spiritual nature, and a diversity of approaches, some scientific, some spiritual and some mystical is central to the articulation of the transpersonal vision. The above note is based on the approach of Les Lancaster (Chapter 15) but the definition of transpersonal, like that of Europe, is broad and perhaps wisely left defined in a number of ways!

2. The Sixth EUROTAS Conference: Citizenship in an Interconnected World – A Transpersonal Approach took place at Regents College, London from Tuesday 17- Friday 20 August 2004. It was organised in the United Kingdom by the Centre for Transpersonal Psychology (C.T.P.) exactly 10 years after Ian Gordon-Brown and C.T.P. led the inspirational Third European Transpersonal Conference in London in 1994. The Conference was sponsored by The European Transpersonal Association (EUROTAS) and its members from 16 European Countries. It was also supported by eminent transpersonal and other associations including the Association for Transpersonal Psychology (ATP) and the Scientific and Medical Network (SMN).

CONSCIOUSNESS, ETHICS AND SOCIETY

1. HEALING THE SPLIT

Beata Bishop

Beata approaches the issue of health in an interconnected world by showing how we need to explore ourselves before having a go at the world. Her subject is the fundamental split between the body and the rest of the individual. Health, whole, holy – are interconnected. We need to add a fourth word, healing, to the list. Beata gives a concise historical overview of how we got to our present position, with only some, like Paracelsus, along the way understanding the difference between medical science and medical wisdom. The dualistic approach of Descartes did wonders as a methodological basis for the exact sciences, but the result of this totally mechanistic-materialistic attitude has sweeping and not always welcome consequences for medicine, research and everyday life.

Should we really "declare war on death" or are there more soulful ways of looking at health and an interconnected life? Is a chemical approach to health the only way, or is there a growing counter-trend led by different disciplines and lines of research, which is creating a new perception of the body and its non-material links to the rest of the individual? Psycho-neuro-immunology (PNI) is now a respectable medical speciality, pointing to new approaches away from the dualistic base of orthodox medicine. Mind-heart-body interaction has now become a welcome medical speciality looking to mending the body-nonbody split which, Beata argues, does not make for an interconnected person nor for an interconnected world.

Beata Bishop *has been working with cancer patients for over twenty years. She is a writer, lecturer and psychotherapist working along Jungian and transpersonal lines. She* *has been running transpersonal workshops and seminars on a wide range of subjects, including the psychosomatic connection, in several European countries and in the USA. Her book, "A Time to Heal", has been translated into seven languages; at present she is preparing a study on the psychological needs of cancer patients.*

We can only be true citizens of an interconnected world if we are interconnected within ourselves, striving towards the kind of wholeness that contains every component of our basic humanity. Jung named the aim of this striving individuation. He also warned that it can never be fully achieved; only approached, but that this approach, this journey taking much of a lifetime, is of the greatest value.

To me, the word "interconnectedness" suggests a pattern of mutually supportive parts moving in harmony; a dance that flows in unity with itself, free from inner conflict or split. How easy is this dance for us as individuals? Can we follow its rhythm? On the principle of "as inward, so outward", we need to explore ourselves before having a go at the world. Are we, am I, interconnected within myself, without split or conflict?

The answer is no, or at least not yet. On the whole most of us do suffer from multiple splits within, even if we are not aware of them; much of our inner work is focussed on trying to heal them. There are splits between head and heart, between the inner masculine and inner feminine, between the desired and the possible, between the virtual and the real, between ego and higher Self. But my subject here and now is the most fundamental split of all, the one between the body and the rest of the individual, between the rider and the horse. It is a long-standing destructive split which today is deeper than ever, and which militates against health in the full sense of the word.

Health, whole, holy – those words are interconnected. And the transpersonal approach to health is based on the agreement of those three words. In order to be healthy and experience the holiness of life itself, we must be whole, un-split, the opposite of what we are now – alienated, often at loggerheads with the body. What we need is the fourth member of that family of words, namely healing. But the first question must be: how did we get into our present predicament? Let me attempt a quick sketchy overview of humankind's chequered and changeable relationship with the physical body.

To go back to the beginning: judging by the traces they left behind, our cave-dwelling ancestors were totally at one with themselves, rooted in Nature, in a primordial world that was full of meaning and mystery. The people who created the cave paintings of Altamira and other sites were interconnected not only with their own bodies but also with the animals and plants around them. They were parts of Nature and Nature was part of them. From millennia later, the archaic Greek statues of the kouros and the kore, the youth and the maiden, radiate a much higher level of wholeness, which moves us through its air of serenity, balance and repose. And even later, in the more sophisticated classical statues of perfectly poised athletes we still recognize bodies permeated by spirit, united without a split.

Roman statues, on the other hand, celebrate strength, majesty, and a high degree of self-consciouness. Here flesh is permeated by intellect and will instead of spirit, which signals the first whiff of a split. But – skipping several centuries – the total split only comes with early Christianity and its profound pessimism about life and the world as a vale of tears. The body is denied, despised and hated, the flesh needs to be mortified; only the soul is of value, which seems slightly blasphemous, since encasing the immortal soul in a mortal body clearly was part of God's plan for humankind. However, this is how St Paul set the mood for all believers: "The Flesh lusts against the Spirit, and the Spirit against the Flesh ... so that you cannot do the things that you would." This set up the kind of polarity which can only lead to paralysis, to being torn in half and remaining stuck in a self-tormenting place with no exit.

It took the Renaissance to dispel the darkness by re-discovering the beauty of the created world, including the human being. Life was no longer a vale of tears. The senses were allowed to function again; there was celebration, pleasure, a flowering of the arts and a brave new wave of enquiry and discovery. The body was loved, enjoyed and restored to the centre of life, but with a sense of poignancy underneath it all, for life was brief and youth and beauty fled fast. The glow and intensity of that period eventually faded and the attitude to the body, especially in Northern Europe, became much less exuberant and unproblematic. The split, bewailed by St Paul, was making a comeback. But in the early 16th Century a man, born several centuries too early, put a positive angle on the body-mind dichotomy. He didn't deny it, but raised it to a level where peace between the two became possible. Ironically, what he said then still needs to be heard today. His name was Paracelsus, and here's what he said:

"There are two kinds of knowledge. There is a medical science and there is a medical wisdom. To the animal man belongs the animal comprehension; but the understanding of divine mysteries belongs to the spirit of God in him." That one sentence sums up the transpersonal approach to health, the need for holism in medicine, and for enough humility to admit how little we know about the mystery of life itself. Unfortunately that potential epiphany didn't last. In 1642 René

Descartes published his revolutionary work establishing dualism, a split of the Universe and all it contained into two: Res Cogitans, a thinking something which has no spatial extension, and Res Extensa, a spatial something which has no psychic qualities. Add to this his famous "Cogito ergo sum", which enthrones thinking as the cause and even the precondition of being, and it's easy to see how the split deepens and becomes respectable and even desirable. From now on thinking is supreme. Everything else, being and existence itself are subordinate to it. The body as a fragile, mindless clockwork that has to be mended when it breaks down, is deeply inferior – this time not on St Paul's spiritual grounds, but in the name of science.

Of course, as a methodological basis for the exact sciences, the principle of dualism is immensely valuable. But if it goes beyond that role, making universal claims, it becomes a fatal error, turning Nature into a huge soulless machine which you can use and subjugate, but from which you are exiled. The human body itself becomes a Res Extensa, dim matter with no psychic non-material properties. (In fact, Descartes mistakenly believed that the sole link between body and soul was the pineal gland.) This universal acceptance of dualism was not what its author had intended, but he was unable to prevent it. The result was a totally mechanistic-materialistic attitude to the created world, including the human body, with sweeping consequences in medicine, research and everyday life. And that is where we are still today, with health itself being in need of healing.

The results are obvious. Medicine today treats the body as nothing but matter, a living flesh and blood machine that can go wrong in countless ways and must be repaired, subdued, sorted out. This attitude is reflected in the military terminology of allopathic medicine which we accept without questioning. It is a language that speaks of heart attacks, painkillers, heroic surgery, aggressive treatments, drugs that fight disease, campaigns against major diseases. This is macho medicine, totally lacking the medical wisdom stipulated by Paracelsus; its sole aim is to beat disease into submission, show Nature who is boss, and ignore the non-material aspects of the patient.

The macho attitude can reach bizarre heights. I recall an oncologist at one of my seminars some years ago who declared in ringing tones, "I have declared war on death." I couldn't stop myself from wishing him the best of luck, which brought the house down; sometimes I wonder how he is getting on. This gung-ho attitude inspired the late Ivan Illich to write in his important yet largely forgotten book, *Medical Nemesis*: "Modern medicine turns the patient into a limp and mystified voyeur in the grip of bio-engineers." Here we can observe yet another split in our already fragmented lives, the split between the all-powerful, all-knowing doctor and the powerless, presumably ignorant patient whose only job is to obey instructions right to the end. Yet blind obedience and a total surrender of individual autonomy are the enemies of self-healing. How is the body to fight for survival if the spirit is scared and weak? One of my saddest memories from my twenty-odd years' work with cancer patients concerns an unknown woman who rang me one day. Judging by her voice she was old, weak and frightened. She had spreading cancer, she told me, and after much fruitless orthodox treatment her doctor had told her that there was nothing more he could do for her. Could I perhaps suggest anything? The only honest non-medical answer I could give was to say that a really good, nutritious diet might make her feel better and stronger, and that I would be happy to help her set it up. Oh no, she said, she couldn't possibly go on a special diet – her doctor wouldn't like that. But since he had nothing more to offer...? Even so. He wouldn't like it, she said with great finality, and rang off. I never heard from her again.

That is an extreme example of how far the surrender of self-determination can go. I've seen many milder ones, though. And the effects of all this go beyond our dealings with doctors: we accept their perception of us, which leads to alienation, to splitting from our own body and from Nature, to which it, and we, belong. So there's not much connectedness here. And the result of this voluntary passivity, this "learned helplessness" is that most of us are unable to take responsibility for our own health, even in small ways. It wasn't always like this, said a woman sitting next to me in a train. She had just been to her GP and was clutching several prescriptions which she had no intention of using. "When I was young," she said, "my mother and grandmother knew how to treat colds and sore throats and stomach upsets and cuts and burns. Now people rush to the surgery with the slightest trouble and take too many drugs. It's wrong," she declared and clamped her mouth shut.

She was right: it is wrong, but this is where we are now. Not only divorced from Nature and disconnected within ourselves, but also in thrall to the modern imperialism of allopathic medicine, which itself depends heavily on its powerful backer and controller, the global pharmaceutical industry. The industry's financial support – for research, medical journals, bursaries, equipment and other facilities – needs to be paid for; the price is reduced medical independence. And that leads to another, more ominous development that must be recognized. For the first time in human history, heavily promoted synthetic chemicals have the power to remove the individual's control of his or her body and mind; all of life's experiences are medicalized, in order to sell more drugs to more people. Menopause? HRT (recently discredited). Bereavement? Prozac. Difficult children? Ritalin. GAD, i.e. Generalized Anxiety Disorder? (American, this one): Paxil. Also useful against

Social Anxiety Disorder, a debilitating form of shyness (ditto). And, most shockingly, last year UK doctors wrote 170,000 prescriptions of antidepressants for children, some as young as two years old. No need to go on.

What it all boils down is an increasing chemical control of people's thinking and feeling functions, the two characteristics that make us truly human, starting at the cradle and growing in intensity as we go through life right to the grave. The underlying aim seems to be to standardize us into manageable citizens, free from intense emotions and irregular, original ideas, creating yet another split within our already fractured selves – an Orwellian prospect indeed, in stark contrast with the transpersonal search for undivided wholeness and body-mind health.

A gloomy state of affairs, but this is where we are starting from. Besides, the gloom is getting thinner, as a counter-trend to all this is gathering strength. What I have in mind is the way in which different disciplines and lines of research are creating a new, infinitely exciting perception of the body and its non-material links with the rest of the individual. The body cannot be seen any longer as a Cartesian-Newtonian clockwork, but as a miracle of cellular intelligence and subtle connections and interactions, all of it fast, precise and co-ordinated. The evolving understanding of the body presents it as an energy field, an information system imbued by consciousness and deep intelligence, which responds to intention and to a range of non-material inputs.

Inputs such as colour, sound, music, light, imagery, prayer and all other varieties of energy medicine, firmly banished from the mainstream variety, are not equally or invariably effective, but they prove that the physical body can and does respond to non-physical therapies. And the powerful effect of mind and heart on matter was allowed in from the cold not all that long ago, with the arrival of psycho-neuro-immunology, PNI for short. PNI is now a respectable medical speciality, not yet widely known and certainly not sufficiently used, since it contradicts rather strongly the dualistic base of orthodox medicine. Put simply, PNI proves that our view of life and of the world, our prevailing mood and outlook have a direct measurable influence on our immune system, and hence on our state of health. Recent progress in the understanding of brain chemistry enabled researchers to recognize the incredibly subtle interactions of hormones, themselves precisely regulated by thoughts and emotions, that either boost or undermine the equally complex immune system. Observe how the circle becomes complete: what healers, psychotherapists, priests and other non-medical practitioners have known for a long time about the mind-heart-body interaction has now become a medical speciality – and most welcome it is, too...

All these separate developments add up to a clear trend and introduce a quiet revolution in which we can all play a part. What we are approaching is a healing of the body-nonbody split, which demands a new relationship with the body as an equal partner and ally whose needs and messages must be respected. This need was clearly defined some twenty-five years ago by the Irish physician Dr John Bradshaw, when he wrote:

"We must look for hope, not to doctors, but to those, whether or not they are medically qualified, who see the need to create a new society, of which health will be an integral part (as ill-health is of ours); and who will search for the philosophy, the religion, needed for the establishment of such a society. The alternative is that the ill-health of our present society, its terrible cancerous disease, will prove mortal to it, and to us and to our children; and will ensure that our children's children shall never be born."

To be interconnected within, we need to reclaim the body and restore our broken link with Nature, of which we are a part. Our bodies contain the same elements as the remains of meteorites: we consist partly of stardust, and our blood shares some of the qualities of sea water (not to mention the striking similarity between the human genome and that of the humble mouse.). Now is the time to arrive at the next twist of the spiral of evolution, where a flowing, unselfconscious unity of body and soul operates. To my mind this is the key to the transpersonal path to health: acknowledging that matter is the densest form of spirit, and spirit is the highest, most subtle manifestation of matter.

It may take a while for this insight and practice to become widespread. But for the moment each of us has an urgent task: to heal the split within and see where it takes us.

2. CONSCIOUSNESS AND SOCIETY: AN ETHIC OF INTERCONNECTEDNESS

David Lorimer

Progress in spirituality – to become more deeply human – is the most fundamental of the cultural progressions of humankind. David develops what he calls the ethic of interconnectedness out of the the science of interconnectedness in physics, biology and psychology. Jung's idea of the collective unconscious posits a unity beneath the surface, and mystics describe an intuitive sense of unity beyond the senses. David reflects on the transpersonal or mystical aspects of the near death experience (NDE), how a unity of consciousness might imply an ethic of interconnectedness and shows how a number of authorities support this concept.

That the focus of evolution has moved from physical to mental, moral or more widely cultural development is well argued over the past century. David follows this thinking from Isaiah Berlin to Toynbee, the Bulgarian sage Beinsa Douno through to Dennis Kucinich in the remarkable campaign for the Democratic Presidential nomination of 2004 and his concept of "evolutionary politics". David sees the challenge of ethical mysticism and our duty to remain optimists in our current actions and to develop an ethic of reverence for life and a feeling of union with the infinite arising from selfless service.

David Lorimer is Programme Director of the Scientific and Medical Network and author of Radical Prince: The Practical Vision of the Prince of Wales *as well as editor of the recently published* Science, Consciousness and Ultimate Reality. *Along with John Drew and Serge Beddington-Behrens he ran the first Inward Bound course in 2003.*

"Three kinds of progress are significant for culture: progress in knowledge and technology; progress in the socialisation of man; progress in spirituality. The last is the most important. Technical progress, extension of knowledge, does indeed represent progress, but not in fundamentals. The essential thing is that we become more finely and deeply human."

Albert Schweitzer

Albert Schweitzer is remembered not only for his medical missionary work in tropical Africa, but also for his gifts as an organist and for his philosophical and theological work. His key ethical principle is 'reverence for life' (Ehrfurcht vor dem Leben), an insight that came to him one afternoon on the river. We are familiar enough with his first category of progress in knowledge and technology, but, as he points out, social progress is more important and progress in spirituality is the most fundamental level. Here he uses the resonant phrase of becoming 'more finely and deeply human', which I take to represent a refinement of consciousness that is reflected in ethically informed action. This means closing the gap between knowledge and wisdom, ensuring that technological and spiritual progress go hand in hand.

Aldous Huxley expressed a similar concern but more strongly in his book 'Ends and Means', published during the Second World War in 1941: 'in the world in which we find ourselves, technological advance is rapid. But without progress in charity, technological advance is useless. Indeed it is worse than useless. Technological progress has merely provided us with a more efficient means for going backwards.' In a Machiavellian world based on power politics, acquisition and use of biological or depleted uranium weapons is a case in point.

A Science of Interconnectedness

Before coming more specifically to what I mean by an ethic of interconnectedness, it is useful to highlight the development of a science of interconnectedness in physics, biology and psychology, disciplines that have until recently been dominated by atomistic conceptions of isolated particles, genes or individuals which put an emphasis on separation rather than unity. This sense of isolation in an indifferent cosmos has led to widespread alienation and loss of meaning. On the other hand, more holistic concepts in science stress participation and belonging as ways of overcoming this sense of alienation. And Arthur Koestler has provided the useful idea of a 'holon', which is at once a whole and a part: cells are individual but form elements of organs; organs are in turn individual but forms part of the body, just as the body is part of the earth and the individual a part of society. And the earth is part of the solar system, which is in turn part of the Milky Way galaxy and so on.

Physicist John Archibald Wheeler has asserted that 'the universe does not exist "out there", independent of us. We are inescapably involved in bringing about that which appears to be happening. We are not only observers. We are participators. In some strange sense this is a participatory universe.' The inseparability of observer from the observed has been a standard element in quantum theory since the 1930s even if many physicists do not share the view that consciousness actually 'collapses the wave function'. The physicist and philosopher David Bohm elaborated a new view whereby unity is prior to separation with his ideas of the 'implicate' and 'explicate' orders (literally enfolded and unfolded orders). For him, reality is 'undivided wholeness in flowing movement' (his best known book is *Wholeness and the Implicate Order*), so wholeness is primary and partness or separation is secondary and derived from this.

Ecology and biology have built on the systems view of the world introduced in the 1940s by Ludwig von Bertalanffy. His key insight is the distinction between open (organic) and closed (mechanistic) systems where the former interact and exchange with the environment in a dynamic way. Life forms and habitats (ecosystems) are both complex open systems. As Fritjof Capra observes, the very principles of ecology are applied in holistic biology: 'interdependence, recycling, partnership, flexibility, diversity, and, as a consequence, sustainability'. The metaphor of the 'web of life' says it all, beautifully expressing both unity and interconnectedness. Other concepts from biology include symbiosis – co-operation between organisms for mutual benefit – and synergy, where individual elements within a system work together for the good of the whole. Then Jim Lovelock's Gaia hypothesis questions the sharp distinction between organism and environment, arguing that organisms regulate the composition of the atmosphere for their own benefit – this is mutuality in action.

In psychology, Jung's idea of the collective unconscious posits a unity beneath the surface while mystics from all traditions describe an intuitive sense of unity beyond the senses. This mystical or transpersonal insight is also reflected in the near-death experience (NDE) and underlies the experience of life review, where people experience events as if they were another person involved in the same episode. In other words the event is not relived from their own vantage point but as if you are another. In this sense, each event has as many aspects as there are experiencers.

Metaphysics and Ethics

In his book *The Crooked Timber of Humanity*, Sir Isaiah Berlin asserts that 'ethical thought consists of the systematic examination of the relations of human beings to each other, the conceptions, interests and ideals from which human ways of treating each other spring, and the systems of value on which such ends of life are based.' These ideas of relation and value rest in turn on a person's world view or metaphysic, thus intrinsically linking metaphysics with ethics. Christian eschatology (or the Last Things) consists of death, judgement, heaven and hell. If death is the end, then there can be no relationship between one's conduct in this life and one's fate in the next. However, to the extent that an afterlife is posited, then the question arises.

I believe that we can gain some insights into this matter from the NDE life review. As already mentioned, this seems to enable people to experience events from another person's angle. This would only be logically possible if there is an underlying unity and connectedness of consciousness, which is also experienced in mystical states. So unity of consciousness implies an ethic of interconnectedness. The experience of the life review takes place within an atmosphere of love emanating from what is usually sensed as a 'being of light' who also embodies the spiritual qualities of peace, joy and compassion. The Bhagavad Gita puts it like this: 'The yogi sees himself in the heart of all beings and he sees all beings in his heart. This is the vision of the Yogi of harmony, a vision which is ever one. And when he sees me [Krishna] in all and he sees all in me, then I never leave him and he never leaves me. He who is in the oneness of love, loves me in whatever he sees, wherever this man may live, in truth this man lives in me.' The yogi understands the unity of life and consciousness that 'we are one another' and it becomes natural to apply the Golden Rule of doing as you would be done by. For me, the NDE life review is a demonstration of the unity of consciousness and hence of the necessity of an ethic of interconnectedness that is also found in the New Testament. Here Christ encourages us to see him in all people and act accordingly: 'for inasmuch as you did it to the least of them, you did it to me'. Love of God and your neighbour is the cornerstone of Christian ethics that is reflected in the NDE life review. It points towards a very considerable degree of personal moral responsibility.

The Evolution of Consciousness

It is a commonplace to argue that the focus of evolution has moved from physical to mental, moral or, more widely, cultural development. The idea of an evolution of consciousness has been put forward for over 100 years and is sometimes related to a scheme that includes reincarnation, as with Rudolf Steiner. Oswald Spengler followed Hegel in applying a cyclical analysis to the rise and fall of cultures, and his book *The Decline of the West* struck a somewhat disconcerting chord when it was published during the First World War in 1917. It represented an internal crisis of confidence in the Western project. Arnold Toynbee followed this up with his massive 12-volume *Study of History* published between 1934 and 1961.

Toynbee was also concerned with the genesis of civilisations, which he attributed to the activities of the 'creative minority' within an existing society. Fritjof Capra builds on this idea in his book *The Turning Point*, arguing that the holistic (and transpersonal) movement represents just this creative minority that is the seed of a new culture. The sociologist Pitirim Sorokin offers a model involving an alternation between what he calls sensate (materialistic) and ideational (spiritually-based) cultures, arguing that our current sensate culture is giving way to a spiritual renaissance, a hope and aspiration also shared by Toynbee. More recently, systems theorist Ervin Laszlo has offered his own idea of a 'macroshift' from 'logos' to 'holos', citing the same kind of data referred to above that point to an emerging science of interconnectedness. Yet another model is offered by Spiral Dynamics, with its characterisation of phases of conscious development moving from blue (conservative) through orange (scientific and technological materialism) to more integrated levels beyond the green of the ecologically sensitive self.

The Bulgarian sage Beinsa Douno (Peter Deunov, 1864-1944) offers his own model of the evolution of consciousness on the basis of a grand scheme of involution (moving from the One to the many, or oneness to differentiation) and the reverse process of evolution from separation towards unity. He distinguishes five stages:
• Primitive collective consciousness (Lucien Levy-Bruhl's
  participation mystique or Owen Barfield's original participation)
• Individual consciousness (towards differentiation, separation)
• Collective consciousness (socialism, communism)
• Cosmic consciousness (the conscious mystical sense of unity)
• Divine consciousness (even wider and deeper)

Current societies alternate between forms of individual and collective consciousness, while in the transpersonal movement there is growing acknowledgement of the significance of cosmic consciousness (also R.M. Bucke's phrase) as a new phase of development.

Beinsa Douno provides two other parallel schemes of evolution. The first is what he calls Four Degrees of Human Culture:
- Violence – force, domination, power
- Law – threat, control (external)
- Justice – universal, excludes privilege
- Love – life for the whole

The reader can see here that the end point of Douno's thinking points towards what he calls a Culture of Love beyond violence, law and justice. Love internalises the universal principle of justice with its principle of dedication to the life of the whole. Likewise, his analysis of four systems runs:
- Clericalism, corresponding to the prevalence of outer ceremony
- Militarism, corresponding to the use of force
- Capitalism, corresponding to exploitation

The shortcoming of all these systems, in his view, is that they all employ the same methods of violence, constraint, control and fear. Only with the application of love – the fourth system – are these contradictions overcome and is a virtuous circle established.

Underlying the philosophy of Beinsa Douno are three fundamental principles:
- Love, bringing warmth to the heart
- Wisdom, bringing light to the mind
- Truth, bringing strength and freedom to the will

In addition, two further principles – justice or equity and virtue – make up the symbolism of the pentagram, which is also danced in Douno's paneurhythmy (literally, universal harmony of movement) for which he also composed the music. The movements of paneurhythmy are replete with symbolism that combines the masculine and feminine principles represented by wisdom and love.

Dennis Kucinich and the Politics of Interconnectedness (www.kucinich.us)

Some readers will be aware of the remarkable forward-looking campaign by Rep. Dennis Kucinich for the Democratic Presidential nomination, which he took all the way to the Convention. Kucinich has been an implacable opponent of the war in Iraq, observing that dichotomous thinking leads to war and a vicious circle of escalating violence. He sees the role of the US president as overcoming divisions through reconciliation and healing, remembering that the motto of the United States – *E Pluribus Unum* – can be applied on a planetary scale on the basis of the following principles: faith, optimism, hope, renewal, justice, non-violence, co-operation, mutuality, courage, integration, transformation.

Returning to the origins of the US, Kucinich observes: ' Whether we look at the first motto of the United States, *E Pluribus Unum* (out of many, one), which is a spiritual principle, or in the latter motto "In God We Trust," we have to recognise the Founders were immersed in contemplation of a world beyond our experience, one of spirit, of mysticism, one which saw the potential of the country as unfolding in a multidimensional way, both through the work of our hands and the work of our hearts.'

Kucinich calls for an evolutionary politics 'of creativity, of vision, of heart, of compassion, of joy; to create a new nation and a new world using the power of love, of community, of participation, to transform our politics, and yes, to transform ourselves', adding ' Let us remake America by reconnecting with a higher purpose to bring peace within and without, to come into harmony with nature, to confirm and to secure the basic rights of our brothers and sisters.'

His proposal for a Department of Peace has received over 40 votes of support in Congress and has been adopted as policy by a number of local Democratic parties. And in 2004, he received the Gandhi Peace Prize for his efforts. Dennis explains: 'Americans have proven over and over again we're a nation that can rise to the challenges of our times, because our people have that capacity. And so, the concept of a Department of Peace is the vehicle by which we express our belief that we have the capacity to evolve as a people, that someday we could look back at this moment and understand that we took the steps along the way to make war archaic. War is not inevitable. Peace is inevitable!'

In a lecture on evolutionary politics, he commented that 'we are in a period of chaos, which is driven by fear, by control, by power, by secrecy, mistrust, fragmentation, isolation, and by policies which use the lexicon of unilateralism and of pre-emption.' However, the power of consciousness is to call forth the new: ' The world is multidimensional. The new vision is a holistic one that understands the power of intention and the power of co-operation, of mutuality, of trust, of seeing the world as one. That vision then becomes our outer reality. Ours is the ability, through our consciousness, to create peace, to create love. The organ of transformation is the human heart because there is nothing – no weapon ever made – that is more powerful than a human heart.' This is an inspiring and visionary message that echoes Beinsa Douno's Culture of Love and is way ahead of our current thinking while giving it a sense of direction.

Ethical Mysticism – Creating the Future

"It is our duty to remain optimists. The future is open. It is not predetermined and thus cannot be predicted – except by accident. The possibilities that lie in the future are infinite. When I say 'It is our duty to remain optimists', this includes not only the openness of the future but also that which all of us contribute to it by everything we do: we are all responsible for what the future holds in store. "

Sir Karl Popper, the Myth of the Framework, p. xiii

I believe that this remark by the philosopher Sir Karl Popper contains a profound moral truth. Pessimists paralyse the efficacy of their own actions in a self-fulfilling loop that entails a passive lack of creative impulse. Moreover, as Kucinich points out in the previous section, if positive intention is a key component of activism, then it becomes a tool to be employed.

Albert Schweitzer's ethic of reverence for life is a powerful formula in the way he defines it: 'just as white light consists of coloured rays, so reverence for life contains all the components of ethics: love, kindliness, sympathy, empathy, peacefulness, power to forgive'. He adds: 'whenever my life devotes itself in any way to life, my finite will-to-live experiences union with the infinite will in which all life is one, and I enjoy a feeling of refreshment which prevents me from pining away in the desert of life'. This is an actual definition of ethical mysticism – the feeling of union with the infinite arising from selfless service. And this is entirely consistent with acting on the Golden Rule which exemplifies the ethic of interconnectedness already explained. In this way there is an expansion of both consciousness and ethics.

The basic dichotomy of the future is the choice between a path of fear and a path of love. The path of fear is a vicious circle that brings power, control, mistrust and alienation. While the path of love is a virtuous circle of participation, trust and belonging. This second path can only be followed through conscious inner intent, while the triumph of fear relies on ignorance and passivity. Let us act with conscious loving intent.

3. CITIZENSHIP IN AN INTERRELATED WORLD: THE TRANSPERSONAL AND EDUCATION AS TOOLS FOR SOCIAL, POLITICAL AND ECOLOGICAL CHANGE

Eva Titus

Eva does not claim to introduce new ideas but, in the light of current global crises, she seeks to make more explicit and accessible existing concepts of interrelatedness, identity, power and ethics which need to be applied to education, civic responsibility and citizenship.

There is so much to do and the tasks seem daunting for us as isolated individuals. What we lack is knowledge and experience of this interrelatedness. We need to know our options and be able to deal also with their darker implications. A historic review of how the different elements of the universe interreact, as perceived by different sages, shows that there have been several world-views, each offering different notions and choices. The technological view of interconnectedness is described. Its limitations are compared and contrasted with the spiritual-philosophical view which produces a flexibility and creativity of the whole interrelating process with a very much changed concept of identity and power.

Identity becomes smaller, as we give up the concept of self as a separate element in the process, but at the same time it becomes larger, like the cell that knows it belongs to a larger body. Power in the technological world view is over or against another, while in the spiritual world view it is power with each other. This "we-power" reduces the sense of being alone and ineffective, and demands modesty and compassion. Transpersonal psychology can make an important contribution through its knowledge and experience of interrelatedness in education, health and healing.

__Eva Titus__ is a psychologist and teacher. She is Co-founder of the Tarab Institute for *the study of Tibetan Psychology and Philosophy (Belgium.) Co-founder of the Flemish Institute for Gestalt therapy (NVAGT). Educational Consultant University of Antwerp. Current activities: teaching, publishing and organising methods for applying the paradigm of interrelatedness to national and international organisations.*

Introduction

My contribution does not pretend to introduce new ideas. It aims to make more explicit and accessible the existing concepts of interrelatedness, identity, power and ethics. I draw on and cite expert sources of Eco-psychology (Roszak), engaged Buddhism (Joanna Macy) and the epistemological studies of Tarab Tulku Rihpoche – as well as gestalt field theory and new-paradigm science.

My motivation for doing so arises from our actual global crisis with its new needs for a different education, civic formation and professional training regarding interrelatedness and planetary citizenship. My hope is to be instrumental in the development of new forms of this citizenship.

The Actuality

We are confronted at the present time with a series of global crises. We live at a very special time: special not because of the existence of these crises but because their global aspect has made evident to everyone, (via global communication systems, technology and politics), that interconnectedness and interrelatedness have become a worldwide issue for us all.

Since September 11th (and Afghanistan and Iraq), we are experiencing in a tragic form what is also a precious reality; we are inevitably interconnected, interrelated and interdependent, on this planet and beyond. There is a new general awareness that we can no longer ignore global events – nor avoid being part of global action. We are confronted with the quality of our own inevitable contribution to this action; not acting is also acting.

But this new general awareness also creates an actual general need, a need to know not only the frightening aspect of our global interrelatedness. Because our first and strongest natural reaction towards our global crisis is fear for our own life and peaceful existence. When confronted with the now inevitable sharing of pain and destruction elsewhere, we know we will also have these concrete consequences with us here.

Fear, anger and even compassion with what happens elsewhere can easily lead to feeling paralysed. We do not know as isolated individuals what to do, how to do it and with what power. Withdrawing without hope from the world comes so naturally.

What is so much needed and what is lacking is the knowledge and experience of the other luminous qualities of being interrelated and interdependent. That is, to know that each of us – as part of an interconnected whole – can also share the immense courage and creativity of that whole – and not only it's suffering. Also to know that this way we can use our knowledge of this total, shared empowerment and hope to realise our potential to evolve together as one living whole towards balance and harmony.

So what is crucial for our reactions to being interrelated is to know what options we have to deal with, both its dark and luminous aspects. We have to explore the possible meaning of this concept – the historical meaning of the philosophical and spiritual concept of interconnectedness between all elements of the universe.

Is there (according to you) a difference between modern cybernetic definitions of interrelating as practised in modern technology and industry and the form of interrelating expressed in the following philosophical wisdom?

"The eye with which I see God is the same eye with which God sees me"

Meister Eckhart

"One in all – and all in one (yet the one remains the one – and the all the all)"

Zen

or

"Unity in Duality"
(or the paradox of meeting while remaining differentiated) as stated in the Buddhist principle of Pattica Samupadda)

"Each element has the capacity to contain, to illuminate and to reflect ... the whole".

Avatamsaka Sutra

Now, if you think there is a difference between modern cybernetic interrelating and the quotes I gave, how do you sense this difference? One of the key differences between the two visions is the difference in cosmology they contain. Each has a different view of how all elements of the Universe interact. Maybe you sensed that in my last quotes these elements are not only interacting but are also interdependent and co-creating each other. In the quotes I gave there is a difference but not a discrimination between these elements.

The perennial spiritual concept of interconnectedness as expressed in my quotes has been manifested at different moments in history. For example, in Buddhism, in early Christian Mysticism, in the Sufi Movement and more recently in Field theory, General Systems theory and new-paradigm science.

Buddhism contains the most extensive epistemological analysis of the interconnectedness paradigm. The core of Buddhism is the principle of interdependency and co-arising of all that exists and appears (Pattica Samuppada or rtendrel in Tibetan). The Tibetan Scholar Tarab Tulku Rihpoche has recently made this principle more accessible for western psychology and science.

Anyway I will use today the Buddhist systemic description – because it is so precise – to make clearer the difference between the technological and the perennial spiritual definition of interrelating. It is important to understand these differences as they allow us to give more insight in our actual global options for interrelating. These options have great implications for many areas of our daily life.

My aim in this comparison is not to establish right or wrong. We have to live on a planet that contains several world-views but each offers different notions and choices. So let me try now to give you an imperfect profile of the technological view and the perennial spiritual view on interrelating. How do they each see the interaction between all possible elements of the universe?

The Technological View of Interconnectedness

In our classic Western technological world-view, the universal interaction between all possible elements is seen as a linear and causal process according to fixed dualistic (yes – no) rules. Interrelating is equated with only mechanical cybernetic forms of interconnecting.

Here the separate elements are interrelated by a process of influencing each other in a certain hierarchical order in 3-dimensional space and time. In this definition there is no mutual but only a serial interdependency between the separate elements.

The total result is seen as the predictable sum of the input of all separate elements, each with its own competing conditions and characteristics. The balance of give and take between the elements is seen as a balance that reflects the tendency of each separate element to maintain a status quo favourable only for its own survival.

My metaphor for this form of interrelating would be an engineer's 3-dimensional topological overview with arrows representing systematic order and dynamic patterns. This interactive system cannot act as one functioning whole that is creating by itself a fundamental change of its own rules without being re-programmed from outside. If cannot produce a fundamental change that allows for the miracle of spontaneous emergence of something totally new, that would make the total interrelating system evolve in a totally new direction.

I invite you now for a little experiment to test the practical application of this technological model. How does this world-view make you see our interrelating in this room?

- How does this model make you see your identity, your relation to me, to others?
- What is it stating about your capacity to be influenced and to make things happen, or to create …?
- In what way do you sense your responsibilities described for what happens here: to the subject, to you, to others?

Now let me switch to the other spiritual/philosophical view on interrelating. This kind of Universal interconnecting is not the predictable sum result of separate elements. My metaphor here is that of one living vibrating whole in constant evolution. And its form and functioning are not limited by the linear time and space-concept. It exists as a whole because all the separate elements are mutually dependent on each other for functioning, existing and evolving. All interaction takes place synchronously across time and space. There is no hierarchical order. There is differentiation but not discrimination between the qualities, and conditions of each element. There is no competition between their separate needs. There are no static dualistic rules for this interaction, nor predictable outcomes. The "rules" have to allow for ever changing conditions, for ever changing elements, that have to create conditions for each others shared existence and growth and evolution – and this all the while forming a unity while acknowledging diversity.

These ever changing conditions demand rules that are also not rules, as they allow for paradox such as the paradox of change and continuity, of meeting the other and remaining oneself. This freedom allows the interrelated whole to change and recreate by itself its own rules, without ceasing to exist and without interference from outside.

It allows for the spontaneous emergence of a totally new evolution of the whole. It is this flexibility and creativity of the whole interrelating process that allows for a flexible balance of give and take between the elements; a balance that can represent the interest of the total situation with all the paradoxes and differences it contains.

Now let us test this theoretical spiritual vision here and now: what does this imply for our way of interrelating at this moment? How can you and I reflect a unity while remaining differentiated? It implies that I am neither a separate self limited by my skin from you, nor am I confluent with you. I am a "flow through" and while you are listening to me this information is already transforming into your personal creative process. Where did this process begin and where is it going to? It started with the light and the landscape in which I grew up – the plants and animals that fed and loved me. It started with my teachers, some of whom I never met alive – with all those who encourage and sustained me to be present as I am. And where is the stream going to? Is it passing through me and then (transformed through you) influencing in ever larger circles, your environment in the future?

As our awareness here is growing, so is the awareness of the web of life, for we are the Universe becoming conscious of itself. Have you noticed how in this worldview the concept of identity and power has changed? As we will now see this different experience will offer new options for experiencing the action of being a citizen in an interrelated world.

Implications of the Spiritual Concept of Interconnectedness

So what has changed in our experience of identity? It has at the same time become smaller and bigger than in the technological vision of interconnectedness. Smaller, as I give up the initiated concept of self in which I can arise, survive and grow as a separate element that has the capacity to function autonomously and independent of the whole. It is an inflated concept in which I can influence my environment, make things happen and create on my own. I let go off this vision because I have become aware that I am just an interdependent part of the larger interaction process. But at the same time my identity becomes larger because we have realised that in this definition of interaction, the energy of the total is in all the particles and so it is also present in me. I am like a cell that knows in its functioning that it belongs to the larger body by which it is influenced and that it is influencing.

This new vision of identity also leads to a new experience of power. In the technological world-view, power is mostly seen as personal and hierarchical: as "power over" or "power against" another. In the spiritual world-view it is "power with each other" coming from mutual adjustment in a balancing process of give and take. This power cannot be switched "on" or "off" by one individual. This power can only function as coming from the total field. It is a power in which I do not act alone; it demands modesty as well as compassionate concern for the whole.

This "we-power" also reduces loneliness and gives strength and courage to act, to make choice and efforts. The "we power" of the citizen of an interconnected world always asks before action: "What small step does the actual situation need now in order to lead to a future positive enduring development of all elements of these fields?" In this way citizenship in an interconnected world leads to ethics and a sense of justice that promotes and encourages participation of all the elements in a balance of give and take. It represents a specific conflict model. It also leads to a sense of civic responsibility that notices when conditions for participation of each element are not fulfilled and then creates positive opportunities to restore the balance.

Conclusion

Transpersonal psychology can make an important contribution because of its specific knowledge of the principle of interrelatedness of all elements of the Universe. It can use this knowledge not only for further self-development of these individual or small groups but also into a larger social context by:
• Exploring and teaching related forms of citizenship
• Promoting and supporting relevant models for conflict-resolving in the economy, ecology, education and health.
• Developing new diagnostic therapeutic tools for actual forms of depression that are not related to pathology nor to an ego-centred concern about our personal welfare in this world crisis. This asks for healing methods that not only heal the individual, but also heal his environment in its largest sense.

4. AWAKENING TO SPIRITUAL CONSCIOUSNESS IN TIMES OF RELIGIOUS VIOLENCE: REFLECTIONS ON CULTURE AND TRANSPERSONAL PSYCHOLOGY

Olga Louchakova

As spirituality and science come together in research and enquiry, a different picture of spiritual awakening emerges. Awakening transforms the lower ego and neutralizes basic drives of power, greed and cruelty. Olga tells about her experience of how awakening differs in different cultures, for example, in Russia and America. Meditation crosses cultural boundaries, as when Margaret Thatcher and Mikhail Gorbachev practise meditation with the spiritual teacher Tich Nath Hann! Spirituality offers some hope in a world where religious violence is widespread. The role of religion in public life may be declining, but it is increasing in personal lives. Olga describes aspects of spiritual awakening and concludes from her own research that it is accompanied by psychological and even physical changes. Awakening is a life-long process.

She identifies the different stages and concludes that advanced spirituality does not make one indifferent to the world and others. Broadly comparing many nations, cultures and expert witnesses, Olga shows that spiritual awakening is not necessarily a path to enlightenment, but may serve very specific purposes and help individuals to make life-changing decisions. In a time of religious violence, it can help us to correctly position our awareness, which is a journey worth taking.

***Olga Louchakova**, M.D., Ph.D., is a distinguished core faculty professor at the Institute of Transpersonal Psychology, recognized spiritual teacher and the founding director of Hridayam® School of Psychospiritual Development and Kundalini Yoga. She holds private practice in spiritual awakening guidance in San Francisco, Bay Area, and* *can be reached by email at hridayam@prodigy.net, or by regular mail at the Institute of Transpersonal Psychology, 1069 East Meadow Circle, Palo Alto, CA 94303, U.S.A.*

"They do not flee their condition, be they caliph or water bearer; sometimes it is their condition which flees them. Their retreat is the crowd; their desert is the public square. Conformity is their asceticism; the ordinary is their miracle…"

Chodkiewicz, 1995, p.1.

Setting the Scene

In spiritual awakening, the knowledge of one's true self begins with the awareness of impasse. Before awakening, the spiritual substance of life is veiled, and the vast Being-ness at its core is obscure to itself. Then, the Light of awareness breaks through the veils, shows through the cracks in personality, and illumines and sheds the fallacies of the false self. One by one, it brings to congruence exterior expressions and interior meanings in a solid masterpiece of a particular personhood. Hidden and esoteric becomes available to reason, "irrational" reveals its impeccable interior logics, and transcendental shows as an intrinsic fabric of everyday life. If only we pay attention…

Over the last 10 years, spirituality has become a subject of many polemics in psychology, philosophy and theology. Transpersonal psychology discovered the phenomena of spiritual emergency/emergence, a.k.a. spiritual transformation. This central concept initially created a revolution in the attitudes towards non-ordinary human experience. However, down the road it absorbed much of a common prejudice against spirituality, turning spiritual awakening into one more myth of modernity. This new mythology treats spiritual awakening as something outstanding, non-ordinary, controversial and infrequent. Spirituality then resonates with super-humanness, otherworldliness, a message of unalloyed happiness, or promise of the full freedom. When spirituality and science come together in true enquiry, a different picture of spiritual awakening emerges. Critical thinking and phenomenological method replace the highly romanticized and misleading, idealistic image of spiritual awakening by the true knowledge of spiritual awakening, how it actually happens in people's lives.

In the lives of saints, spiritual advancement may be concealed both within a brilliant destiny and an obscure life. For example, in the life of the holy Amir abd-al Kader, spiritual awakening happened in a context of a life of a swordsman. Amir practised the lofty gifts of non-dual wisdom while a military commander of the Ottoman

Empire, and was later betrayed and imprisoned by the French as a political captive. Like his spiritual predecessor Ibn-al-Arabi, the spiritual Master par excellence, Amir had to carry on his spiritual transformation within the milieu of Islamic fundamentalism (Chodkiewics, 1995).

Hindu saint Valmiki, Christian saint Sergii of Radonesj, great Indian visionary Sri Aurobindo, and many others have agreed that awakening to spiritual consciousness changes one's moral choices in life. Spiritual awakening transforms the lower ego, and neutralizes the animalistic tendencies such as drive to tyrannical power, greed, and cruelty. The life of abd-al Kader is the perfect example of it. His pure and modest lifestyle, his fairness to inferiors and enemies, his equanimity with superiors, the absence of cruelty in warfare, and care of his associates, make him different from the traditional image of the military commander in service to the fundamentalist Islamic monarchy.

Marguerite Porete, the French Beguine mystic of the 12th century, reveals the same non-ordinariness of character. Her book *The Mirror of the Simple Souls* contains no traditional medieval-times apology for being a woman who trespassed on the male terrain of writing about highest things. One of the few writers who explicitly described the stages of the soul in the process of spiritual awakening, Marguerite became a victim of political struggles. She accepted the sentence of being burned at the stake with uncommon placidity. She was acknowledged by historians and philosophers as a person of "great heart" and "noble courage". Marguerite Porete called the awakened soul a "phoenix" – a definition which could be easily applied to Porete herself (Lerner, 1993, pp. 1-3).

According to oral teachings of Malamatia Sufism, spiritual transformation serves to balance the expressions of inter-cultural violence and injustice in "hot" places of the planet (Shaikh Yasin of the Malamatia Sufi order, San Francisco, 1999, personal communication). Spiritual concepts of "enlightened rulership", and "enlightened craftsmanship" imply that spiritual awakening brings out positive changes in character that find expression in positive social action. Some forms of Christianity, and all of Islam, posit that spiritual consciousness harmonises the life of the community. Therefore, the focus should be not on the individual, but on community spiritual advancement. The concept of Buddhist "engaged spirituality" directs the practice of spiritual values into everyday life. The concept of "chivalry" in Islam and Christianity, or "sacred warriorship" in Buddhism, Hinduism, and Taoism, assumes the spiritually infused moral conduct in battle, and dignified moral choices in life. According to Islam, personal changes in the overall process of spiritual unfolding result in a "noble character structure". Contrary to the popular view of spiritual awakening as a process transcending personality and culture, real life spiritual awakening causes profound changes in the person, and affects all spheres of life.

Spiritual Awakening and the Cultural Self

For the author of this article, attention to culture-specific ways of spiritual awakening grew out of the personal experience of cross-cultural teaching of spirituality. Practices and approaches that worked in Russia didn't work in Estonia, Moldova or America. While meditation skills advanced in a similar way, the changes of personality in Russians, Americans or Turks in spiritual awakening were radically different. Methodological cul-de-sacs begged for the creative alliance of transpersonal and cultural psychology.

Indeed, culture and mind, and more specifically, culture and self, mutually constitute one another. The web of rituals, myths, cultural practices such as sex, childbearing, family life, dying, socializing, worshipping etc. happen via the medium of human self. The mutual making of culture and self causes cross-culturally diverse patterns in cognition, emotion, motivation, moral reasoning, psychopathology, and altered states of consciousness. People embody and practice their ethnic identities, which affects the embodied aspects of consciousness and energy such as chakra system (Louchakova & Warner, 2003). So, it is in this continuum of the self-body-culture that the spiritual awakening happens. Internal and subjective processes of spiritual awakening at a certain critical mass have a potential to transform the cultural systems (Louchakova, 2004, June).

Migrations associated with spiritual search and the cross-fertilization of spiritual traditions change western eurocentricity. Satsang, the gathering of people who receive the teachings of self-realisation from the self-realised master, became a highly "elite" spiritual activity in the West. When the Hindu saint Sri Ranjit Maharaj holds his international spiritual dialogue (Satsang, from the Sanskrit) in the Ketwadi slums in Mumbai, is this just a caprice of destiny, or is something meaningful and purposeful going on? As a researcher of consciousness, the author thinks that satsang is needed, especially in places of great suffering. It changes the "psychic atmosphere" of the hellish environment in the slums. Those coming to satsang will bring consciousness of satsang to other parts of the world. Here is the other, different globalization going on: spiritual consciousness transcends the frames of one culture and becomes the agent of a positive global change.

Some cultural theorists, applying the principles of critical theory to cultural power dynamics, consider that polarization, opposition and conflicts are inherent in culture as such (Cushman, 1995). We live in a divided world of antagonistic forces: mind versus body, the war on terrorism, the war against Iraq, the war of genders, the conflicts of "majorities" and "minorities"...In the mind, the "inner child" fights against the "inner parent". Inside the "inner parent", the "bad" parent tries to split off the "good" one... In order to be stable, the common psyche needs an enemy. It's an attempt to gain internal stability by externalizing tensions in resistance to the external opponent. This is the world of religious fundamentalism, the antagonizing world of exclusion. On the contrary, spiritual awakening brings out the innate wholeness of the self. "Good [spirit, God, innate Goodness] unifies and holds together what has been separated, evil clearly divides and corrupts what has been unified," says St. Maximos the Confessor, Christian mystic of the 6th Century A.D. (1981). The wholeness of the human self reflects in the holistic attitude to the world, in stability through the web of non-oppositional, dialogical connections.

When the Vietnamese Buddhist monk Thich Nhat Hanh teaches the silent walking meditation to state leaders Margaret Thatcher and Mikhail Gorbachev in San Francisco Presidio, this is not just a satisfaction of their personal stress-reduction pursuit. Something larger is going on, which may affect the lives of thousand people on the planet. Meditation brings awareness to subconscious, opens Kundalini energy, and over time changes the structure of personality. The antagonistic divisions, such as superego-ego-id tensions, give place to the more unified, wholesome psyche (Washburn, 1994). Consciousness changes from within, it becomes more stable, more inclined to search for dialogical, non-violent solutions.

Acknowledgment of the spiritual awakening in the world, where religious violence is becoming a commonplace, is neither a pacifist emotion-based practice, nor a wish-fulfilling New Age way of thinking. These are, as current research shows (Louchakova & Warner, 2003; Wall & Louchakova, 2002), reflections on natural events within overall human development, and a mechanism by which consciousness balances its own violent or destructive extremes. We can posit a connection between spiritually awakened politicians and better politics, as well as a connection between spiritual awakened peace activists and better conflict resolution (Burdge, 2004). Likewise, there is a correlation between spiritually based ethics and a better psychological climate in business (Yan, 2003). As scientists, we can research, evaluate and confirm the "real life" effects of spiritual experience, as manifestations of the most essential part of who we are (Wildman & Brothers, 1999; Louchakova, 2003, 2004 July-August, 2004 August) as individuals, nations, races or civilizations.

Spiritual and cultural realms within the psyche are very close. The call is for transpersonal psychology to become a more real life engaged enquiry into human consciousness that has the flexibility to contribute to a better and global psychological climate and more humane international politics.

The Conundrum of the "Closet Spiritual Awakening"

Surveys show the increasing frequency of spiritual experience in contemporary westerners (Marty, 1993; Roof, 1999) (no data available for non-industrial countries). For example, in United States, religiosity over the last 20 years shifted from the quest for group identity and belonging to a social group to the quest for an authentic inner life and personhood. Activated more at the inner level, Americans are asking questions such as, "Does religion relate to my life?" "How can I find spiritual meaning and depth?" and "What might faith mean for me?" While the influence of religion in public life declines, it is increasing in personal lives (Arnold-Magnum, 1994). Inner experience takes over from learned dogma. The leading factor in a religious experience is a change of perception (Louchakova, 2004, July-August). Many of those who have the experiences of expanded perception do not know how to conceptualise, share them or relate to them (Palmer, 1999). When perception changes rapidly, people may think they are crazy. At the same time, there rises an undeniable sense of sacred. Is sacred crazy? How did we get to think that our intrinsic, inborn capacity of spiritual perception is "crazy"?

The Western world is a secularized world (Cox, 1990). Our architecture, art, science, values, healing systems and daily rituals constitute a materialistic culture. The soteriological meanings are alienated from life, and are segregated into the special reservations nicely called "spiritual retreats". By the decree of behavioural psychology, the range of normality in everyday emotional life is limited to several (up to ten) basic emotions such as fear, anger, joy, sadness, disgust, surprise, shame, interest and the like (Ekman, Levenson, & Friesen, 1983), and the "entrained" cognitive schemas keep attention directed outward. Spiritual emotions as "true joy", sacred weeping or devotion are considered to be an emotional problem. Emptiness of the self is common (Cushman, 1995), loss of meaning escalates, and the level of suicide skyrockets (McKenna, 2004). Spiritual experience is not "us", it is a "thing" acquired, and in a manner one acquires a car, a partner, or a new job. With globalization, spirituality can be imported from India, China or Japan. There are different packages and deals, such as a weekend workshop, week-long seminar, a spiritual tour or a session in a spa. The rise of inward perception, and the change of self-identity, inherent to spiritual awakening, challenge this artificial social consensus.

The teacher of non-duality Robert Adams experienced spiritual awakening in his tender teens in New York. After he reported his experiences to his parents, they took him to see a psychiatrist. The psychiatrist, by a lucky chance, was a follower of a great Indian saint Paramahamsa Yogananda. He referred Robert Adams to Yogananda. Yogananda examined the boy and sent him to the other saint, Sri Ramana Maharshi. Robert stayed with Ramana, and then returned to the West to teach. This is a lucky case scenario. In less lucky cases, people get treated for the assumed "loss of self" which frequently gets misinterpreted as a psychiatric condition.

After centuries of denial of our inherent spiritual-ness, we know very little about it. Some of the fallacies are:

1. Spiritual awakening is rare
2. Spiritual awakening is a separate event, not a life-long process
3. In order to be spiritually awakened, one needs to have a transmission of something from somebody else
4. Spiritual awakening is about spirituality only, and has nothing to do with psychology
5. Spiritual awakening makes one renounce the world
6. Spiritual awakening makes one weird
7. Spiritual awakening makes one happy
8. Spiritual awakening makes one miserable
9. Spiritual awakening doesn't exist
10. Spiritual awakening cannot happen to me, etc. etc.

It is in this environment that the frequency of spontaneous spiritual experience increases (Louchakova 2004, July-August; Wall and Louchakova 2002). The conflict between the reality of spiritual awakening, and inadequate beliefs, causes psychological complications. The author's research involving more than 500 informants over 15 years shows that spiritual experiences do not stand isolated. They are accompanied by necessary psychological and even physical changes. They are a part and parcel of a special life-long developmental process, which does not correspond to the biological aging of the body. The Templeton Foundation research links religious experiences to stages in gradual personal transformation throughout one's lifespan (Wildman & Brothers, 1999). Fowler (1981) considers that religious conversion depends on the innate ontogenic structures that unfold invariably throughout life. Grof and Grof (1989) insisted that spiritual awakening is a long term process. In spite of this, the separate peak-experience oriented view of spiritual emergency has received predominant attention in transpersonal psychology. As of now, there are no developmental clinical approaches that would allow us to successfully navigate the process of spiritual awakening.

We finally have to admit that spiritual awakening is an ontological, normal, inherently human process of maturation. It happens to people spontaneously, like ripening of a fruit, often uncalled for and unwarranted by any spiritual practice. The "glorious" or troublesome exceptional experiences are but a small part of the process. A complete picture consists of a slow, gradual, life-long process of psycho-spiritual transformation, involving stage-specific correlations of individuation, religious/spiritual experiences, modalities of embodied awareness, changes in perception, self-awareness, self-identification, values, attitudes and character structure. It is the overall life-long change in the self.

Growth of requests for spiritually competent therapy and counseling shows that the process of natural spiritual awakening is much more common in general population than we generally think. The need for crisis counseling is only a small part of these requests. The majority are in need of longitudinal non-pathologizing growth oriented counseling, incorporating dimensions of spirituality. Something our "civilized" western culture is, as yet, unable to provide.

A Life-Long Process of Spiritual Awakening

Understanding of relationships between spiritual experiences and human development acquires additional importance with the growing evidence of spontaneous awakenings outside traditional religious or spiritual frames. The social impact of this phenomenon is not researched, but can be significant. In Russia, for example, the underground spiritual awakening movement helped to overcome the Soviet regime (Kungurtsev & Luchakova, 1997). Spiritual elder and scientist Antonov used Kundalini Yoga exercises to enhance people's spiritual awakening. His research shows that people in a spiritual awakening process changed the strategies of conflict resolution from violent to dialogical and non-violent. Aggressiveness and fear decreased, and the capacity of strategic decision making increased, the rate of psychosomatic health problems went down, the use alcohol and drugs decreased. People report being happier and their lives become more meaningful (Antonov & Vaver, 1989).

In 2002, Wall and Louchakova showed that the everyday consciousness of Americans right after the September 11, 2001 catastrophe contained many elements of evolutionary and non-dual spiritual experiences (Wall & Louchakova, 2002). It is important to notice that the research of spiritual awakening doesn't easily surrender to straightforward statistical methods, and requires complex, integral and imaginative methodologies typical for innovative qualitative research. Because of the complexity of the phenomenon of spiritual awakening it is impossible to say whether in case of "9/11" this is typical part of the post-traumatic response, or the evidence of the evolution of consciousness, but it is clear that elements of spiritual, and even non-dual consciousness, are engrained in the fabric of our everyday life. That which is eternal and real shines through the gaps in the impermanent and relative.

Lifespan long spiritual awakening can be averagely "healthy", or can be associated with psychological or health problems (Louchakova, 2004, July-August). In this context, spiritual experiences of a client may be interpreted by the therapist as indicators of particular developmental stages in spiritual awakening and the overall development of the ego. The psyche, undergoing spiritual awakening, also changes as a result of spiritual experience. For example, the experiences of non-dual consciousness serve as developmental catalysts (Louchakova, in press). However, occasionally, rapid spiritual openings can be traumatic and lead to developmental arrests unless there is an additional work of integration (Louchakova, 2004, July-August). Our research also shows that overall character of the process of spiritual awakening differs in regard to the focus on self-actualization, self-knowledge, creative expression, sexuality and/or development of bodily awareness. Marker religious/spiritual experiences signify the overall changes in the self, and are associated with specific changes in self-awareness, self-identification, and motivation. In a non-problematic development spiritual experience leads to balanced character structure associated with the sense of wholeness and well-being. The overall psyche responds to the instances of non-dual consciousness by the enhancement of individuation (Louchakova, in press). Thus, spiritual experiences are the essential components of the healthy human "self," and are associated with particular psychological changes and subtle shifts of bodily awareness. The Indian chakra model provides a map for the developmental changes of bodily awareness happening in spiritual awakening (Louchakova & Warner, 2003). Conventional ego development may switch to spiritual development as an advanced form of cognitive functioning early in life.

Stages of spiritual awakening may last for many years. Our clinical research involving people in self-identified spiritual awakening over a period of more than 15 years shows that there are stages of spiritual awakening, clearly defined through the lifespan. The clinically important first stage includes paranormal experiences and the spontaneous actualization of the access to subconscious. The second stage is associated with the growth of self-awareness, spontaneous deconstruction of the "false" self and actualization of the true psychological self. Marker spiritual experience here includes the gestalt of oneself as pure consciousness, and other variants of spiritual experiences of the Self. Stage three involves the shift from in-depth psychological work to deeper existential issues, heightened discrimination and authenticity. Stage four is characterized by the spontaneous awareness of archetypes and deep character transformation. Marker spiritual experiences include "transcending the root of the ego", "uncreated" light and cosmic psyche (described in detail below). All informants report their increasing sense of life satisfaction and well-being over time. This research indicates that life-stage psychology should account for at least two different developmental tracks (i.e., conventional and spiritual), one of them requiring non-traditional counseling and psychotherapy.

Non-Dual Dialogue and Global Psyche – Means for Cultural Healing

Contrary to the popular opinion that advanced spirituality makes one psychologically immune to the world and others, there are many examples where spiritual awakening over time brings out more engagement with life and relatedness. Here is the life story of a woman in her mid 40s. As many undergoing a spiritual awakening process, she shared it because her experience seemed significant enough to affect people's lives. For several years she practised Kundalini Yoga[1] under the guidance of an Indian master of the ancient and well respected lineage. Her latest practice was the repetition of Divine Names in the centre of the subtle body, called the Spiritual Heart[2]. She did not consider herself a strong practitioner, so what followed came as a surprise. She experienced strong anxiety and aches in the left side of her body, predominantly the chest. It was during the night time, and she and her husband thought that she was having a heart attack. She thought though that the condition may have been related to her spiritual practice, and decided to wait before calling an ambulance. The condition worsened, anxiety turned into a strong fear, pain increased, but something inside told her to surrender to her condition.

Suddenly, after several hours of turmoil, her state shifted to the consciousness of omniscience. She perceived with absolute clarity the experience of every living being. She was insects and animals, whales and angels, her children and her ancestors, saints and killers, extraterrestrials and beings yet to be born. There was delight, and pain, and insights, and terror, and love, perils and paradise, births and deaths, and everything imaginable. This continued for some time, and then subsided. Indeed, it would have been very difficult for her to continue living in this condition of expanded awareness. If one's own life can be hard to cope with, how much harder it is to be present to the life experience of all beings! So she saw it, and remembered, and changed her life, so she would work with people and tell them about the sentiency which lives in the heart of everyone and contains the whole universe.

Experiences like this one are not rare, but quite characteristic of a certain stage of spiritual awakening. The observations in the author's clinical practice here are supported by the evidence found in spiritual literature. They have enormous transformative impact. Spiritual awakening implies at least two types of transcendence – vertical and horizontal (author's unpublished research). Vertical transcendence takes one away from diversity, into pure awareness which is the substance of Being. Horizontal transcendence is of the kind described above – the cosmic form of all existences within one Being (Louchakova, in press). This is the Cosmic Christ, the Perfect Man of Sufism, and the Cosmic Form of Krishna in Bhagavat Gita (Srimad Bhagavat Gita Bhasya of Sri Sankaracarya, 1983, p.347-383).

A precise phenomenological description of the experience of the cosmic psyche comes in the famous hadith given through the prophet Mohammed "Heavens and earth contain Me not, but the heart of My faithful servant containeth Me" (Chittick, 1989). This kind of experience stretches consciousness to embrace polarities. The range of acceptance widens, tolerance and inclusiveness grow. One intuits directly the oneness and indivisibility of all existence, the need for confrontation subsides, and aptitude towards dialogue and inclusiveness increase.

When the enlightened mystics of different traditions agree on the nature of reality, does it mean that their experience of reality is the same? Not necessarily. It rather means that they can deeply share the understanding of reality. Spiritual advancement does not annihilate individual differences. Advanced spirituality understands, empathizes with and appreciates the other. Self-definition of a spiritually evolved person is by inclusion, not by exclusion. Spiritually developed character is antithetical to egotism and narcissism. This kind of consciousness would allow for the culture which doesn't need to create enemies in order to be stable, and does not need to be on the top of a power pyramid in order to feel safe.

Spiritual consciousness, inclusive of opposites, manifests itself in the most benign ways in cultural dialogical practices. Dialogue about spiritual consciousness helps to find non-violent political solutions. Talking practices also play an important role in strengthening resilience to cultural stresses such as the ongoing threat of terrorism

(Burdge, personal communication, September 21, 2004; Wall & Louchakova, 2002). Sohbet, sincere and egalitarian talking practice, was cultivated in Islam. Sohbet has to come from the place of "egolessness", receptivity, loving friendliness and the conformity with the sense of the whole called the ethiquette, "adab" (from Arabic). Successful sohbet actualises one's sense of self. It also can bring out the shared group experience of the universal Self. The co-experienced insight into the non-dual consciousness is the pinnacle of sohbet. In non-dual consciousness, the resolution of opposites happens to attain the new synthesis, and the group reaches satisfaction. Moods of depression, angst, concern or confusion shift to states of clarity, empathy, joy, delight, highly positive experience of the self and total connectedness.

A form of communal dialogue called veche (root base "vech" connects with speech, eternity and knowledge, from Old Slavic) was used by ancient Slavs at the times of the military attacks of Mongols in the 13th century. The turning point in Veche was the communal experience of the direct intuition of "Truth", searched for and valued as the means of resolving complexity.

The talking practice of Indian satsang also opens access to non-dual consciousness and causes the assimilation of complicated meanings. Satsang (in Sanskrit, association with the Truth, or Being) is a flow of the questions and answers between seekers and teacher established in non-dual consciousness. Bhagavat Gita gives the famous example satsang between Arjuna's and Krishna. The psychological emphasis of satsang is on the internal conflict resolution and peace, resulting from the emergence of the non-dual consciousness.

Upwards and Onwards or Back to Wholeness?

The common understanding is that awakening to spiritual consciousness is a "step up", a development towards higher levels of consciousness. However, the nature of these spontaneous spiritual awakenings may vary. Much depends on the timing and on the context.

An old Indian story tells about the cow of dharma, a metaphor for the order of things. In the first quarter of creation, the cow of dharma has all four legs. In the young creation the elements are in harmony, human self is whole and complete, and everybody attains spiritual completion in the course of life. There is no "spiritual awakening", because there is no prior spiritual "sleep".

In the second quarter of creation the cow of dharma loses one of her legs. There is a bit of disharmony, a cruder, harsher life. Spiritual substance of life gets slightly obscured. The self is more opaque to itself, veiled to its own awareness. To attain the gestalt of one's nature, and spiritual completion, original transparency and wholeness of the self needs to come back. The practice of rituals becomes the means to balance the disorganized elements of creation. Human capacities are less, obstacles to self-knowledge are more. Spiritual awakening however is common, and has a natural developmental character.

In the third quarter of creation the cow of dharma lost two of her legs. In order to be whole and attain spiritual completion one has to practice yoga and meditate. Meditation and yoga integrate the disbalanced self, and spiritual awakening happens to those who manage to attain this integration. Spiritual awakening happens to some people, but not to others.

In the fourth quarter of creation three legs of the cow of dharma are gone, and things get completely out of sync. In the old body of creation elements are out of order, both in nature (such as earthquakes) and in the human mind (such as violence, wars, and insanity). The human self deteriorates, personality disorders become the common problem. Self-alienation grows in the divided world. Then, even spiritual practice is not enough. Wholeness and completion have to happen from within, from the internal, sentient Ground of Being, from the realms beyond the egoic separateness of the individual mind. Since creation is cyclical, there is a need for the process by which it would return to its original, transparent condition. According to Indian metaphysical chronology, this is our historical period. This can be seen as the context of our contemporary spiritual awakenings. Through the cracks in the self the energy from within "glues" together the fragmented pieces. Spiritual awakening is restorative of intrinsic humanness, of wholeness which allows us to see who we really are. It is a return to the self.

In meeting and interviewing many people in spiritual awakening in many countries, it became clear that spiritual awakening is not necessarily "enlightenment". It may be serve a very specific life purpose, such as catalyzing the decision to move to another geographic location, enrol in higher education, change profession, enter growth oriented therapy, get out of depression, emigrate etc. It helps to mourn the loss of a close one, to heal abuse issues, or to choose a right life partner. The applications are numerous. For some people, spiritual awakening can unveil non-duality, some fall in love with God, some become Gnostics. But there is a common ground shared by all alike: this is an open-ended process, which transforms the person and deepens as long as the body lasts, and maybe even after that.

Cornel West, Professor of Religion and African American Studies at Princeton University, and one of America's most gifted, provocative, and important public intellectuals, once said: "We live to position our awareness correctly". Spiritual awakening in times of religious violence helps us to correctly position our awareness. Then, it is a journey well travelled.

NOTES

1. Kundalini Yoga is a spiritual system that works with specific energy in the human body, so called Kundalini, intimately connected wiith spiritual awakening.

2. For teachings on the Spiritual Heart Centre contact Olga Louchakova through her website (www.hridayamyoga.org). This knowledge, passed to Olga in the Russian spiritual underground, is part of a book in progress.

REFERENCES

Antonov, V., & Vaver, G. (1989). *Complexnaya Systema Psychophysicheskoi Samoregulatsii (A handbook of complex system of psychophysical self-regulation)*. Leningrad, Russia: Cosmos. (All books by this author are available from him directly; Do vostrebovania, Sanct Petersburg, Russia).

Arnold-Magnum, E. (1994). Spiritual America. *U. S. News and World Report, 116*, 48– 59.

Burdge, S. (2004). Learning from exemplary peace activists in the Middle East: The role of culture and religion in moving towards peace. Unpublished manuscript, *Institute of Transpersonal Psychology*, Palo Alto, California.

Chittick, W. (1989). *The Sufi Path of Knowledge*. Albany: State University of New York Press.

Chodkiewicz, M. (1995). *The Spiritual Writings of Amir 'Abd al-Kader*. New York, Albany: State University of New York Press.

Cox. H. (1990). *The Secular City: secularization and urbanization in theological perspective*. New York: Collier Books.

Cushman, P (1995). *Constructing the Self, Constructing America*. Reading, MA: Addison-Wesley.

Ekman, P., Levenson, R. W., & Friesen, W. V. (1983). Autonomic nervous system activity distinguishes among emotions. *Science, 221*, 1208- 1210.

Fowler, J. (1981). *Stages of Faith: the psychology of human development and the quest for meaning*. San Francisco: Harper & Row.

Grof, S., & Grof, C. (1989). Spiritual Emergency: understanding evolutionary crisis (pp.1-26). In S. Grof & C. Grof (Eds.), *Spiritual Emergency: when personal transformation becomes a crisis*. Los Angeles: Tarcher, Inc.

Kungurtsev, I., & Luchakova, O. (1997). The unknown Russian mysticism: pagan sorcery, Christian yoga, and other esoteric practices in the former Soviet Union. In T. R. Soidla and S. I. Shapiro (Ed.), *Voices of Russian Transpersonalism* (pp. 7-15). Brisbane, Australia: Bolda-Lok Publishing and Educational Enterprises.

Lerner, R.E. (1993). Preface. In M. Porete, *The Mirror of Simple Souls* (pp.1-4). New York: Paulist Press.

Louchakova, O. (2003, August). Psychospiritual development through the life-span. Paper presented at the 111th annual American Psychological Association Convention, Toronto, Canada. Retrieved 9.26.2004 from http://www.hridayamyoga.org/papers/complete.html.

Louchakova, O. (2004, June). Towards the comparative history of esotericism: Kundalini awakening in the West. Paper presented at the First conference of the Association for the Study of Esotericism "Esotericism From Europe to North America", Michigan State University, East Lansing, Michigan.

Louchakova, O. (2004, July-August). Spiritual Tracks in Life-Span Development: Restoring the Human Person. Paper presented at the 112th annual American Psychological Association Convention, Honolulu, Hawaii. Retreived 9.26.2004 from http://www.hridayamyoga.org/papers/complete.html.Honolulu, 2004.

Louchakova, O. (2004, August). Spiritual Life-Span Development as Restoration of the Human Person. Eurotas conference, London. Retreveed 9.26.2004 from http://www.hridayamyoga.org/papers/complete.html.

Louchakova, O. (in press, 2005). Ontopoiesis and Unity in the Prayer of the Heart: Contributions to Psychotherapy and Learning. In A. T. Tyemeiniecka (Ed.), *Logos of Phenomenology and Phenomenology of the Logos.* Analecta Husserliana, v. 91. Dordrecht: Kluwer.

Louchakova, O. & Warner, A. (2003). Via Kundalini: Psychosomatic excursions in transpersonal psychology. *The Humanistic Psychologist, 31*(2-3), 115-158.

Marty, M.E. (1993). Where the Energies Go. *Annals of the American Academy of Political and Social Science, 527*, 11– 26.

McKenna, J.F. (in press, 2005). The meaningfulness of mental health as being within a world of apparent meaningless being. In A. T. Tyemeiniecka (Ed.), *Logos of Phenomenology and Phenomenology of the Logos.* Analecta Husserliana, v. 91. Dordrecht: Kluwer.

Srimad Bhagavat Gita Bhasya of Sri Samkaracarya. (A. G. K. Warrier, Trans.). (1983). Madras, India: Sri Ramakrishna Math.

Wildman W. & Brothers, L. (1999). A neuropsychological-semiotic model of religious experiences. In R. Russel, N. Murphy, T. Meyering, & M. Arbib (eds.), *Neuroscience and the Person. scientific perspectives on divine action* (pp.347-416). Berkeley, CA: Center for Theology and Natural Science.

Pamer, G. T. (1999). *Disclosure and Assimilation of Exceptional Human Experiences: Meaningful, Transformative, and Spiritual Aspects.* Unpublished doctoral dissertation. Institute of Transpersonal Psychology, Palo Alto, California.

Roof, W. C. (1999). *Spiritual Marketplace: Baby Boomers and the remaking of American Religion.* New Jersey: Princeton University Press.

St. Maximos the Confessor. (1881). First century of various texts. V. 49. In G.E.H. Palmer, P. Sherarrd & K. Ware (Eds.), *The Philokalia,* p.174. London: Faber & Faber.

Yan, J. (2003). *Spirituality and Business: the next movement?* Paper presented at the Chief Brand Officers' meeting, Amsterdam, January 17, 2003. Retrieved 9.26.2004 from http://www.jyanet.com/cap/2003/0117fe0.shtml.

Wall, K. & Louchakova, O (2002). Evolution of consciousness in responses to terrorist attacks: towards a transpersonal theory of cultural transformation. *The Humanistic Psychologist, 30*(3), 252-273.

Washburn M. (1994). *Transpersonal Psychology in Psychoanalytic Perspective.* Albany, New York: State University of New York Press.

5. REFRAMING THE CONFLICT IN FIJI: ECONOMIC AND TRANSPERSONAL FRAMEWORKS FOR PEACE

Harris Friedman

The world is filled with conflicts between peoples who hold on to narrow identifications. Harris shows through the case study of a situation in Fiji a microcosm of the wider conflicts that are most globally threatening. Islands are more natural laboratories for studying social change as external influences are often less apparent because of the physical boundary of the sea. Harris speculates about the potential worth of reframing (a psychological technique) such conflicts into transpersonal perspectives with a view to assessing their relevance to conflicts elsewhere.

Fijian problems have been commonly attributed to racial and ethnic divides that are not easily amenable to change. Harris provides an alternative understanding of these conflicts as competing economic models. The scientific transpersonal perspective is present as another alternative framework especially applicable to religious conflicts

This contribution shows how a serious study of an island population can lead to pointers of extending such a study to conflicts in a wider world thus leading to better understanding of some of the challenges of an interconnected world which is not always one joined by love and compassion but by real economic and spiritual differences which also will need to be reconciled if the vision of global citizenship is to be held and worked towards.

Harris Friedman is Professor Emeritus at Saybrook Graduate School and Professor of Psychology (Courtesy) at University of Florida, as well as a licensed psychologist. His current research interests include scientific approaches to transpersonal psychology and facilitating cultural change. He authored the Self-Expansiveness Level Form, a measure of *transpersonal self-concept, served as guest co-editor of a special issue of The Humanistic Psychologist on transpersonal psychology and a special issue of the Journal of Transpersonal Psychology on transpersonal measurement, and has co-edited the International Journal of Transpersonal Studies since 2003. He was recently elected a Fellow of the Division of Humanistic Psychology of the American Psychological Association. Correspondence may be addressed to Harris Friedman at 1255 Tom Coker Road, SW, LaBelle, FL 33935 or to harrisfriedman@floraglades.org.*

Watzlawick, Weakland, and Fisch defined reframing as "to change the conceptual and/or emotional setting or viewpoint in relation to which a situation is experienced and to place it in another frame which fits the 'facts' of the same situation equally well or even better, and thereby changes its entire meaning" (in Segal, 2001, p. 90). Reframing has been used in many counseling and psychotherapy interventions, most notably Eriksonian approaches, and has important implications for facilitating peace. When oppositional sides become polarized to the point where violence is seen not only as a viable but perhaps the only available option, the underlying dynamic is often an impasse in the worldviews of the participants in the conflict. These require more than mere bargaining in which conflicting sides are compromising. Rather they require solutions changing the dynamics from lose-lose, which are always part of mutual compromise, into win-win outcomes. Reframing is a technique that can provide such synergy.

One research approach to understanding how this can operate stems from the classic model proposed by Lewin (1951) in which successful change involves three stages: "unfreezing ... moving to the new level ... and freezing" (p. 228). Vallacher and Wegner (1985) expanded this notion into action identification theory in which an existing equilibrium, such as a stable worldview, must first be disrupted in order to have a meaningful change that allows regaining a new equilibrium. A recent example demonstrating how this can be applied is the work of Davis and Knowles (1999) in which reframing is shown as effective in influencing behavioural change.

In this paper, I discuss reframing as a psychological tool to address some of the complex difficulties in Fiji, a nation demographically polarized and torn by resulting conflicts, in order to facilitate peaceful solutions of its many problems. The approach offered stems from my research (e.g., Van Deusen, C., Mueller, C., Jones, G., & Friedman, H., 2002) and consulting involvements over the past decade in Fiji, including from my involvement as one of the founders of an organisation in Fiji that has provided intensive training to the majority of the current Fijian cabinet members, as well as to many of the country's top business leaders. This consulting has focused on designing and implementing appropriate models for economic development at the local and national level. I also speculate about the possible role of transpersonal psychology in providing an overarching perspective through which reframing religious conflicts, some of the most daunting bases of global strife, could lead to a more peaceful world. Finally, I discuss how the type of solution applied in Fiji can be expanded, for example to the Israeli-Palestinian conflict, in ways that could be similarly useful.

Background on Fiji

Fiji has a bifurcated ethnic composition in which a little more than half of the population are native Fijians and slightly over forty per cent are Fijian Indians, based on an estimated population of under a million people. There are also various minorities, including Chinese, Europeans, and other Pacific Islanders. These demographics are the consequence of British colonialism in which indentured Asian Indians were brought to Fiji to work in agriculture and other industries – since the native Fijians could not be coerced into such roles. Native Fijians typically resisted Westernization, pursuing more traditional village ways, while the Fijian Indians emulated the British – resulting in the emergence of two divergent Fijian cultures.

When the British left Fiji, many conflicts ensued. For example, the Fijian Indians became, as a group, more Western in culture and controlled the majority of professional and business endeavours in the nation. However, the majority of native Fijians retained their traditional village lifestyle, as well as collective ownership by villages of more than 80% of the land. This disparity provided the basis for much of the ongoing national conflicts. Although the majority of the Western press, as well as many Fijians (both native and Indian) attribute the various crises in Fiji to racial and ethnic tensions, there are other more useful interpretations.

It is undeniable, however, that racial and ethnic factors are at play in these conflicts. For example, the differential appearance of the two peoples is striking. Though both tend to be dark skinned, the native Fijians are a large people in which males are commonly heavily muscled and females are admired for their size. In contrast, the Fijians Indians are, on average, a small and slender people. This lends to ready stereotyping across the two cultures. Also, despite that there are some noteworthy cultural similarities; ethnic differences are often magnified by members of the two groups. For example, both cultures share in the rich religious tradition of fire walking. However, this is often seen as a source of contention rather than being perceived as common ground. Specifically, rather than mutually respecting the similarities of their rituals, I witnessed both sides frequently disparaging the other's fire walking as inauthentic – for example, there were accusations from the native Fijians that the coals used by the Fijian Indians were prepared in a way such that they were not really very hot (by being covered with ashes) and corresponding accusations from the Fijian Indians that the native Fijians used a protective balm on their feet.

When first visiting Fiji while involved in consulting to the hospitality industry during the early 1990s, I met a group of Fijian hotel workers and immediately hit the impasse between the two cultures. When in a team-building group I was facilitating, I referred to a Fijian Indian using the term, "Fijian Indian," I was rebuffed, as follows: "Sir, I am not a Fijian Indian, just a Fijian. My family has lived in Fiji for many generations." In contrast, a native Fijian replied, "I partially agree – you are not a Fijian Indian. You are an Indian whose ancestors were brought to my country by the British. And you are a guest in my land who must recognize you are neither Fijian nor Fijian Indian, just Indian." Similarly, I noticed how the prevalent division of labour in hotels mirrored rifts in Fijian society. For example, tourists who come to Fiji are often greeted by native Fijians in traditional garb with warm "Bulas," the indigenous hello and good-bye. Likewise, the majority of the front office workers, waiting staff, and others who interact directly with visitors are native Fijian – communicating the sense of "place" to tourists. However, the Fijian Indian workers who perform the majority of the professional and technical functions mainly worked behind the public scene.

With the recent coup in Fiji, in which a democratically elected Fijian Indian leader was replaced with a native Fijian, conflicts have reached precipitous proportions. Without going into the complex dynamics behind the change in government, it is sufficient to state that the situation there is extremely difficult and both sides of the divide have legitimate concerns and grievances.

Reframing the Fijian Conflict

When problems are blamed on immutable racial categories, there is no room for reconciliation. Similarly, when difficulties are blamed on ethnicity, the situation is also change resistant. In the case of Fiji, if the conflict remains defined as one of race and ethnicity, little positive is likely to emerge – since these are deeply ascribed characteristic not amenable to change. One potentially useful strategy is to reframe these problems into a less emotional discourse through looking for common ground to propose synergistic solutions.

Much of my work in Fiji has focused on reframing the fundamental differences between the Fijian Indians and native Fijians as due to culturally different and competing economic models – since such models can be discussed relatively dispassionately, and reconciled, whereas discussing racial and ethnic attributions is typically counterproductive. This has occurred in a variety of setting, including in one-on-one coaching, small groups, and large workshops. Specifically, I have advocated that the primary differences between the Fijian Indian and native Fijian groups are better seen as due to a conflict between individual and collective capitalism (Friedman, Glover, & Avegalio, 2002). In this sense, the traditional collective economy of the native Fijian village, despite the ever-growing influence of modernism, is currently a form of collective capitalism. In contrast, the Fijian Indians have assumed a British individualistic form of capitalism. These competing economic models result in many conflicts that are too easily misattributed to racial and ethnic causes.

I previously illustrated this in a case study through describing how a Western expatriate manager in Fiji perceived problems with the native Fijian work ethic (Glover, Friedman, & Jones, 2002). The manager stated he had asked a local village chief to send three men to clear a field with each man to receive a payment for eight hours work. However, the entire group of 10 able-bodied men from the village showed up. The expatriate wanted only three and consequently asked the chief to send the remainder back to the village. The chief, however, requested that all 40 could do the work quickly and the payment could be made to the communal fund that helped all in the village collectively. Not understanding this collective approach, the expatriate sent all the men away and, instead, hired three Fijian Indian workers from the city who were more comfortable with an individual model of capitalism, illustrating the clash of different work values and productivity models. The result was that the manager's selection of the Fijian Indians fueled mutual resentments – from the native Fijians toward both the manager and Fijian Indians whose competing labour deprived the village of needed resources and back from the manager and Fijian Indians who perceived the native Fijian behaviour through the stereotypes of Western culture as laziness (i.e. not individually willing to do a "full day's work for a full day's pay").

Adding to the problem of competing economic models is a deep Western-based ethnocentrism that tends to deprecate native Fijian culture. I previously illustrated this in a case study comparing native Fijian ways of fishing with that of modern ways embraced by Fijian Indians (Friedman, Glover, & Avegalio, 2002). Traditionally, the entire able-bodied members of a native Fijian village will collectively go into the ocean, forming a large circle as the tide recedes. Gradually they close their circle, trapping the fish as they become stranded with the withdrawing tide; then, all that is needed is to gather the fish. This method provides much greater yield than using individual fishing poles and is likely one of the world's most productive resource gathering techniques. Yet many Indian Fijians scoff at this "primitive" fishing technique.

Valuing cultural differences, rather than devaluing them, is essential for the type of reframing that can lead to peace. In Lewin's (1951) model that starts with unfreezing, first the ethnocentric belief that "my way is the best way" has to be challenged. Again, it is easier to challenge, or unfreeze, economic models that are less central to core worldview than assumptions about race or ethnicity. However, I am not implying that these are easy to confront, since they are implicitly held, but they are less value-laden than attributions based on race or ethnicity.

Applying reframing, during Lewin's second stage of establishing change, I have advocated that Fiji needs to free itself of the burden of other cultures' economic models and create its own unique unifying model that is sustainable among all of its constituents (Friedman, Glover, & Avegalio, 2002). This is quite different than accepting uncritically the extant Western models that are culturally inappropriate for Fiji. I have illustrated this by presenting a number of alternative economic models to those prevailing in the West – such as ones demonstrating success in non-Western cultures (e.g., the government directed capitalism of Singapore) or that are emerging with promise of success (e.g., the modified Communist model in the People's Republic of China). Hopefully, as a uniquely Fijian economic model emerges, the divisiveness within Fiji will ameliorate, facilitated through reframing the bases of Fijian conflict as primarily economic.

Reframing Using a Transpersonal Perspective

Economics, however, is not the whole story. The role of spirituality is also crucial to any successful reframing of Fiji's conflicts. For example, Williksen-Bakker (2002) recognized that, though economic differences underlie many of Fiji's conflict, this has to be viewed in a wider frame than economics as usually understood in the West. For example, the importance of the native Fijian sense of "vanua" emphasizing a spiritual connection between people and the land has to be considered in contrast to the more Western notion of land held by most Fijian Indians which views it primarily as a resource from which to profit. The implications of these differences are profound when it comes to decisions such as whether or not to timber old growth forests.

Similarly, Ewins (1998) emphasized how the Fijian conflicts have roots in deep traditions more than on race or ethnicity. Likewise, Brison (2001) discussed how native Fijian identity is constructed through such traditions, particularly the kava ("yaqona") ceremonies – and, incidentally, how native Fijians use reframing as a traditional way of reconciling regional, tribal, and social class conflicts. Bosson (2000) also explored the role of traditions, mainly through festivals, as part of nation building and reconciliation in Fiji. And Norton (2000) discussed how reconciliation at the Fijian national level must occur through dialogue that allows for accommodation of contending worldviews. Thus there are a number of convergent strands of thought pointing in a common direction for healing the rifts in Fiji, namely through the use of reframing emphasizing the role of spirituality.

I speculate that transpersonal psychology, which addresses spirituality from a scientific perspective, provides a possible avenue for establishing the most solid common ground on which to deeply reframe Fijian conflicts. The focus of transpersonal psychology involves an expansion of the perceived self as being "beyond (trans) the individual or personal to encompass wider aspects of humankind, life, psyche, and cosmos" (Walsh & Vaughan, 1993, p. 3). Grof, for example, discussed his view of transpersonal psychology as involving a temporal-spatial expansion of the self beyond that of the corporeal-physical boundaries of the "skin-encapsulated ego existing in a world of separate beings and objects" (1992, p. 91). After reviewing 37 definitions of transpersonal psychology, Lajoie and Shapiro (1992) concluded they commonly focused on "the study of humanity's highest potential, and with the recognition, understanding, and realization of unitive, spiritual, and transcendental states of consciousness" (p. 91). Braud (1998) aptly described the meanings of "trans" in transpersonal psychology with a metaphor:

> The visible parts of trees in a dense forest seem to be separate entities until one looks beneath the surface of the earth and finds the extensive, interconnected root systems that bind the trees together. The peaks of mountains shrouded in mist seem isolated and unconnected until the mist melts away, revealing the common lower continuities that previously had been obscured. (p. 39)

Congruent with these approaches to transpersonal psychology, I proposed a transpersonal construct called "self-expansiveness" to both describe the potential of personal identity to expand through self-conception and to provide a corresponding empirical method to research the self-concept from such a perspective (Friedman, 1983). This has lead to a number of studies supporting the scientific utility of this construct (e.g., Friedman & MacDonald, 2002; MacDonald, Gagnier, & Friedman, 2000).

I have become increasingly convinced that the human capacity to construct itself in ways that transcend individualistic limitations is salient to addressing Fijian conflicts. Specifically, there are no limits to how we conceptualize ourselves. As we can identify with only our isolated selves, as biological beings, we can also narrowly identify with our allegedly racial or ethnic roots. Alternatively, we can learn to identify in more expansive ways, such as with a sense of national patriotism – which could unify a conflicted nation such as Fiji.

The construct of self-expansiveness also allows understanding how to expand our identity beyond the limits of what is typically understood as the personal self, and even beyond the collective self of national identity, in a way that can have profound implications for peace. The model I developed for understanding this uses space-time cartography. From this approach, individuals can identify in the present with just their own behaviours, thoughts, feelings, and physical bodies, the usual Western sense of isolated self. They can, however, also expand their identification in enlarged or contracted spatial ways. One could manifest an enlarged spatial identification through, for example, embracing others as a component of one's sense of self, as in love, or could manifest a contracted spatial identification through feeling resonant with body parts, such as identifying with one's heart feelings.

Individuals can also expand their identification in temporal ways, through feeling identified with their pasts or with their anticipated futures. When such identification, either spatial or temporal, goes beyond connections with the individual as customarily understood in the West, it may be said to transcend the isolated individual level and enter into a transpersonal domain. Examples of such include identifying with possible future descendants who might be citizens of a unified world or even with the environment as a whole that sustains all life on earth. This transpersonal perspective allows for a way to reframe narrow identifications fueling much of the pain in the world. Consequently, a transpersonal reframing could involve native Fijians and Fijian Indians finding ways of honouring their past identifications, or differences, without rigidly holding on to them, leading to an expanded transpersonal identification which would include but also transcends the more limited identifications.

In the case of Fiji, there are strong extant spiritual traditions, both among the native Fijians who now are mostly Methodist Christian but also adhere to many traditional beliefs (Katz, 1999) and the Fijian Indians who are mostly Hindu, Muslim, and Sikh. These are clearly related to their other prevailing worldviews, including competing economic models, and germane to the nation's conflicts. One clear advantage of a transpersonal perspective is that it could lead to reconciliation based on a scientific integration of religious divisiveness through providing a common ground. Many have called for seeking peace through scientific understandings (e.g., Fliestra, 2002) and some have hypothesized how this could possibly happen (e.g., Burnell, 2002).

Transpersonal psychology has made significant progress in scientifically exploring some areas (e.g., MacDonald & Friedman, 2002) and I have previously suggested how this could occur more broadly, including its potential practical applications to areas such as peace (Friedman, 2002). Cortwright wrote, "Transpersonal psychology is in the unique position of being the only psychological approach to human experience that can be more than just integrative but fully inclusive" (1997, p. 242). Similarly, Krippner (1998) stated, "There is an urgent need in today's fractious world for integrative transpersonal perspectives, especially if presented in ways … able to be linked in contemporary scientific and practical concerns" (pp. x-xi). In this vein, perhaps reframing the most daunting cultural dilemmas into transpersonal perspectives would facilitate the emergence of peace in Fiji.

Conclusion

I have discussed the potential of the psychological technique of reframing for addressing cultural dilemmas in Fiji related to resolving conflicts and achieving peace. I presented my efforts in Fiji to reframe differences widely perceived as based on race and ethnicity into being seen as due to competing economic models, enabling a less divisive discourse to emerge. I also presented what I consider the widest possible lens that can be used to reframe conflicts threatening peace, the transpersonal perspective. When I think about the many current conflicts that are leading to so much suffering, I surmise that it is time to begin to reframe antiquated identifications into more universalistic understandings. I advocate unfreezing and reframing these identifications in ways that support innovative dialogue, equally honoring the narratives of different peoples as both true – but in limited senses that need to be transcended to find a deeper commonality.

The discussion about reframing these dilemmas in Fiji can also apply more broadly. For example, similar conflicts are found in other South Pacific nations (including in Papua New Guinea, the Solomon Islands, and Vanuatu). In addition, conflicts based on similar dynamics also occur in other societies in which the British introduced indentured Indian labourers, such as in Trinidad and Tobago. Finally, perhaps all conflicts that are currently framed as ethnic or racial can be seen in similar ways. Using the Israeli-Palestinian conflict as an example, as long as Israeli Jews somehow see themselves as part of a distinct Jewish state or promised Jewish homeland, they separate themselves from their Palestinian brethren in ways that cannot be sustained, and vice versa. One possible approach is to look for common ground within the divergent Jewish Israeli and Muslim Palestinian views of history and destiny so that each side can come to appreciate the differences of the other.

It is asking a lot, however, to encourage simultaneous belief in contradictory stories or respect for one's story that demeans another's. For example, the current Israeli-Palestinian conflict has been widely seen as due to religious differences, though both sides have essentially the same scriptural base and worship the same deity. Some have argued that the similarities of the traditions should be stressed, for example, through focus on the common agreed upon ancestor, Abraham, to facilitate peace (Biema, 2002). Unfortunately, both traditions interpret Abraham's role in mutually disadvantageous lights. Instead, perhaps an economic reframing of the two traditions might be more useful, similar to what I have used in Fiji. Clearly Westernized Jews who are dominant in Israel have different implicit economic models than the Muslims who are dominant among the Palestinians. Likewise, both sides are economically suffering due to the continuing conflicts – which could provide a powerful motivational basis for accepting such reframing. However, for the most potent reframing of this conflict, I suggest a transpersonal perspective in which both sides can be encouraged to understand a deeper view congruent with the highest teaching of both traditions.

The world is filled with conflicts among peoples who hold on to narrow identifications. In some ways, Fiji is a microcosm of the wider conflicts that are most globally threatening. As an insular nation, it is somewhat less subject to the immediate influences of adjoining nations and, in this sense, I have come to appreciate island nations as natural laboratories for studying phenomena related to social change, particularly involving issues such as social justice, sustainability, and peace – since external influences, though always present, are usually less pressing. Consequently, extrapolating from the methods of reframing I have used in Fiji, and my speculation about the potential worth of reframing into transpersonal perspectives, may have relevance to conflicts elsewhere. It is my hope that reframing in this fashion could lead to reconciliations among those most threatened in our greatly challenged world, namely all of us.

REFERENCES

Biema, D. (2002). *The Legacy of Abraham*. Time, September 30, 64-75.

Bosson, C. (2000). Festival mania, tourism and nation building in Fiji: The case of the Hibiscus Festival, 1956-1970 [Electronic version]. *The Contemporary Pacific*, 12, 123-154.

Braud, W. (1998). Integral inquiry: Complementary ways of knowing, being, and expression. In W. Braud & R. Anderson (Eds.), *Transpersonal Research Methods for the Social Sciences: honoring human experience* (pp. 35-67). Thousand Oaks, CA: Sage Publications.

Brison, K. (2001). Constructing identity through ceremonial language in rural Fiji [Electronic version]. *Ethnology*, 40, 309-327.

Burnell, J. (2002). The peace hypothesis. Science and Spirit, September-October, 37-42.

Cortright, B. (1997). *Psychotherapy and Spirit: Theory and practice in transpersonal psychology*. Albany, NY: State University of New York Press.

Davis, B. & Knowles, E. (1999). A disrupt-then-reframe technique of social influence. *Journal of Personality and Social Psychology*, 76, 192-199.

Ewins, R. (1998). *Changing their Minds: traditions and politics in contemporary Fiji and Tonga*. Christchurch, NZ: MacMillan Brown Center for Pacific Studies.

Finin, G. & Wesley-Smith, T. (2001). More than ethnicity behind Fiji's unrest [Electronic version]. *Population Today*, 29, 10.

Fliestra, R. (2002). World religions seek peace through science. *Research News & Opportunities in Science and Theology*, 3, 1 & 28.

Friedman, H. (1983). The Self-Expansiveness Level Form: A conceptualization and measurement of a transpersonal construct. *Journal of Transpersonal Psychology*, 15, 37-50.

Friedman, H. (2002). Transpersonal psychology as a scientific field. *International Journal of Transpersonal Studies*, 21, 175-187.

Friedman, H., Glover, G., & Avegalio, F. (2002). The burdens of other people's models: A cultural perspective on the current Fiji crisis. *Harvard Asia Pacific Review*, 6, 86-90.

Friedman, H. & MacDonald, D. (eds.) (2002). *Transpersonal Measurement and Assessment*. San Francisco: The Transpersonal Institute, 2002.

Glover, G., Friedman, H., & Jones, G. (2002). Adaptive leadership: When change is not enough—Part One. *Organizational Development Journal*, 20, 15-31.

Grof, S. (1992). *The Holotropic Mind: the three levels of human consciousness and how they shape our minds*. New York: Harper.

Haley, J. (1973). *Uncommon Therapy: the psychiatric techniques of Milton H. Erickson, M.D.*, New York: Norton.

Katz, R. (1999). *The Straight Path of the Spirit: ancestral wisdom and the healing tradition in Fiji*. Rochester, VT: Park Street.

Krippner, S. (1998). Foreword. In D. Rothberg & S. Kelly (Eds.), *Ken Wilber in Dialogue* (pp. ix-xi). Wheaton, IL: Theosophical Publishing House.

Lajoie, D., & Shapiro, S. (1992). Definitions of transpersonal psychology: The first twenty-three years. *Journal of Transpersonal Psychology*, 24, 79-98.

Lewin, K. (1951). Frontiers in group dynamics. In D. Cartwright (Ed.), *Field Theory in Social Science* (pp. 188-237). New York: Harper.

MacDonald, D. & Friedman, H. (2002). Assessment of transpersonal and spiritual constructs: State of the science. *Journal of Humanistic Psychology*, 42,102-125.

MacDonald, D., Gagnier, J., & Friedman, H. (2000). Transpersonal self-concept and the five-factor model of personality: Evidence for a sixth stable dimension of personality. *Psychological Reports*, 86, 707-726.

Norton, R. (2000). Reconciling ethnicity and nation: Contending discourses in Fiji's constitutional reform {Electronic version]. *The Contemporary Pacific,* 12, 83-122.

Segal, L. (2001). Brief psychotherapy. In Corsini, R. (Ed.). *Handbook of InnovativeTherapy* (pp. 86-94). New York: Wiley.

Vallacher, R. & Wegner, D. (1985). *A Theory of Action Identification.* Hillsdale, NJ: Erlbaum.

Van Deusen, C., Mueller, C., Jones, G., & Friedman, H. (2002). A cross-cultural comparison of problem solving beliefs and behaviors: Helping managers understand country differences. *International Journal of Management and Decision Making*, 3, 52-66.

Walsh, R. & Vaughan, F. (1993). On transpersonal definitions. *Journal of Transpersonal Psychology*, 25, 199-207.

Williksen-Bakker, S. (2002). Fijian business—a bone of contention. Was it one of the factors leading to the political crisis of 2000? [Electronic version]. *Australian Journal of Anthropology,* 13, 72-87.

*An earlier version of this chapter was published in the **International Journal of Transpersonal Studies.***

6. THE ART OF ALLOWING ALL-THAT-IS TO WIN

Lisinka Ulatowska

Lisinka looks at the two forces tearing our lives apart – globalization and war in all its aspects. She sees a further, gentler force which has always been there but is not always recognised. It is seen as divine by some and technological by others.

She talks about the evolutionary waltz which dances as an energy change leading first to chaos and then to a new stable pattern. It is a waltz encountered at every leap of creation. We have been dancing it from tribes to cities to nations. Now nations through the force of globalization have to change. The challenge is how we can live together as individuals in a global society of interconnected citizens.

The all-win principle is proposed and this can only exist if people follow their hearts rather than their heads. People throughout history have followed their hearts but the efforts have been thwarted by the centralization of power and hierarchy. From the birth of the International Telecommunications Agency in 1865, global organisations have developed leading eventually to the United Nations and its agencies. It does not have all that much power but it works in an all-win form of decision making.

We can apply the all-win principle to our own lives. Lisinka explains and elaborates on her own personal path and from it deduces a wider opportunity for all-win relationships which will span the globe. She shows how ecosystems, social systems, educational systems and economic systems, business and commerce, national governments – all can form stable all-win rather than win-win partnerships. It is an art which can be learned like writing or singing. An all-win network could be a power for good and perhaps this could be at the top of Maslow's pyramid which is the need for individuation. It is a visionary approach which is all the more important in these days of despair, frustration and concern with the shadow side of life. Many chapters in this book stress the positive aspects of the future, both because saints and sinners have always done this, and also because the downside is pessimism and despair – and after all we have to live our lives positively.

Dr. Lisinka Ulatowska is a transpersonal psychologist and represents three organisations at the United Nations, with which she has been affiliated since 1969 and where for several years she chaired an NGO Task Force on Financing. She taught a student centered approach to Transpersonal Psychology at Columbia Pacific University. In 2001, she organized a conference, Seeds of Wholeness: Science, Systems Spirit which developed a systems approach, which, when applied to the conference process, can help scientists and other participants to communicate transdisciplinarily and transculturally and together to come to grips with complexly interrelated global problems. She received her doctorate from the student centered university, now called the Union University and a Masters from UC Berkeley, both in the USA. Her most recent book, so far published in Dutch under the name, "Samenzwering Samenspel. Naar Spiritueel Wereldburgerschap", shows how the all-win principles can help a global community to emerge. This book, which is accompanied by a World Citizens Handbook (available in English, Dutch, German, and Chinese), has resulted in a number of action groups. An objective is to work with governments at the UN on implementing the all-win principles to education and governance.

Introduction

Two powerful forces seem to be wrenching our lives apart. There is the march towards globalization. In its wake, the second: a whirlwind of chaos and confusion – war, terrorism, crime, depression, burn-out and a snake pit of global problems, which wreak havoc with our personal lives and with the fabric of Nature herself.

Among the ruins left by these two forces, a third one is attempting to emerge. This one is often overshadowed by the other two, for it is gentler. Yet it is equally strong. This third force seeks to find ways in which each woman, child and man can come into her or his own potential, without harming others; in which each plant and animal is revered for its function within the whole and Mother Nature is reinstated as our personal ally as she bestows and transforms life. This third force has existed since the beginning of time. It embraces the two more obvious ones and can, if we let it, bring them to rest. It is particularly useful to get to know this third, gentler force in this period of human development, because the timing is perfect.

I should like to share with you what I am learning about this gentler force, the ways in which it has manifested itself from the beginning of time, and how each of us can tap into it. Some people see it as a divine principle, others as a scientific one. I should like to begin by illustrating it in a simple experiment. Then I shall show how the principle can be applied to our lives.

Seeing Evolutionary Forces at Work – The Evolutionary Waltz

So let's pretend we are in a cinema. The lights go out and on the screen we see a glass container filled with water. Floating on top, layers of different coloured paint. The narrator of the film says: "And now we run an electrical current through the whole at a stable frequency".

Chaos on the screen. Water and different coloured paint mill around in the container. Then out of the chaos we see, as in a kaleidoscope, a pattern emerge. Dots and patches of colour offset one another so that each particle of paint is shown off to perfect advantage. The pattern remains stable.

The narrator says, "And now we change the frequency and so the electrical field in the container changes again." Once more chaos. Then another, quite different pattern appears and becomes stable.

This process is repeated again and again. With every change of frequency, a different pattern emerges. Every time we discern the same three steps:
1. An energy change;
2. Chaos; and
3. A new stable pattern, which emerges out of the chaos, in which each particle of paint is shown to perfect advantage.

The narrator concludes: "I call this the Evolutionary Waltz."

The All-Win Relationship – a Point of Rest in the Dance

Let us look more closely at these three steps. First the energy changes. Second each particle of paint is thrown into confusion. And then, propelled from within, each particle finds its own place into a whole different set of relationships with all other particles in the container. Some blotches of red go to one part of the pattern, others to quite different parts. Each particle of paint knows its new place in the emerging pattern. It is a movement determined from within the individual particle. Not imposed from the outside.

As this second step stabilizes, we notice that each particle has found its way into a constellation of relationships which allow it to shine in individual splendour and at the same time it brings out the inherent beauty in each other particle of paint. Each of these new associations of all the particles of paint can be called all-win relationships. An all-win relationship is one in which each part benefits from its association with all others. All win relationships are for (they benefit) all and are against (harm) none.

In the third and final step the pattern completes itself. Each particle comes into its own and through its very existence allows all others to come into their own. The final pattern is dynamic because it is brought forth by the promptings from deep in each particle. It is also stable because it is based on the self interest of all the parts. Finally this governing pattern allows the whole to be much greater than the sum of the parts. And it tends to remain stable until new influences from outside once again change the energy.

Patterns that have evolved according to these three steps from the beginning of time have often been stable for millennia. Examples are: the solar systems and galaxies; atoms and molecules; and the cell. The cell has remained the building block of life from when it first emerged, even though it is constantly combining with other cells to form the most extravagant bacterial, plant and animal types, it remains a basic building block of life.

We encounter the evolutionary waltz at every leap creation makes, starting with the big bang, followed by the formation of mass into regular solar systems and galaxies, then as we move from mass to life and every time a new species is born; and now as the human species is attempting to become one harmonious whole.

At Which Phase is Humanity in its Evolutionary Waltz?

Human beings have been dancing this evolutionary waltz as they moved from tribes to cities to nations. With each new form of community, there was a change of atmosphere as the expansion took place, followed by chaos as new forms of living together were worked out. Such communities remained stable to the degree they emerged out of the innermost desires of its citizens and served all citizens. In other words, they were based on all-win relationships.

Now, nations are forming into a global community. The forces of globalization are at work. We find ourselves in the chaos/confusion phase with the final governing pattern seeking to emerge. Our challenge: to discover a way of living together as one humanity in which each person can come into her or his own and where each of us can be nurtured by the relationships we are in. In other words, we are being challenged to apply the all-win principle. If we work with the all-win principle at this crucial point in our evolution, where the human species is becoming a global community, we are working in harmony with the forces of evolution and Mother Nature herself.

The All-Win Principle and our Daily Lives

This movement toward a unity by which all that is wins exists only because individual people, like you and I, follow our hearts, our innermost urges, and each in our own way allow our full passion for life to speak. When we follow our hearts, we feel happy, creative and are in touch with our whole potential. In other words we are functioning from our point of greatest personal power.

As we feel centred in our own greatest strength, we feel alive and grateful and want others to experience the same sense of joy. This prompts us to create relationships based on the all-win principle, each of us, of course, implementing it in our own personal surroundings. As a parent, for instance, we have a deep effect on the lives of each family member. Here our challenge is to discover ways in which each can follow her or his own life's path without stunting others in the process. Others seek to implement the all-win principle as teachers, lawyers, gardeners. Each one of us can do it in our own field. Since the all-win principle sets out to allow all to follow their own hearts, we find ourselves surrounded by people who are grateful for our support and who often, in return, want to support us in following our innermost yearnings. All-win relationships are self-perpetuating.

The Emerging Governing Pattern

Throughout the ages people have followed their hearts, so humanity has become inter-linked in myriad ways through a dance of letters, telephone calls, emails, and networks within which cars, boats and planes flit around, weaving a cocoon of communication threads. This has changed the energy on our Planet. Each of us experiences this by the greater intensity with which activities take place and our growing numbers of connections.

In this dance, larger and larger constellations of people have formed, until in 1865, with the birth of the International Telecommunications Union (ITU), governments created the first global organisation. This was followed in 1885 by the World Postal Union. These both became part of the United Nations (UN) after its birth in 1945. Now the UN helps to coordinate and regulate all issues that transcend national borders. The UN helps to make it possible for people to work or be educated in foreign countries, to combat epidemics, to salvage cultural sites which are of value to the whole of humanity and to gather global statistics. The UN deals with all issues that go beyond national borders and are therefore beyond the capacity of any one government to deal with.

The United Nations is emerging as a governing pattern, the most comprehensive one that exists. It is a response to the connections we forge. At the same time, it makes it possible for new connections to form at a dizzying rate. The United Nations has very little power in an outer sense: no army, a whole batch of agreements and laws, but very few means to enforce them. Its central organ, the General Assembly, makes around 85% of its decision by consensus. This is in essence an all-win form of decision making. The United Nations, like any evolutionary governing pattern, exists by virtue of all-win relationships. It will reach its full potential when each person follows her or his heart and empowers others to do the same.

The United Nations Universal Declaration of Human Rights

The United Nations has many tools which we can use. In 1948, for instance, it adopted the Universal Declaration of Human Rights, which lists the rights and freedoms which make it possible to develop our full personality while encouraging others to do the same. The 30 articles of the Universal Declaration of Human Rights apply to every child, woman and man on Earth. It is moreover incorporated into most countries' legal machineries. There, unfortunately, our human rights are too often ignored, because many do not know these fundamental rights and freedoms exist, and those that do ignore them. It would be very hard for those who want to suppress or discount others to do so be it politically, economically or through social status, if each of us were used to standing up for our rights.

Applying the All-Win Principle to our own Lives

When we discover the force that makes our hearts sing, creativity is unleashed that we never suspected existed, and with this we come into our greatest strength. I first discovered this inner capacity when, at 23, my first husband died and life as I knew it came to an end. For a couple of days I lived in a highly sensitive state in which I saw how everything and everyone was interconnected by energy streams which affected their every movement. Later I discovered that this Zero Point field had been discovered by Professor Hal Puthoff. Usually invisible, it has become a concept which modern science is increasingly working with. When I discovered it experientially, it became clear that observing the level of my own physical/mental and spiritual energy was a way of discovering how to develop my fullest potential.

This is how it works for me:

Where possible, I allow myself to follow my innermost urges by, for instance, eating a certain food, reading an article or a book that catches my eye, cultivating a new friendship, or just doing something that feels good. As I allow myself to follow hunches, sensings, gut feelings, I notice that some actions increase my energy. They make me feel as if I am plugging into some Universal energy field. Yet other actions deaden me. There is no outer rule I can apply. Sometimes even eating a pound of dark chocolate with nuts and raisins, or spending an evening just zapping in front of the television might actually make me feel more energized, even though these actions more often than not have the opposite effect. As I develop the art of following my heart, I notice that I am led into situations and relationships which are deeply nourishing. All-win relationships have a way of spreading from one person to another. My own life is embedded in a network of all-win relationships that spans the globe.

I am convinced that, as more and more of us find one another in all-win relationships, the governing pattern that is trying to emerge from within us all and is expressing itself in the activities in the United Nations will finally come to rest in its point of greatest stability.

Our Challenge as Human Beings

Unlike other animals, human beings have the ability to ignore their innermost urges and so the all-win phase and governing pattern is having difficulty in uniting human beings. There is a danger that instead of breaking through, the all-win governing pattern will break down and that humanity as we know it will cease to exist.

All-win relationships exist wherever we look. From the cells in the body where each cell is able to function because it is nurtured by all others, as well as the body as a whole. There are ecosystems where plants and animals provide habitat, food and the means for one another to thrive and procreate in dynamic yet stable relationships, and these are embraced by the systems of nature where wind, sun, soil, water and air allow systems within systems to nourish and embrace one another.

Beside natural systems there are also ones which have been created by human beings: systems of roads, air and waterways, educational, economic, political, cultural and social systems. All these are effective to the degree they are based on all-win principles.

Businesses that have overemphasised the bottom line in order to survive are now contending with absenteeism, burn-out, and cut-throat competition. They are realizing that unless human beings are given the possibility to express the fullness of who they are, the business will be eroded from the inside as well as swallowed up by more powerful mammoths. Powerful organisations which have breached the all-win principle are increasingly running into difficulties.

Many organisations, be they businesses, local and national governments, as well as the United Nations itself are now looking to their employees or constituents to provide a creative life force. They use tools such as Open Space meetings where everyone, from cleaners to directors, from clients to providers are invited to work at fashioning the business in ways that would work better for them.

In the United Nations, Secretary General Kofi Annan has developed a Global Compact whereby businesses undertake to obey and enforce nine international agreements. In so doing, they tend to diffuse the wrath of anti-globalizationists and win the goodwill of customers.

Some schools include their students in policy decisions. Others teach young students peaceful conflict resolution. In Berkeley in a couple of Montessori schools, for instance, children as young as 6 years old are given the tools to resolve their own conflicts in all-win ways. When a conflict erupts the students concerned are invited to sit on the peace carpet outside the room, after each choosing a fellow student as support. Together the little group will solve the conflict among themselves. In the meantime the teacher and the rest of the class are free to continue the lesson. The conflicting parties are welcomed back once they have resolved the issues. And so students, teacher and school benefit and so does society, because along with reading and writing students learn the skills of all-win relationship, the tools to build a dynamic, stable human community.

Forming Stable All-win Relationships

There is much talk about win/win relationships and "doing as thou wouldst be done by". These are each important first steps. The Evolutionary Waltz and the three steps of the All-Win Principle show that we are working with a larger process, which comes to rest once the individual parts (people) have evolved all-win relationships with everyone in a specific situation and an over all governing pattern has emerged. So when working with the concept of all-win, it is important to see that all steps are honoured.

Tools at our Disposal

Religious, Cultural and Spiritual Disciplines

The all-win relationship is an art that can be learned, like writing or singing. Once a simple vocabulary (say the word, all-win) is commonplace and the simple three step process is understood, then a vast range of resources become available to us.

The Evolutionary Waltz and the three steps of the all-win principle can be seen as the grammar of durable relationships, while the wealth of different approaches, theories, disciplines and tools, developed by religions, cultures and spiritual organisations can be seen as the languages which help us scale the heights and plumb the depths of relationships, which work. If the wealth of existing theories and approaches could be understood in terms of this grammar, they would be come more easily accessible and people would find it easier to assess them and then make a choice.

Life would be more harmonious if every child learned the art of all-win relating along with reading, writing and arithmetic at school.

Summary of Tools

We each have many tools at out disposal:
• First and foremost: our own inner knowing which in many cases we must learn to respect
• Our ability to determine what gives and what deadens energy
• The outline above about how the process works: the
  Evolutionary Waltz and the three steps of the all-win relationship itself
• Our ability to nurture the emerging unity which seeks to bring us together through the all-win aspects of the United Nations

- There are a myriad of people and organisations dedicated to one or all aspects of this process. Working with others who are exploring an all-win way of life provides us with nourishment, strength, insight and support
- Learning to discriminate between which of these learning situations is best suited for our person and fully honours the process as a whole is a part of learning the art of all-win relationship
- And finally, the United Nations Universal Declaration of Human Rights.

The All-Win Network

The All-Win Network promotes the all-win concept. It consists of people and organisations who are dedicated to fostering the all-win principle in human relations. At present it is collecting examples of all-win relationships, all-win problem solving tools and all-win solutions to common problems as a resource for anyone who can use them. They are also collecting a listing of organisations, approaches to education, examples of curriculum and names of organisations which are dedicated to the all-win principle so that others can benefit from what they have to offer.

The All-Win Network offers lectures and workshops on the all-win principle and is beginning to develop a network of think tanks. These think tanks consist of people who wish to gain mastery of the all-win principle for their own personal lives and work and in some cases also to help Governmental representatives at the United Nations become more familiar with the uses and advantages of the all-win approach. At UN conferences, representatives of the All-Win Network work for a part with governments directly and for a part at a distance via think tanks connecting to the UN via email. You are welcome to join this action. This All-Win network can be reached via its web site, www.allwinnetwork.org. Or via its Secretariat, Zweerslaan 31, NL 3723 HN Bilthoven, the Netherlands. Tel/Fax +31 (0)30 228 6173.

A Deep Need for All

Abraham Maslow, an influential psychologist, designed a hierarchy of needs. At the top of the pyramid was the need for "individuation", which we could describe as a need for personal development by following our own hearts. At humanity's present phase of evolution, we notice that a new need has emerged: the need to help the whole of humanity to transform itself into a global community based on the all-win principle. Once this is achieved, people's desire to follow their hearts and live in all-win relationships will become more commonplace.

7. THE IDEA OF A SPIRITUAL UNIVERSITY

John Drew

John describes the history of the university in Europe and how we have reached the twofold crisis of today. He is not concerned here with the important issues of funding, communicating, regulating, educating and training at different levels. His theme is the more fundamental issue of the role of the university in matters of wisdom, spirituality and values.

His experience of working with managers on personal development leads him to discuss the growing awareness and acceptance of new responses to the profound changes of the next decade. His concept is of the Three Circles which surround our economic, social and inner lives. A closer and more sensitive integration of the Three Circles could be a responsive framework to these challenges.

He suggests that the spiritual and ethical vacuum of our Western society is particularly evident in our universities. Traditional role models no longer provide a relevant framework as they did when Cardinal Newman and Humboldt helped bring about the reform of Universities in Europe in the 19th Century. This vacuum is being partly filled through the rebirth of a personal, (transpersonal?) and spiritual dimension to our lives. It is random and uncoordinated, but could lead to individuals becoming responsible for their own personal and inner development.

Universities could again provide a framework for discussing the issues of how economic, social/family and inner values are better integrated in the interests of society as well as the individual. How can the spiritual aspect return to university life? Could universities help bring spirituality, transpersonal values, planetary and environmental concerns back into the mainstream of teaching and research? The aim would be to help students acquire broad and cross-disciplinary wisdom to address these fundamental societal issues.

John links these thoughts to the pioneering work of a wide variety of organisations and in particular refers to the creative and informational work described by Janice Dolley in Chapter 8.

***Professor John Drew** works with groups and individuals on their personal and spiritual development through the integration of their economic, family and personal lives. A former President of EUROTAS, he is a Council Member of the Centre for Transpersonal Pychology. He was a UK and European diplomat and director of a multinational company. He has held professorial posts and written extensively on European Management in UK and foreign universities.*

"All who have meditated on the art of governing mankind have been convinced that the fate of the world depends on the education of youth"

Aristotle, 384-322 BC

The University in History

Universities originated in the 12th and 13th centuries in Europe in such places as Bologna, Paris, Oxford, Padua and Naples. They were created by those seeking truth and practical training, free from external, especially ecclesiastical, domination and control. They often replaced institutions such as the monastic schools and were committed to teaching, study and the pursuit of knowledge and truth.

The Early Modern University developed between 1500 and 1800 and was differentiated by a significant change in spatio-temporal awareness. The present was seen as 'new' relative both to Antiquity and the Middle Ages and was exemplified by empirical observation in the sciences, the emergence of the ideals of civility and civilisation and their recognition, often formally by the civil authorities, as places where knowledge was concentrated. While their purpose became more defined in terms of initiation into life, professional training and leadership, their curricula adapted to a changing world of experiment, critical examination and new advances in mathematics and physics. They became a network across Europe and also part of a wider higher education system, with emphasis on faculties and college communities.

The Late Modern University which developed in the Eighteenth and Nineteenth centuries was characterised by increasing state interest, dissociation from theological orthodoxy and concern for the totality of knowledge, the combination of research and teaching and considerations of competitive examinations and rising standards of teaching.

Two great reformers of the Nineteenth Century, Wilhelm von Humboldt in Germany and Cardinal Newman in England, had a profound influence, both enabling modern changes to our traditional universities and facilitating the emergence of new universities in the late Nineteenth and early Twentieth centuries.

Our Universities in Europe are direct descendants of this span of eight hundred years. They face two problems as they seek to adapt to a world which is changing faster than ever before in history. My concern here is not the first problem, important though it is for society - funding, communicating, regulating, providing and encouraging education and training at different levels and at different times in people's lives. It is rather with the second more fundamental issue about the role of the University in matters of wisdom and ethics.

The Three Circles and the Idea of a University

Before discussing values, may I introduce you to the Three Circles? They are relevant to us all and relevant to the changes Universities will need to make during the next decades.

I work with managers on their personal development. My thesis is: a deeper awareness and a different approach to personal development may be required to respond to the profound changes the next decades will bring to the Three Circles of our economic, social and inner lives. A closer and more sensitive integration of them will be necessary to respond to the challenges of these changing times.

We can be certain of few things except death, taxes and, during the next ten years, rapid, dramatic and often unforeseen changes in European and global civilization. These changes will be more condensed in their impact than at any other watershed of history.

Our civilization is paradoxically becoming at the same time more global and more individual. This leads to a two way tugging at our national roots – in one direction by steps towards European and global government and in the other by the demands of local communities and individuals for greater freedom of action. We experience the steps towards European and global government with the development of the Single European Market, the Euro and the growing importance of the United Nations, the World Trade Organisation, the International Monetary Fund and the World Bank.

There are three circles in our lives:

The first is the economic or earnings circle, the second, the social circle which includes friends and family and the third is our personal circle which may also be spiritual and which is what we are really about on this sparrow's flight from the cradle to the grave.

Many of us find that the economic circle squeezes up the other two. Yet many managers are seeking permission to debate the "soft" subjects of management – personal development, ethical responsibility, creativity, innovation and intuition, while continuing of course to seek new ideas in the "harder" subjects such as strategy, financial control, accounting, marketing, information technology and production. What has brought about this sea change?

Some argue we have explored our outer world during the Second Millennium and we need to explore more our inner world during the Third. We now accept ideas such as artists in residence in financial corporations, poets working with top management in multinational companies such as Boeing, of the verse of Irish poets woven into the fabric of aircraft seats on Aer Lingus. The President of Coca-Cola recently laid out his own personal beliefs and inner development to the whole of his corporation worldwide. Some organisations are encouraging yoga and meditation for stress relief and to improve creativity among their managers.

How to explain this gradual change in attitude to the three circles? Even Chancellor Kohl failed to forecast the fall of the Berlin Wall and the subsequent collapse of communism was as unforeseeable as is much of our future. We are hurtling in three decades into a new information, communications and technology based civilisation. Our society is becoming global while individuals seek freedom to develop their personal agendas uncluttered by the restrictive laws and customs of the past.

We demand freedom, which also means choice. Since the earliest times, we discovered our gods in animals, trees and rivers and our beliefs in the mysteries of the universe or buried in the shadow side of our souls. Over the last two thousand years, the great faith religions with their scriptural traditions – Judaic, Christian, Islamic –– have proclaimed universal and eternal truths. They integrated and largely replaced the village gods of antiquity. The Enlightenment during the Eighteenth Century led to a gradual and partial revision of traditional religious attitudes caused by developments in the natural sciences, the growth of historical understanding and the widespread acceptance of critical thinking. Its effect has been to erode the influence of traditional religions, leading to individual disappointment, disenchantment and dispossession.

Our role models – the family, the church, the state, work groups, schools, universities and others have weakened as sources of authority. This vacuum is being filled by the rebirth of a personal, sometimes spiritual dimension in our lives. It is random and uncoordinated at this stage, but could lead to individuals attempting to better organise, direct and take responsibility for their own personal management and inner development. Increasingly we shall need to look to our own values and those we perceive for society.

How can we as individuals respond to these challenges? We cannot just walk away from them. Perhaps we should try to understand more the nature of change, to have some effect on the unfolding of events through studying the past, understanding the present and seeking a framework to discuss the future. We need to widen and deepen the debate and to thicken the thin veneer of the managerial stratum of society, which Jung described as: "fairly intelligent, mentally stable, moral and moderately competent – but do not overestimate its thickness". We can work on closer integration of our economic, social and personal spheres so that they look more like this:

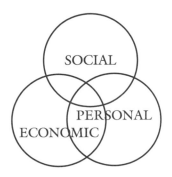

We need to understand the components of each circle and how they might vary from one part of the world to another and from one organisation, one individual, to another.

- Economic Circle: National – European – Global
- Social Circle: Family – Friends – Professional Contacts
- Personal Circle: Health – Values – Inner Self – Spiritual Self

Perhaps spirituality lies at the intersection of these circles. Understanding change, widening the debate and thickening the veneer would go some way to managing that part of the future that we can influence. Rather like the tennis player awaiting a serve, we must train to be on our toes. The future is careering towards us like the serve coming over the net. We do not know at what speed it will be delivered or whether with top or back spin it will swerve to left or right. Being aware and keeping mentally on our toes would give us a better chance of managing change. St. Exupery wrote in The Wisdom of the Sands: "As for the future, your task is not to foresee, but to enable it".

Tolstoy suggested that all philosophy and life could be reduced to two statements: "how to live and what to live for." It may be that we, in the materially richer countries, are beginning to understand the "how to live aspects" which leaves the "what to live for" uppermost. This is relevant as we look at the changes which must take place in our concept of the University

The Idea of a Spiritual University: Do We Need It?

In his Preface to "The Idea of a University" Cardinal Newman states his aims and values for the university which: "is a place of teaching universal knowledge. This implies that its object is, on the one hand, intellectual, not moral; and, on the other, that it is the diffusion and extension of knowledge rather than the advancement." Newman did not want moral issues to be discussed at universities because he saw this function as the role of the Catholic Church. He continues: "If its object were scientific and philosophical discovery, I do not see why a University should have students; if religious training, I do not see how it can be the seat of literature and science." … "it cannot fulfill its object … without the Church's assistance." Newman wrote for an age when the Church was one of the great pillars of society and Universities another.

This was fine in Catholic Ireland where his first five lectures were given. The world is wider now. We may need to study other religions – Judaism, Islam, Hinduism and Buddhism, for example, and perhaps equally important other formal and informal associations concerned with the inner self, which may help us to better understand our values and spiritual dimension. If we agree with Newman that universities are concerned with the intellect and their role is the diffusion and extension of knowledge, then should not considerations of spirituality, morality and citizenship be part of what a university means and even commands through its courses and examinations? A university should not tell us what to do, but it should provide the knowledge and teaching to help us strive towards wisdom.

Over the last century the faith traditions have not played the central role that Newman envisaged for them. Our role models – the family, the faith traditions, the state and others groupings and associations – have weakened as sources of moral guidance and authority. Peer groups, the media, mega-stars through mass communication have become important influences. We lack serious forums for the discussion of personal and citizenship issues.

There is a spiritual and ethical vacuum in many parts of our Western society. The conditions which existed in Newman's day no longer appertain as none of the traditional role models provide an effective and relevant framework as he hoped they would do. This vacuum is being partly filled by the rebirth of a personal, often spiritual and sometimes ethical dimension. It is random and uncoordinated, but could lead to individuals attempting to better take responsibility for their own personal management and inner development.

Could universities provide such a framework? How can economic and social/family and inner issues come together in the interests of individuals and society? Can we bring the spiritual (not necessarily the religious) back into university life? Could we ask universities to take into their teachings the study of spirituality, of the transpersonal, of ethics, of concern for the planet and the environment? Newman perhaps did not distinguish sufficiently between religion and spirituality. He and others encouraged the detachment of religion from universities, little realising that spiritual and moral issues might also find themselves left drifting in space.

Mary Warnock in *"An Intelligent Person's Guide to Ethics."* (Duckworth 1998): "I want to try to show that ethics is not only possible, but essential to our lives...we can and must interest ourselves in handing on, from one generation to the next the idea of ethics ... The morality that lies behind all efforts to improve things in the world at large, to defend human rights, to pass generally acceptable laws, to seek peace and justice, is essentially that of private standard-setting and of private ideals to be pursued." What she is saying is that ethics and spirituality are personal. What I am saying is that if they are personal, then a context must be found for addressing them and that context could be the university.

I have discussed the history of universities, my approach of the Three Circles to respond to the growing number of people reflecting on their work/life balance and my concerns that universities no longer see their role in spiritual and ethical terms. Things could change and a university based on fundamental spiritual concepts could return as both scientists and mystics approach spirituality from different sides even thought the spirituality is the same.

The Idea of a Spiritual University: What is Being Done?

My thesis is that there is a spiritual vacuum which has occurred as a result of religion being taken out of the university context, because it was felt in the 19th Century that it was stifling the growth of intellect in universities. Newman and others thought that religion, especially the Catholic religion, would continue to influence the University through a faith tradition as they had done in the past. Perhaps matters were changed by the failure of faith traditions to change their style, more than their content

As a result we find ourselves at the beginning of a new millennium without a coherent spiritual framework, and this during decades of the most profound changes in society the world has ever experienced. Many attempts are being made to fill the vacuum, but they are uncoordinated. Some stem from our deepest spiritual beliefs and feelings, sometimes they grow out of existing religions, others take the best from different religions, but in a world where small is beautiful and decentralisation and delegation are the key words, it is difficult for what is becoming a widespread and wide felt movement to be recognised for what it is – a possible change in our attitudes to the individual and to society and citizenship.

Sir George Trevelyan followed a mystical path from being an agnostic to becoming one of the leading visionaries of the 20th century. In the early days of his journey he said: "It is very clear that many minds are now questing for deeper meaning and a new understanding of the great oneness of life ... we may in a true sense be preparing for what might be called a ' University of the Spirit.' "

Across Europe there are a growing number of mostly small organisations which are reacting against the 'culture of accountability' with its emphasis on vocational and technological competence, with teachers as technical enforcers and testers of centrally determined teaching regimes. They believe in the need to bring into education such qualities as development of human consciousness, spiritual intelligence, a holistic and integrated world view which includes awareness of spirit, spiritually based values and ethics, inner- or self-directed and self-organised. They are seeking to discuss a context for education within the journey of life, the soul's journey or perhaps the hero's journey and of course not only at University level. These qualities encompass such aspects as love, empowerment, mutual support, the transpersonal context, holism, self-reflection and faith as reflected in ethics and values.

These concerns and what is being done about them are described in Janice Dolley's Chapter 8. While none of the initiatives is large, perhaps they should not be. Small is beautiful as we hope the EUROTAS London Conference was. The President of EUROTAS in Poland, Tanna Jacubowicz-Mount quotes: "When we drop our little mind like a stone into vast and quiet waters, the stone will disappear in the depths, but the circles will grow ever larger." Charles Handy in his book, *The Empty Raincoat*: "Change comes from small initiatives which work; initiatives which imitated become the fashion. We cannot wait for great visions from great people for they are in short supply at the end of history. There is a role and perhaps a duty for every one of us".

So what is the way forward as we begin to look at the idea of a spiritual university? It might well involve functions such as:

1. Developing new and incorporating existing programmes to provide opportunities for learning about 'spirit' and 'spirituality'.
2. Influencing mainstream education to bring in spiritual values.
3. Informing, researching, guiding and mentoring
4. Quality controlling – recognition, accreditation and co-ordination of efforts. Use of the internet for communication,
5. Developing the concept globally
6. Ensuring that the vision is developed and the co-ordination sustained
7. Keeping the idea of a university for the spirit embryonic with simple structures, to enable resolution, avoiding codified standards and restrictive committees

Our discussion at EUROTAS in London involved seeking to work towards a culture that sees inner development as important, recognises there is a conjunction of eastern and western approaches – of the rational analytical and the imaginative intuitive; crosses traditional disciplinary boundaries; encourages the spiritual and ethical dimensions of all activities; is wide ranging in its choices; is non-hierarchical in structure and that helps people find their own spiritual path. The interface with mainstream religions needs careful thought. Partnerships and collaborative efforts are fundamental.

The Way Ahead

There seem to be three ways ahead for the idea of a spiritual university:

1. Encourage the successors of Newman and Humboldt to discuss the issues and take a lead.
2. Collect and disseminate the work already being done by different organisations and individuals, so they recognise they are not alone.
3. Encourage the development of the ethical and spiritual aspects of university teaching and learning.

Jean Monnet, one of the founding fathers of Europe, said: "Europe se fait par des petits pas" and it is true even more so for European spirituality, that it will be made by small steps.

8. SPIRIT OF LEARNING: SOUL IN EDUCATION

Janice Dolley

Janice Dolley begins by reflecting on her experiences at recent 'Soul in Education' conferences that reflect a new spirit in education to match the inner aspirations of a new generation of children. The impulse behind these conferences goes back to the 1960s and early 1970s, which saw the founding of the Open University and the establishment of the Findhorn Community and Sir George Trevelyan's Wrekin Trust. These initiatives encouraged a more feminine and intuitive approach to knowledge and development.

More recent manifestations of this unfolding movement are the self-development course called 'The Quest – Exploring a Sense of Soul', the Soul in Education meetings already mentioned and the community formed by the University for Spirit Forum. The educational field is putting up its own new shoots with Human Scale Education, home schooling and Education Otherwise along with other initiatives for young people like WYSE (World Youth Service Enterprise). Janice's vision is for the rivers of religion and education to flow into new forms based on a more subtle perception and understanding of reality.

__Janice Dolley__ was a lecturer at the Open University for 30 years and is now the Executive Director of ther Wrekin Trust and co-ordinator of its key project - the 'University for Spirit Forum'. She was a co-founder of the 'Soul in Education' international series of conferences, co-founder of the Bridge Trust and CANA (Christians Awakening to a New Awareness) and trustee of both the Findhorn Foundation and WYSE International. She is co-author of 'The Quest – Exploring a Sense of Soul' *and of* 'Christian Evolution; Moving towards a Global Spirituality' *and is currently working on a book on death, dying and the continuity* *of consciousness. Her grandchildren bring her delight and a passion for engaging with the learning needs of the young generation.*

Introduction – Education for the Soul

A casual visitor to any of the international conferences on 'Soul in Education' might ask why so many people travel so far, at their own expense, to meet others and share ideas for several days, much as they did to the EUROTAS Conference in August 2004 that inspired this book Several answers spring to mind.

A first answer might be a growing awareness that we are living in rapidly changing times as a new world is now arising from the increasingly crumbling ashes of the old. Those who are waking up to this view ahead of the majority have often been labelled weird or heretical, and hence feel isolated in a society still bent on "getting & spending – forgetting much of nature that is ours". We gain strength by joining up and sharing ideas and learning in a supportive community. We find we share a vision of another way and by linking our own networks to other networks we can encourage each other to *"become the change we want to see in the world"* (Gandhi).

A second answer might be that they, or their children, shared the anguish of our youngest daughter who cried every night for the first few weeks at Secondary School, *"Mummy, the teachers don't know anything"*. Of course, they knew about biology, history, mathematics, but, *"They don't know about things that matter and they don't see me; they just want to open my head & stuff facts in"*. Her plight has been explained more clearly by Flavio Cobobianco who was born in the early 1980s in Argentina and in his book, "Vengo del Sol"[1] wrote, *"New children are being born, they are different human beings, although they don't look different. I am just one of them, one of the first ones. Humanity is changing. The connection with the spiritual world becomes more open. All children can now maintain the one-ness with their essence"*.

New world views, new children, yet an education that has retrogressed into a straightjacket of old views, old approaches and constant quantification of things the teachers know but the children do not see as important to learn. What they yearn for instead is a soul-based approach to the things that matter: the inner needs of their deeper selves, or souls. Yes, they need the 3R's and vocational and professional training, but they also need the inner laws of the 'game' on planet earth – the universal laws of nature and spirit, the values for well-being and happiness and how to create a culture of love. For lack of this approach it is no wonder, perhaps, that a recent survey[2] has shown that in the last 25 years the emotional and behavioural disorders of 15-year-olds have doubled. We also know that the second largest killer of young people, after road deaths, is suicide. As one journalist has put it:

> *"Childhood has been infected by a highly supervised managerialism loaded with targets and statistics – developmental outcomes, tests, league tables – and perhaps we need to put back centre stage an old dream: happy children. What is just as important as a clutch of exam certificates is their emotional resilience to deal with what life will throw at them. It's a troubling possibility that our teenagers are like the canaries they used to take down the mines to detect gas. Their acting-up is acting out a much bigger problem."[3]*

The young bear out Wordsworth's assertion, *"Trailing clouds of glory"* do we come from God who is our home and whilst *"heaven lies about us in our infancy, shades of the prison house begin to close upon the growing boy"*. This process seems to be a natural aspect of an earthly incarnation, but modern pressures seem to have speeded up this closing down beyond one which is naturally sustainable. Deep down young people still have a connection with: *"The Soul that rises with us, our life's star"* but so often find their parents and teachers seem more like those in Martin Armstrong's "The Cage".

> *"Man, half afraid to be alive,*
> *Shuts his Soul in senses five . . . . .*
> *Ah, how safely barred is he*
> *From menace of Eternity."*

Young people are aware of a multi-dimensional world amidst so many of the older generation "shut in by senses five". One young person told me she has seen angels since she was young and described their response to the singing in the opening ceremony at the conference in Budapest we were attending. But she hasn't yet 'come out' about this. No wonder, perhaps, that so many people are keen to come together to seek ways to build a spiritual foundation for learning so that the next generation may be equipped to face the challenges they have inherited and build a sustainable future for a caring and sharing global family.

His- and Her-Story

Since the Sixties there have been signs that some people, young and old, have been seeking a new way of understanding and living in our world that is both spiritual and sustainable.

"It's still a question of story. We are in trouble now because we do not have a good story. We are in between stories. The old story, the account of how we might fit into it, is no longer effective, yet we have not learned the new story."

Thomas Berry *(Dream of the Earth)*

The new story will not just be his-story, it will also be her-story, i.e. it is from the wellspring of intuition – from inner knowing through insight and heart connection that the new 'story' is now being more clearly articulated. It is the feminine aspect of ourselves, silenced for so long in the face of a prevailing cognitive and over-structured approach to learning, which is affirming that new knowledge often arises first in an inner way and is then affirmed and shaped by research, study and intelligent discourse. When the Open University received its Charter in 1969, the then Chancellor, Lord Crowther, declared:

"It has been said that there are two aspects of education, both necessary. One regards the individual human mind as a vessel of varying capacity, into which is to be poured as much as it will hold of the knowledge and experience by which human society lives and moves. This is the Martha of education – and we shall have plenty of these tasks to perform. But the Mary regards the human mind more as a fire that has to be set alight and blown with the divine efflatus. That also we take as our ambition . . ."

This twin vision inspired those of us who joined the staff of the Open University in those innovative early days when subjects were studied in an inter-disciplinary style curricula and academic tutoring was combined with educational counselling – the cognitive and affective coming together in a 'confluent' way to bring both intellectual development and personal transformation. But under economic and political pressures "shades of the prison house" often hem in growing institutions much as they do the "growing boy". And whilst the Open University continues to bring inspiring learning opportunities to so many some of this early vision seems to have given way under economic and other pressures. The models it pioneered may well be taken up elsewhere in different forms.

As the new story emerges more clearly from the wellspring of intuition – from inner knowing through insight and heart connection – it is now being more clearly articulated. It is the feminine aspect of ourselves, silenced for so long in the face of a prevailing cognitive and over-structured approach to learning which is affirming that new knowledge often arises first in an inner way and is then affirmed and shaped by research, study and intelligent discourse.

One place where new knowledge has first arisen in an inner way is at the Findhorn Foundation in Scotland. Since the Sixties it has been offering thousands of people each year an educational experience that raises consciousness and helps them to embody spiritual qualities in their lives. For forty years the Foundation's aim has been *"to discover and demonstrate a new vision of the divine potential in each of us; to help answer the hunger in humanity for new ideas and concepts that are positive, constructive, uplifting and demonstrably practical through having been lived and proven in action".* They find that by offering an opportunity for people to spend time in silence to connect with their deeper selves and to share with others at the level of the transpersonal they re-discover a sense of their souls and reconnect with the inner world they knew as children, before they were shut in "by senses five".

Early Initiatives

Both the Open University and the Findhorn Foundation were inspired and initiated during the spiritual wave that flowed through the Sixties. At the same time Sir George Trevelyan was pioneering the introduction of spiritual themes into the residential programmes at Attingham Park in Shropshire where he was Warden. These attracted such large numbers of students that when he retired he set up The Wrekin Trust – an educational charity – to continue the work. His conviction was that *"We are in the second Renaissance. In the first, our ancestors explored the seas and discovered new Continents. In this present age, we are setting out to explore the cosmos and reality."* For about twenty years about ten thousand people a year from diverse disciplines and viewpoints studied leading edge topics in a non sectarian way and in 1982 the Wrekin Trust received a Right Livelihood Award for its work *"forming an essential contribution to making life more whole, healing our planet and uplifting humanity".*

Realising that the "new story" will not just drop on us like a comet from the skies but is for us, humanity, to envision and create, pioneers emerged from amongst those learning from these earlier initiatives so that by the time of the millennium a second wave of initiatives was under way.

One of these initiatives that is part of our shared exploration for a 'new story' is "The Quest – Exploring a Sense of Soul". This started with a small group from the Open University, with a background in writing inter-active open learning materials, coming together with a small group from the Findhorn Foundation to share their own versions of the emerging "story." Eventually "The Quest" was written by an independent group in collaboration with the Findhorn Foundation, The Quest (www.thequest.org.uk)

has provided a framework for individuals and groups to explore a growing sense of Soul. People find that it helps them to "dig deep within" to "develop my own individual spiritual awareness and an opportunity to share that journey with others". As more people share their journeys and the different ways they connect with the "sacredness of life" so the eternal truths at the core of all the world's religions and wisdom, tradition, can be explored, experienced and integrated. Feedback from people in over 25 countries thus far and, again, after its paperback version in Spring 2005 (John Hunt Publishing) and links with a TV series in Canada and USA, will offer further contributions to a "new story" for the twenty-first Century.

Another initiative has been an international series of conferences on the theme of 'Soul in Education'. The first conference was envisioned and organised by a small group and was held in Scotland in October 2000 in collaboration with the Findhorn Foundation. Since then this impulse has been taken up by a courageous few and has flowered in Hawaii, Holland, Poland, Australia, South Africa and now Hungary. The next will be in Colorado, USA. Running through the many themes that are explored are two golden threads. The first is a growing recognition of the essential one-ness of all life. For some this derives from a visionary experience of seeing the energy of Life flowing through all and manifesting in a variety of forms. For others it derives from an understanding of the insights of quantum physics that sub-atomic particles cannot exist as separate from each other. We now know that matter is not fixed in empty space but rather that space is an ocean of microscopic vibration of particles and waves which move into and out of form in a continuing dynamic cosmic dance. We know, as all the great faiths have told us, that the universe is permeated by a subtle energy which is beyond the range of our 'senses five'. So filled are we with today's noise that most of us have not yet been sufficiently quiet and still inside to develop the inner ears to hear and the inner eyes to see. At these conferences we have explored spiritual intelligence, non-violent communication, the role of the heart in learning; we have been shown how vibrations of sound and colour can heal and seen from photographic research how crystals formed from frozen molecules of water change shape in response to music, words and human emotions. No doubt this is the kind of curriculum to which our youngest daughter and presumably, Flavio Coboblanca, would have responded.

But soul-based learning isn't just about a new curriculum, it is also about the second golden thread that these conference participants share. It is about the underlying matrix of love from which our world has been created and a growing knowing that to live in harmony with this, we need to establish a culture of love. So, soul-based learning is not about special schools and colleges, though the pioneering work of Steiner Waldorf Schools and a wide range of small schools and holistic education centres are pilots we might follow. It is more about an atmosphere in which deeper level learning can happen and a holistic approach that meets all levels of student need – physical, mental, emotional, and spiritual as well.

University for Spirit Forum

The apparent need for a holistic approach to education was one of the motivations for the Wrekin Trust to consult with colleagues in the field of spiritual education and in September 2000 to set up the first steps towards a 'University for Spirit' as a counterbalance to the prevailing materialistic orientation of so much of mainstream learning. The University for Spirit Forum (www.ufsforum.org) now comprises about 70 organisations and individuals who have come into association around a common aim "to explore, provide and promote spiritual education". They come from different settings – small centres in universities, small initiatives in schools, centres devoted to the new consciousness, open centres, networks, publications and individuals carrying a torch in places still deeply stuck in the old rationalistic and materialistic paradigm. An annual Round Table represents this variety and acts as a mixing pot where different perspectives are exchanged and potentially divisive identities loosened. The shared spirit bubbling between the growing cracks in the walls flows with channels of co-operation and co-creation. A first foundation programme 'Embodying Cosmos' is one of several collaborations emerging and we are beginning to see how this holistic initiative fits within a newly emerging holistic framework of learning appropriate for 21st Century "Planetary Citizens".

Even today, the word 'spiritual' seems to evoke a mixed response. In popular imaginations, this is often equated with religion or confused with spiritualism. Contemporary spirituality is moving beyond both these aspects. When the Wrekin Trust, which was founded by Sir George Trevelyan in 1971 (www.sirgeorgetrevelyan.org) to provide spiritual education of a non-sectarian kind, set up steps towards a 'University for Spirit' it was agreed that the description by U. Thant was the nearest we could find:

> "Spirituality is a state of connectedness to life,
> It is an experience of being, belonging and caring,
> It is sensitivity and compassion, joy and hope,
> It is the harmony between the innermost life and the outer life,
> or the life of the world and the life universal,
> It is the supreme comprehension of life in time and space, the

*tuning of the inner person with the great mysteries and secrets
that are around us
It is the belief in the goodness of life and the possibility for each
person to contribute goodness to it.
It is the belief in life as part of the eternal stream of time, that
each of us came from somewhere and is destined somewhere,
that without such belief there could be no prayer, no
meditation, no peace and no happiness."*

As Secretary General of the United Nations, (1961 - 1971) U. Thant was in touch with so many cultures, traditions and expressions of the One Spirit we all share and in order to establish unity from amidst diversity tried to express the universal aspects of the different traditions. So, too, has Dr Robert Muller – former Deputy Secretary General of the UN. In 1971 at a Community Education Conference in Trinidad he declared: "Either the 21st Century will be a spiritual Century or there will be no 21st Century at all". Though now in his eighties, Dr Muller continues to inspire daily on his site www.goodmorningworld.org.

His declaration was, for me, an affirmation that the streams of endeavour we then knew to be incorporating ideas of community, experiential learning and emotional intelligence into mainstream education across the World would begin to flow together and then converge with the stream that was bubbling to re-enliven the 'Spirit of Learning' and "transform learning institutions into places where we can draw on the Soul in a spirit of community" (Clarence Harvey, initiator of the Soul in Education programme).

New Shoots

Before flowing together, streams meet and mingle a little. There is a point of confluence in Brazil where the Rivers Negro and Amazonas meet. Each river is a different temperature and a strikingly different colour - the one dark brown, the other beige. So over many miles, these colours are distinct but after a while they start to mingle, then slowly blend until eventually they become the mighty Amazon River which supports so much life in its lengthy journey to the sea. Might this be a metaphor for the worlds of learning and religion for today? As they meet and blend, might a great new river flow forth?

For not only the field of education but also the many world religions have tended to reduce the vastness to the seemingly manageable, replacing truth by many lesser truths. If these streams could flow more closely together might we then find that the research of the external world and "me-search" of the inner worlds were all part of the same exploration of that which is 'universus', turned towards the One.

Early shoots of change are already showing in the wider educational field. The home schooling movement is one sign of new shoots growing, linking through the 'Education Otherwise' and the 'Human Scale Education' movements. Some parents and teachers are seeking alternatives convinced that *"Education has become an institution whose purpose in the modern world is not to make culture, not to serve the living cosmos, but to harness humankind to the dead forces of materialism. Education as we know it, damages the Soul"*[4]. This extract was quoted by Dr Jack Millar from the University of Toronto who asserts, *"by reclaiming my Soul, we find that any educational encounter takes on a new vitality and purpose – students and teachers no longer go through the motions but, instead, feel alive and nourished by what they do. In a word – learning becomes soulful . . . We recognise Soul in people when we see their eyes light up, when their speech is animated, when their body moves with grace and energy"*.

As well as alternative ventures new shoots are also growing in complementary ways. Summer Camps (eg, www.wyseinternational.org, www.universalpeacecamps.org.) renew young and old by participating in the sacred through community, beauty, nature and all that brings delight. Retreat centres provide oasis of quiet, and restore souls depleted by the images from TV and computer screens and stress from 24/7 schedules. Conferences, workshops, and electronic connections, bring meeting points for kindred spirits seeking to link at the level of the transpersonal. Spontaneity and creativity, wisdom and loving kindness can flourish again through such connections.

Researchers of the future might also spot the emergence of new forms from small innovative endeavours not yet connecting up to form a wider picture. Local learning groups meeting to study the wisdom teachings, to share 'contemplative fire' to celebrate full moons and seasonal rhythms, to create a 'million circles for peace' - to name just a few, are pointing to the same value of connection through local learning groups that the Open University discovered in its early years and the home school movement promotes today. Teachers are needed but no longer do they need to pour out knowledge from their over-crowded heads.

Knowledge, which itself is changing so fast, is readily available in libraries and learning resources centres, and through the Internet. Educators need, instead, to be facilitators of learning – helping students of all ages to not only engage with knowledge but also to draw forth their own wisdom, thus learning from both their own experience and the discoveries of others. Teachers need the space and support to re-connect with their own Souls and they need the freedom to design learning environments that are appropriate for the needs of their students. These might be farm centres, space research stations, theatres, and classrooms -- provided not only by concrete walls but also by the remaining forests, parks and wilderness which have for so long been the learning spaces for indigenous cultures. Preserving these from pressures of housing and corporate pursuit must surely be an urgent task for our time and earth literacy as high a priority as technological literacy.

It may be the glaring need to protect the Earth, its finite resources, diversity and beauty that is the wake up call to the world faiths to drop their sectarian separatisms and connect with the golden thread of 'do unto others that you would have them do unto you' that was the teaching of all the founders of religions. For a key theme in the emerging new 'story' is that we are part of a vast evolving universe and that humanity's role within it is to care for the myriad of life forms as a sacred trust. William Bloom in his recent book "Soulutions"[5] cites recent research by the University of Michigan World Values Survey Team which shows that a new form of spirituality is emerging in post-industrial societies as they shift from traditional faiths to a form of spirituality that he terms 'Holism' (www.holism.info). He suggests that this new spirituality is "open-hearted and open minded, welcomes diversity, connects with and experiences the wonder and beauty of all life, perceives connections and inter-dependence and respects diverse ways of exploring meaning, purpose and mystery".

The UN Earth Charter that Bloom also cites proclaims:
"We stand at a critical moment in Earth's history, a time when humanity must choose its future . . . to form a common partnership to care for the Earth and one another or risk the destruction of ourselves and the diversity of life. Fundamental changes are needed in our values, institutions and ways of living. We must realise that when our basic needs have been met, human development is primarily about being more, not having more."

The Charter echoes the voices of the prophets: "Without vision the people perish," said an ancient prophet (Isaiah). More modern prophets also warn: "We are now too clever to risk living without wisdom" (Dr E. F. Schumacher); "Souls have shrunk terribly due to this machine cosmology." (Matthew Fox) And an inspiring modern poet, Kathleen Raine: *"This is not a rehearsal but the thing itself, for which we have all been summoned into this mysterious and sacred world . . . in order to bring about the changes without which this poor, beautiful earth will die, not only Nature, but the Soul of the World"*.[6]

It seems a long struggle from the present to the possible, just as it is from a caterpillar to a butterfly. Both involve a dissolving of what has gone before, a transformation of the former cells to create the new. Those who recoil from and even scorn these ideas are reckoning without two things. They are discounting the power of love – "The love that moves the Sun and the other stars" (Dante) and they are reckoning without those quantum moments when the timeless breaks through into time and when envisioned waves of possibility break through into actuality. This is what Gregg Braden calls "The Isaiah Effect".[7] "The expression of an ancient science stating that we may change the outcome of the future through the choices that we make in each moment of the present." For quantum science suggests the co-existence of many possible futures with each future lying in a state of rest until it is awakened by choices made in the present. Choices made by a relative few acting with wisdom, insight and concerted intent. If we are to develop the wisdom and insight we need, then some educators are realising that we need to work from deeper levels of intelligence.

Most of us see through the eye of rational intelligence (IQ) using analysis, logic and reason to figure out the challenges of our time. Others learn to see through the eyes of emotional intelligence (EQ) and develop the sensitivity and empathy to contribute to our world in caring and compassionate ways. A few are beginning to perceive through the eyes of spiritual intelligence (SQ) where purpose is shaped from deeper values, the best path selected through wise discernment and the action to bring the new into being is directed with spontaneity, flexibility and creativity. These are the attributes for which, deep down, our children and grandchildren yearn.

As I stood with others during the closing moments of a recent conference, I recalled a moment at a Peace Conference in The Hague in 1999, when a beautifully choreographed dance of young mothers – with babies in their wombs, in their arms and on their backs raised their arms in yearning together. Then, I knew why we worked as we did in what feels like one long landscape of here and now with the future of the world in each of our hands: I knew why we have to transcend the struggle of hard work, of budgets, and badgering. I knew why Spirit has to be restored to learning. There are frequencies beyond the range of those we see and hear. A conscious intelligent mind that is the matrix of all matter is awaiting our co-operation and can flow in at-one-ment with all we think and do if we so choose. The rivers of education and religion might flow together – they might, just might, restore the Soul of the World.

NOTES

1. Cobobianco, Flavio, (1991) "I came from the Sun".

2. "Time Trends in Adolescent and Mental Health" *Journal of Child Psychology and Psychiatry*, Nov. 2004.

3. Bunting, Madeleine, "The Guardian" - 13 Sept. 2004

4. Sardello, Robert (1992).

5. Bloom, William, (2004), "Soulutions – The Holistic Manifesto", Hay House Inc.

6. Quoted by H.R.H. Prince
   Charles at Kathleen Raine's Memorial Service and published by the Temenos Academy.

7. Braden, Gregg, (2002), "The Isaiah Effect" - Hay House Inc.

CONSCIOUSNESS, SPIRITUALITY AND GROWTH

9. TRANSPERSONAL PSYCHOLOGY

Ian Gordon-Brown

Ian wrote this article over twenty-five years ago. It is included in this book as a tribute to his special contribution to the development of transpersonal psychology over this period and also because it offers a crystal clear account of the foundations and development of the subject.

It explains how behaviourism and psychoanalysis, which dominated psychology for nearly 100 years, met a new emerging force in the 1950s – humanistic psychology. The pioneering role of Abraham Maslow and others is explained as well as the connection with encounter groups, co-counselling and gestalt, and a wide range of body therapies.

But humanistic psychology failed to fulfil all the hopes of its founders, who were increasingly interested in the spiritual dimension of consciousness. This led to the development of transpersonal psychology, and those who were fundamental in bringing it into existence are succinctly described to complete the Western side of the picture. There was also a move to integrate Eastern and Western approaches to psychological understanding and human growth. "So what", asks Ian "is the practical use of all this high-blown stuff?" He was always ready to get down to the practicalities of what can be done in an interconnected world that will be directly relevant to individuals and through them to society. Transpersonal psychology is not for everyone, he concludes, and some will be happier within a Freudian, behaviourist or other frame. But the transpersonal perspective enlarges our understanding of life in all its aspects. There are millions of people seeking new meanings in life and for some of them, he maintains, transpersonal psychology can be a lifesaver.

Ian gives ideas behind the concept of transpersonal psychology – maps to explore, the idea of the energy centre of self – not to be confused with personality, for it is something more profound; the yearning for wholeness, for self-fulfillment, but with an acceptance of relativity rather than exclusivity.

Ian Gordon-Brown *(1925-1996) was an Industrial Psychologist, with a deep interest in the spiritual side of life, an interest he deepened by acting as Secretary to the Lucis Trust (Alice Bailey's work) for 12 years. In 1973 he and Barbara Somers founded the Centre for Transpersonal Psychology in London. In 1977 he helped Barbara establish the Centre's training, and continued to carry the growing workshop programme. In 1995 he was elected President of EUROTAS, a position he filled with a characteristic blend of warmth, humour and authority. He died, suddenly and peacefully, in October 1996. Ian was an excellent innovative therapist, an original thinker and an inspiring teacher.*

Perhaps his greatest contribution was to the hundreds of people who were directly influenced by him when developing their inner lives in an outer world, without trying to take over or run or lead anything. "As for the future," said Le Petit Prince of St Exupery, "your task is not to foresee but to enable it", and this is what Ian in his thoughtful and special way was able to contribute to his many students.

Psychology today is in a state of flux. Behaviourism (or first force psychology as it is sometimes called) has lost much of its appeal, for despite its immense contribution to human understanding, it persists in treating man as if he were a machine. Likewise, the psycho-analytical stream (second force) is suspect. It too has had a tremendous influence, especially in opening up the whole question of unconscious factors in the psyche and in human behaviour. But many psychoanalysts persist in treating the peaks of human experience as deviant and as signs mental imbalance. This is bound to lose them credibility in an era of the 'explosion of consciousness'.

Behaviourism and psychoanalysis have dominated psychology for nearly 100 years. But in he 1950s, a new force – humanistic psychology – began to emerge. It was pioneered by men like Abraham Maslow, who at the time as relatively unknown but who later became president of the American Psychological Association. Humanistic psychologists sought to put ordinary human beings and the full range of human experience back into the centre of the psychological stage. Since that time humanistic (third force) psychology has grown rapidly and now embraces a wide range of perspectives and techniques. It is strongly experiential and the 'growth movement' and humanistic psychology are now largely synonomous. Encounter groups, T-groups, sensitivity training, co-counselling, transactional analysis, gestalt, and a wide range of body-therapies and techniques are all found within its orbit. It is now well established as part of the psychological scene, accepted in a growing number of universities, and influencing large numbers of people.

But humanistic psychology failed to fulfil all the hopes of its founders. Abraham Maslow, his closest colleague Anthony Sutich and others, were profoundly interested in the spiritual dimensions of consciousness, and the capacity of people to transcend their limited everyday awareness, and to explore the 'peaks and mountain tops' of the psyche. They wanted psychologists to investigate the 'farther reaches of human nature', to discover the conditions in which altered states of consciousness could be entered or induced, and to map the relationship between these transhuman states and the world of ordinary reality.

But by the middle of the 1960s, humanistic psychology was so concerned with helping people to rediscover their feelings and their bodies, and to stop working everything out with their heads, that it seemed unlikely that the trans-personal dimensions of the psyche could receive adequate attention within the humanistic movement as it then existed in the United States. So, in 1969, after several years of preparation, Maslow, Sutich and others launched a *Journal of Transpersonal Psychology*, and eighteen months later formed an Association for Transpersonal Psychology, both based in California. Today, the trans-personal movement (fourth force) in psychology is growing rapidly in North America. In the last four years it has begun to put down roots in Europe.

What then is transpersonal psychology? Definition is not easy, for transpersonal or fourth-force psychology was intended to be perspective and to provide an eclectic and informal umbrella for people who shared basic attitudes, but whose opinions on specific questions might differ widely. The factor of greatest significance is that within transpersonal psychology a number of major strands, woven by giants in the psychological field, are coming together to form a recognisable over-all pattern and tapestry. Any selection of these strands is bound to be a personal one, and therefore arbitrary. But I give my own as a way of illustrating the new synthesis that I sense is now emerging within psychology.

First, *Abraham Maslow,* with his special interest in gifted people, in peak experiences, and his emphasis on the processes of self-actualisation and self-realisation, as dynamic motivating factors in human growth. Maslow began to explore these questions in the 1940s.

Second, *Roberto Assagioli*, an Italian psychiatrist, founder of a system known as psychosynthesis. Assagioli started to develop his ideas in the 1920s, and is significant for his mapping of higher consciousness states, ways of being in touch with and entering these dimensions, and his emphasis on the spiritual or transpersonal self as the essence and ultimate direction and monitor of the psychological energy system of the individual.

Third, *Victor Frankl*, founder of logo-therapy. Frankl spent time as an inmate of Nazi concentration camps during the Second World War. He found that those whose lives had meaning, or those who could invest their lives or the experience with meaning, stood the best chance of survival. The will-to-meaning became the keynote of his psychological system and his methods of psycho-therapy.

Fourth, and most important of all, *Carl Jung* and his immensely gifted group of followers. They have not only underlined the importance of unconscious factors, both individual and collective, in the human growth process, but have shown how individuals can become whole, and fulfil all sides of their nature, through the process they call individuation.

Note two things: how recent is the formal emergence of what we call transpersonal psychology; and how long ago the key strands from which it is being developed were started.

So far, I have mentioned only the western half of the picture. One of the most significant aspects of the transpersonal perspective is that it is beginning to relate and integrate both eastern and western approaches to psychological understanding and human growth. Down the ages mystics of all the great religions and philosophies have pioneered the exploration of transcendental states. Transpersonal psychology today embraces and applies the perspectives of religious and esoteric schools, and such eastern disciplines as yoga in its various forms, Zen, Tao, Buddhist teachings and others.

It may be asked at this point: what practical use is all this high-flown stuff? How does it help ordinary people live better in a complex and often difficult world?

Firstly, transpersonal psychology is not for everyone. There are those for whom humanistic approaches are best. Others will be most at home and most helped within the Freudian frame. Some will fit best into the attitudes and style of behaviourist psychology. And many will not feel comfortable in psychology at all, and should turn elsewhere.

Secondly, the transpersonal perspective enlarges our understanding of life in all its aspects – higher consciousness and how it relates to ordinary life. A wider understanding is always practical.

Thirdly, there are millions of people today seeking new meanings in life. As they explore and search within, often as a result of some crisis in their lives, they become aware of unexplained impulses within the psyche, of unusual intuitions, and ideas that do not fit a rational picture. They break through into new dimensions and do not know how to handle their discovery. Such problems are now widespread. For such people transpersonal psychology can literally be a life saver.

I have said that any tight or rigid definition of transpersonal psychology is undesirable, and out of keeping with the spirit of its pioneers. But as we have seen, a very real synthesis is beginning to emerge from the blending and interrelationship of the different psychological traditions. Certain key ideas provide the nucleus around which this synthesis is being built. None of them is new. What is new is that growing numbers of psychologists testify to the experiential and existential reality of these ideas and are working with them in practical ways and in terms of the psychology of quite ordinary people.

I give six ideas:
1. The idea of a field or continuum of consciousness comprising many different potential dimensions of awareness and states of being. Jung's collective unconscious (unconscious because at any one time we can only be aware of a fragment of this reality) together with oriental notions of planes of consciousness and Assagioli's concept of different levels of awareness within the psyche, provide us with the initial maps to explore and chart the consciousness field.

2. The idea of the self, that there exists in every person a factor, energy or centre – the individual's essence –which is the core of his being. Whether we call this essence self, soul, transpersonal centre, Atman, matters not. It is the central energy of the psychological system, the key to growth, integration and expansion of awareness. Transpersonal pyschology is the only branch of psychology that conceives the self in this sense.

3. This self is not to be confused with personality, or the 'personal I'. It is something other, deeper and more profound. It is experienced in many

different ways: through peak and transcendental experience: in 'big dreams'; through the activity of intuition and inspiration; at moments of crisis and desperation; in the urge to create; in the impulse to useful action; in relationships. It can also be noted as a factor in the life patterns of those who have little conscious experience of it. The following verse of Alan Watts expresses precisely the distinction between the personal I and the self:

There was a young man who said through
I think that I know that I know
What I would like to see
Is the I that knows me
When I know that I know that I know.

4. The fundamental urge of the psyche towards wholeness, to become what it is, to actualise its full potential, to realise the nature of the self, the inside and the outside to become one.

5. There are many different ways of growth to self fulfilment. Human beings are infinitely diverse, with widely differing growth needs. What is ideal for one may be totally unsuited for another.

6. The idea of relativity. In no sense does transpersonal psychologt deny the usefulness of the many different psychologies extant today. Indeed, the transpersonal psychologist will use a variety of approaches as and when appropriate. Transpersonal psychology is not in sympathy with those who assert the exclusive primacy of any single school of thought.

Finally, to give readers a flavour of the areas that are currently of interest to transpersonal psychologists, let me list topics written up in the *Journal of Transpersonal Psychology* and discussed by practitioners: altered states of consciousness; education for transcendence; mysticism and schizophrenia; cultivating intuition; states of consciousness and the chakra system in yoga; height psychology (Assagioli) and depth psychology (Jung); meditation as therapy; guided imaging; masculine and feminine principles; identity and dis-identification; myths and symbolism; archetypes; archetypal psychology; LSD and experimental mysticism; voluntary control of internal states; physiology of meditation; biofeedback; LSD-assisted therapy; the encounter with death; astrology and cycles of growth; samahdi and nirvana; synthesis and the will; paradox; actualisers and transcenders; mid-life crisis; letting 'It' do it; transpersonal counselling and psychotherapy.

10. PSYCHOLOGY, RELIGION AND SPIRITUALITY

David Fontana

David gave the Ian Gordon-Brown Commemorative Lecture at the EUROTAS London Conference in August 2005. He argues that there is evidence, apart from his own personal experience, for a spiritual dimension to life. This dimension has played such a crucial role in human history and society in general that we should not neglect its study.

The study of spirituality and religion (which are not the same) is important for psychologists and psychotherapists as well as for society in all its aspects. In this article he examines the differences and overlaps of spirituality and religion and explains their important associations with mysticism. He covers carefully the way in which the relationship of mind and brain has been studied through history. He shows how recent scientific developments, while they may not provide evidence of how brain can generate mind, yet the way the non-physical mind may be able to influence the physical activity of the brain cannot be dismissed so readily. Quantum mechanics is too complex to discuss here but, near death experiences (NDEs) suggest that mind can exist outside the physical body. David gives a comprehensive overview of research and activities in this field and cites evidence from para psychological research including the Stargate Project financed by the US government to the tune of $20 million

He shows how the study of certain aspects of the mind, thanks to transpersonal psychology, is now beginning to return to its rightful place within mainstream psychology. He concludes that if mind is non-physical, this provides the notion for a spiritual dimension to existence and also to the possible survival of physical death.

These findings and suggestions have profound implications for us all in the fast developing world of the 21st Century.

*   **Professor David Fontana** *is a Distinguished Visiting Fellow of Cardiff University and a professor at two universities in Portugal and of Transpersonal Psychology at Liverpool John Moores University. He was co-founder of the Transpersonal Section of the British Psychological Society. "Psychology, Religion and Spirituality" is the title of one of his recent books.* "Is There an Afterlife?" *was published in March 2005.*

Why the Study of Religion is Important for Psychology

Religion has been one of the major formative influences upon human thought and behaviour throughout recorded history. It has had a profound effect upon the lives of individuals and upon groups and cultures, inspiring some of the most noble acts of self-sacrifice and altruism and stimulating much of the world's greatest architecture, finest sculpture, and most sublime painting and music. It has motivated men and women to develop moral and ethical systems, to philosophise on the nature of self and on the meaning and purpose of life, and to speculate on the destiny that awaits us beyond the grave. It has stimulated the development of techniques for altering consciousness such as meditation, contemplation, ritual, and prayer. It has been associated with mystical states that raise major questions as to the nature of mind and consciousness, and it has provided countless millions with psychological comfort and solace and with a reason for living. It has spawned institutions that have grown into universities and hospitals, and has gained and exercised political power at the highest levels. It has inspired learning, literacy and scholarship, and has been a powerful force behind the growth of banking and of business and commerce, amassing vast wealth in the process. Hardly any part of modern life has not been touched and influenced at some point by religion and by its manifold institutions.

In addition, throughout its history and particularly in more recent years in response to the advance of reductionist philosophies and scientific materialism, religion has addressed the fundamental question are we biological accidents, machines programmed by the random mutations of the evolutionary process and cast adrift in a universe without meaning and purpose, or has life some richer value? Are we destined for extinction at the end of our short lives, or do we pass from this world into some higher form of existence? It is a question that psychology, with the advent of behaviourism in the 1930s and its search for scientific acceptance (Wilber 1998 puts it that 'modern science gleefully denies virtually all of the basic tenets of religion in general.') dropped from its agenda more than half a century ago, as noted by Sir Cyril Burt, whose status as a thinker is undiminished by the claims that he mishandled some of his later data on the inheritability of intelligence, puts it that in the course of its development from a philosophy to a science psychology first lost its soul and then lost its mind. By this he meant that it had come to focus upon the physical and the observable at the expense of the inner world of spiritual and mental events, despite the fact that it is within this inner world that we each have our individual psychological being. The loss to psychology occasioned by this development has been incalculable, and it is only now, with the advance of transpersonal psychology, that we are able to acknowledge this loss and to take steps to remedy it. At the level of personal belief the psychologist may reject all the tenets of religion, but what he or she cannot do without impoverishing psychology is to ignore the profound effect the subject has had upon human thought and behaviour.

This effect has of course been negative as well as positive. If religion has brought out the best in humankind it has also brought out the worst – or should we say that, like political creeds, it has been used as a tool to manipulate humans into doing their worst. Religion has been used as an excuse for ferocious wars, for intolerance and victimisation, for the subordination of women and children, and for the exploitation of animals and the natural environment. At an individual level its misuse has led to the generation of individual psychological problems such as sexual repressions, excessive guilt, the disintegration of families, and various other forms of social dysfunction. But these harmful negative effects only add to its importance for the psychologist – and particularly for those psychologists involved in clinical, therapeutic and social work – since they demonstrate the power that religion and religious belief have over hearts and minds, over emotions, attitudes, self-concepts, motivation and activity.

What Do We Mean by Religion and Spirituality?

Just as psychology largely ignored religion for most of the 20th Century, so it ignored spirituality. Religion and spirituality are not necessarily the same thing. Religion implies a set of doctrines and of rules and regulations to follow, whereas spirituality can imply something more personal and experiential. Thus they require separate definitions. Argyle and Beit-Hallahmi (1975) consider that religion is 'a system of beliefs in divine or superhuman power, and practices of worship or other rituals directed towards such a power', but this may sound too orientated towards a divinity for non-theistic religions. Individual religions not only differ considerably from each other in their understanding both of God or the gods and of the soul (see e.g. Smart 1989 for a survey) but in a number of other important ways. Theistic religions teach the existence of a creator who brought the universe into being; non-theistic religions either consider that knowledge of a first cause is beyond human comprehension, or that the universe existed from 'beginningless time'. Even within theistic religions, some belief systems see the creator as eternally outside – though close to and involved in – his/her creation (i.e. as transcendent), while others see him/her as implicit in, and as in fact manifesting this creation as an aspect of his/her own being (e.g. as imminent). These differences are so extreme that we may question whether all the traditions concerned should come under the one category of religion (a point stressed by Wulff 1997). Another difficulty is that all religions contain an esoteric as well as an exoteric side. The latter is concerned with outward observances and dogma, the former with inner practices and with teachings that are often only imparted to an elite (such as a priesthood) or only discovered through inner explorations by those who wish to penetrate more deeply into the mysteries hidden beneath the surface (see e.g. Fontana 2004 for a fuller discussion of these and related issues). Taking these various difficulties into account, together with all the many attempts in the literature to define religion, we can narrow things down to three basic tenets that appear indispensable if a particular tradition is to be regarded as a religion, namely:

- belief in a spiritual, non-physical dimension to existence
- observance of a set of rituals or practices
- adherence to a doctrine of ethical conduct arising from the teachings of founders of the religious tradition concerned.

The first of these factors would seem to be the most important historically. Belief in – and claimed experience of – a spiritual dimension has been the guiding principle behind the founders of all significant religions. Many individuals in fact accept this first factor while ignoring the other two, and these we can call spiritual rather than necessarily religious, and distinguish them sharply from those who call themselves religious yet reject or are uncertain about the first of them. We can suggest in addition that spiritual people claim to recognise the non-physical dimension as an integral part of their own being, and that the more this dimension is experienced the closer one is to the divine principle that animates existence. Walsh (1999) describes this developmental experience as a process of inner change and development, and lists many metaphors for it such as awakening, de-hypnosis, enlightenment, freedom, metamorphosis, and wholeness. The clear suggestion is that without this inner change, we are incomplete as human beings, living in only a small part of ourselves, with our deeper potential left untouched.

The Place of Mysticism

Both religion and spirituality have their origin in, or are closely associated with, mysticism, another area much neglected by modern psychology. As a profound state of altered consciousness, mysticism is of particular interest to transpersonal psychologists because of its life-changing effect and the insight it appears to give into levels of the mind untapped by other experiences. Mysticism appears to take two distinct forms, transcendent (or theistic, in which God or the divine consciousness is recognised as other than oneself and as the object of love and devotion) and immanent (or non-theistic, in which this consciousness is experienced as one's own true nature). It is the inability to recognise this distinction, and to and to respect both forms of mysticism, that is largely responsible for the schism between Eastern non-theistic religions such as Buddhism, Jainism and some forms of Hinduism and Western theistic religions such as Judaism, Christianity and Islam. Both forms of mysticism contain many similar features such as the following.

- a sense of spiritual – i.e. non-physical or supra-physical – reality.
- a bright light or lights
- profound guiding or calming insights
- beatification of the surroundings and feelings of bliss
- a sense of the underlying unity of all things, and of peace and security
- loss of all awareness of the limited and limiting self
- loss of all fear of death
- a sense of certainty, timelessness and enlightenment
- a realisation that the ultimate reality behind all existence is love

Attempts to explain mystical experiences such as these as brain anomalies (e.g. frontal lobe malfunctions as in epilepsy) do not stand up to a study of the literature on mystics and mysticism (see e.g. James 1960, Staal 1975, Grant 1985, Underhill 1995). Which brings me, logically enough, to a brief discussion of the brain itself, since the question of whether all mental experience arises from the physical brain, or whether mental events – in short the mind – are non-physical and simply interact with the brain is central to the transpersonal psychologist's interest in religion and spirituality. If mind is no more than brain, then it is difficult to see how there can be room for a spiritual dimension or for its survival of death. If mind is no more than the activity of brain, then when brain dies mind dies, and we are indeed no more than biological accidents and all talk of spirituality is a form of self-deceit.

Mind and Brain

As I said earlier, there are compelling reasons for all psychologists to take an interest in religion and spirituality, even though they may themselves reject any notion of belief in a non-physical dimension to humankind. However, the transpersonal psychologist goes further and asks questions as to the reality or otherwise of this dimension, since it is by definition an integral part of what is meant by the transpersonal (i.e. psychological states beyond or transcending the personal). In addressing these questions it must be stressed at the outset that the popular notion science has somehow 'disproved' the existence of the soul, of a God, of survival of death and disposed of any suggestion that mind is not created by brain, is incorrect. Space allows us to look at only the last of these misconceptions, but since the brain-mind relationship is crucial to the whole issue of our true nature, it is the obvious point at which the psychologist must begin any debate on the reality or otherwise of a spiritual dimension to life.

It is argued quite rightly that modern brain research has located with great precision the areas in the brain that are associated with specific mental events, but the conclusion commonly drawn from these findings, namely that the former are therefore the 'cause' of the latter, is unwarranted. The association discovered between brain events and mental events is simply one of correlation, and correlation tells us nothing about which is cause and which is effect. Certainly if brain 'causes' mind then we would expect this correlation, but it is equally true that we would expect it if mind was distinct from and worked through brain, (a process in some ways analogous to the way in which a television signal is distinct from yet works through the circuitry of a television set). The supporters of the view that brain is responsible for mind point to the fact that we do not know how mental events can activate the electro-chemical processes of the brain, but the reply to this is that we do not know how the electro-chemical activity of the brain can give rise to mental events. This point was strongly emphasised by Nobel Prizewinning neurophysiologist Sir John Eccles (1980 and 1989), one of the 20th Centuries most distinguished scientists, who after many years of brain research concluded that 'Regardless of the complexity of electrical, chemical or biological machinery' in the brain there is in 'natural laws' no statement as to how the mind can emerge. The "self-conscious mind" must have some nonmaterial existence'. In his view, the mind influences the body through the exercise of free will, and the body influences the mind by providing sensory information, which the mind integrates into perceptual experience.

Eccles' conclusion supports in effect what is sometimes called the 'substance dualism' position enunciated by Plato in the 4th/3rd Century BCE and by Descartes in the 17th Century CE, namely that the universe consists of two fundamental kinds of stuff, material stuff which goes to make up the physical world, and the stuff of consciousness, the latter associated with soul and spirit. The suggestion that when we come to know more about the brain we will find the areas or processes responsible for generating mind appears untenable in the light of current knowledge. We already know enough about the brain and its processes to recognise that there are no secret places and no secret processes awaiting discovery. The brain, as a physical organ, is no longer a scientific mystery.

The materialist may attack Eccles' form of substance dualism by arguing that we can now produce computers capable of mimicking and vastly out-performing the intelligent behaviour of the human mind. In the future new generations of computers may even be able to take their own decisions and so demonstrate free will and apparent self-consciousness, and to design new computers cleverer than themselves. What then will be the difference, if any, between the human mind and the mind of a computer and what will become of the argument that material objects working on electrical energy cannot generate mind? One answer to this is that I know I am not a computer, but a computer does not know that it isn't me unless I tell it. Even a small child, without being told, knows the difference between a human being and a computer, thus outsmarting the latter on one of the most basic of tests.

Another answer is that, unlike the human brain, we can switch off the computer's brain by disconnecting it from the current that feeds it. Other answers are that the computer depends for its existence upon software programmes initiated by the human mind, and that whereas it works on binary processing (the electric current that determines each mathematical calculation by the computer does so by either being on or off) the human brain works on parallel processing (myriads of different processes are carried on at the same time). A further answer is that even if we can build a computer which is modelled on the neural networks of the human brain but operating trillions of times faster, we still could not programme into it the subjective feeling of what it is like to be alive and to experience colour, beauty, music, art, love, painting, architecture, nature, parenthood, happiness – all the things in fact that go to make us human. There may be people somewhere in the world who would prefer to be computers than humans – clever machines rather than flesh and blood – but in the final analysis I suspect they are probably few in number.

The argument that we have no evidence on how brain can generate mind therefore still holds good, but the contrary argument that we have no evidence the non-physical mind may be able to influence the physical activity of the brain and may be able to operate independently of it can no longer be dismissed so readily. There is a hint arising from some interpretations of experimental results in quantum mechanics that consciousness may indeed directly influence the behaviour of physical matter (see e.g. Goswami 1993), while research into the experiences of those who have clinically died yet on resuscitation report the continuation of consciousness suggest that mind may be capable of functioning outside the physical body. Quantum mechanics is far too complex and problematic a subject to be pursued here, but the experiences of those who have clinically died and report the continuation of consciousness (i.e. those who have undergone so-called near death experiences or NDEs) can certainly be discussed, since these experiences suggest strongly that mind, complete with sensory awareness, self-awareness, memories and emotions (in short replete with all its usual faculties) can exist outside the physical body.

Near death experiences have been reported since antiquity (one of the earliest accounts is given in Plato at the end of The Republic). Brought to popular attention by Moody in 1983 (drawing upon his medical experience), although earlier and more extensive collections of such experiences were published by Crookall in a number of books (e.g. 1961 and 1978), while a range of subsequent studies conducted by medical doctors, neuropsychiatrists and psychologists (e.g. Sabom 1982 and 1998, Ring 1984, Ring and Valarino 1998, Ring and Cooper 1999, Fenwick and Fenwick 1995), indicate variously that between 12 and 40 per cent of those at or near clinical death report going through NDEs prior to resuscitation. Reports typically suggest that during the NDE consciousness appears to be located outside the body, and that sometimes accurate details of the medical procedures carried out on the body during the NDE are observed and later accurately reported, even though these procedures would not have been visible from where the body was lying at the time. Sometimes there are also accounts of traveling to 'paradise' conditions and of meeting deceased relatives or 'beings of light' who are instrumental in sending the wandering consciousness back into the physical body. Usually re-entry into the body is said to occur with great reluctance and even repugnance. Most people claim they would prefer not to return, and only do so either because they are given no choice or because they have responsibilities in physical life that they cannot abandon.

Neuropsychiatrist Dr. Peter Fenwick concludes from his study of 300 NDE cases and those given in the literature that attempts to explain the NDE as generated by the chaotic activity of the dying brain, by oxygen starvation, by a build-up of carbon dioxide in the blood, by hallucinations consequent upon the action of medical drugs or of the body's release of endorphins do not appear to be adequate for a range of carefully explained medical reasons (Fenwick and Fenwick 1995). Fenwick's reasons for rejecting the above natural explanations accord with those advanced in medical detail by Morse (Morse and Perry 1990), by Griffin (1997) and others, and supported by Dossey (2000).

If normal explanations for the NDE appear unsupportable, it can still be argued that as those experiencing NDEs are subsequently resuscitated they cannot actually have died. The medical profession accepts that the exact moment of death is becoming more and more difficult to establish. However, by all the currently accepted criteria of death, many of the patients reporting NDEs appear to qualify. But our main concern when assessing the relevance of NDEs is whether or not the brain shows any vital signs during them. Certainly there may be cellular processes going on within the brain even when it appears moribund, but there is no suggestion that these purely autonomic processes could be connected with the generation of consciousness. In a recent case reported by Sabom (1998), which involved a pioneering and risky operation to correct an hemolysis (ballooning) of an artery at the base of the patient's brain, the blood supply to the brain was medically shut off while the patient's body temperature was lowered to a level of suspended animation. However, despite the fact that all the vital signs in the brain were deliberately switched off by the medical team the patient, Pam Reynolds, reported on resuscitation having experienced an NDE, even giving an accurate description of some of the clinical procedures carried out on her brain during the absence of any detectable brain activity.

As with mystical experiences, NDEs appear to be life-changing events for those who experience them. Ring (1984) found that as a consequence of their NDEs his sample had typically lost their fear of death, worried less about past grievances and future problems, had increased feelings of self-worth together with increased acceptance of others and concern for their welfare, had often changed their life goals and values in less material and more spiritually attuned directions, had come to place more emphasis upon the overriding importance of values such as love and compassion, and tended to seek a deeper understanding of life, particularly at the spiritual and religious level. Even those who had had their experiences many years previously reported that the experiences still remained fresh in their minds, as did the firm conviction that they had died during the NDE and now knew the reality of survival.

Interestingly, expectation appears to play no part in whether or not individuals near death have NDEs. NDEs are as likely to occur to those without religious belief and/or belief in life after death as to those with these beliefs, a finding that substantially weakens the argument that NDEs are purely imaginary experiences brought on by wishful thinking. Further evidence for this is provided by paediatrician Morse (Morse and Perry 1990), who studied NDEs reported by a sample of 12 children after cardiac arrest, many of whom he considers too young to have absorbed cultural beliefs on death and dying, and who found striking similarities between these reports and those given by adults. In a follow-up study ten years later, Morse found that, as with adults, NDEs in children appear to have life-changing effects in that his sample had become 'special teenagers with excellent relationships with their families, [sharing] a wisdom that is humbling'

The fact that mind cannot operate through the brain while the subject is clinically dead helps answer the point that since brain damage affects mental faculties, brain must be the generator of mind. If the mind, although still active in and of itself, cannot work through a brain that is briefly clinically dead, then it seems reasonable that we cannot expect it to work properly through a brain that has suffered damage (at least until other areas of the brain, by a process that remains unexplained, can take over some of the functions of the damaged parts).

Jansen (1996) claims that ingestion of the drug ketamine can reproduce NDE-type experiences, and it is possible that drugs such as this may lead to so-called out-of-body experience (OBEs), a frequently-reported state in which it is maintained that the consciousness leaves the body for a short time in perfectly healthy individuals and one which may be comparable in some relevant respects to the NDE. His argument appears to imply that OBEs at least may be due to brain states. However, even if an association between ketamine and OBE experiences is established through more detailed research, this may not indicate they are brain induced. On the contrary, it may be that the drug inhibits those brain functions that help maintain the brain-mind connection. There are obviously excellent evolutionary reasons why this connection should normally be maintained during physical existence. The vulnerability of a physical body from which the consciousness was frequently withdrawn is too obvious to require comment.

The best way of establishing whether or not consciousness does leave the body during an OBE is to present the subject with some task that can only be successfully accomplished from a position remote from the physical body. Experiments to this end are currently being conducted by Drs. Fenwick and Parnia, from London University and Southampton General Hospital respectively, but the best evidence we have to date come from Professor Charles Tart, then at the University of California in Davis

(Tart 1968 and 1996). Professor Tart arranged for a young woman who claimed to have OBEs virtually at will to pass four nights in his sleep laboratory at the University and to attempt to read a five-figure random number placed out of her sight in the laboratory (and changed each night). On the first three nights the subject was unable to find the number, but on the fourth night, while wired up to electronic equipment that prevented her from leaving her bed without detection, she read and correctly reported it. The odds against getting a five-figure random number correct at the first attempt are 100,000 to one, which leaves us secure in concluding she really was out of her body (the argument that she may have read the number by clairvoyance while remaining in her body seems unconvincing; in the absence of other evidence the young woman herself is the best judge of what went on).

Evidence from Parapsychological Research

NDEs and OBEs support the view that mind, which we might wish to equate with soul and/or spirit, is distinct from brain, and that there is indeed a spiritual dimension to life. This view has received further support from another branch of science, namely parapsychology, the branch that devoted to studying allegedly paranormal phenomena such as telepathy, clairvoyance and precognition (to give them their old but still widely used terms). The charge that, since it seems to fly in the face of known scientific laws, the extreme claims of parapsychology require extreme levels of proof is certainly justified, but for those familiar with it (and most critics and sceptics are not) the evidence for the reality of these phenomena has now been established beyond reasonable doubt over more than 70 years of experimental work conducted with a rigour that far outstrips that employed in most other areas of science (Sheldrake 1999, Watt and Nagtegaal 2004). And if these phenomena are genuine, there is no doubt that they provide further potential support for the idea of a non-physical quality present in the human mind. The results of parapsychological research are too extensive to be summarised here beyond one recent example, but there are excellent surveys in Broughton (1991), Beloff (1993), Stokes (1997), and especially Radin (1997), who also summarises attempts to answer all the criticisms levelled at the methodologies used in parapsychology.

The example concerned is the so-called Stargate Project, funded to the tune of some $20 million by the US Defence Intelligence Agency, the CIA, the US military and NASA. Briefly the project, which ran from 1970 to 1994, was designed to ascertain whether or not it was possible to obtain information about distant locations by paranormal means (clairvoyance, now referred to as remote viewing or anomalous cognitions). Analysis of the results yielded by the project produced odds against their being due to chance of 1020 (one in a hundred billion billion). Utts, the Professor of Statistics on the Supervising Committee appointed by the funding bodies to review the results, wrote (Utts 1996) that:

> It is clear that anomalous cognition is possible and has been
> demonstrated. This conclusion is not based on belief, but
> rather on commonly accepted scientific criteria. (page 30)

Even Professor Ray Hyman, the leading sceptic on the Committee, was forced to conclude that the experiments were 'well designed ... and eliminated the known weaknesses in previous parapsychological research', and that the results 'probably cannot be dismissed as due to chance'.

The Stargate project is the largest study into parapsychology funded by public money yet attempted, and would seem to show that the mind can operate outside space (results were as good when attempts were made to remote view locations thousands of miles away as when viewing locations near at hand). Results from other studies (see above references for details) also point to the reality of precognition, the ability – without clues or other guidance – to gain information significantly beyond chance expectancy of events yet to happen. This suggests that in addition to operating outside the constraints of space the mind can also operate outside those of time. Since the physical world is bounded by the space-time continuum, these abilities point towards the non-material nature of mind – and since physical death means coming to an end in the space-time continuum this also supports the notion of survival of physical death (see e.g. Fontana 2005 for a full examination of the evidence in favour of survival).

Conclusion

The reasons why psychologists should take a professional interest in religion and psychology appear to be clear and compelling. This is not to argue that psychologists need necessarily have religious or spiritual beliefs of there own, but simply that they should recognise the enormous impact that religion and spirituality have had down the centuries upon psychological and social life. However, I have attempted to show why the study of certain aspects of mind – a study which thanks to transpersonal psychology is beginning to return to its rightful place within mainstream psychology – suggests strongly that mind may not be generated by brain, but may be non-physical and work through brain. I have also suggested that if research is correct in demonstrating that under certain conditions the mind can leave and return to the physical body, and seemingly operate outside the constraints of the space-time continuum, then the evidence for the non-physical nature of mind becomes increasingly strong. Finally, I have suggested that if mind is non-physical this provides support for the notion of a spiritual dimension to existence, and also to the possible survival of physical death.

If, as I think the evidence (quite apart from person experience) undoubtedly shows there is a spiritual dimension to life, and that this dimension has played a crucial role in human history, then psychology – and society generally – neglects the study of it at our peril.

REFERENCES

Argyle, M. and Beit-Hallami, (1975). *The Social Psychology of Religion*. London: Routledge & Kegan Paul.

Beloff, J. (1993). *Parapsychology: A Concise History*. London: Athlone Press.

Broughton, R. (1991). *Parapsychology: The Controversial Science*. London: Rider.

Dossey, L. (2000). Immortality. *Alternative Therapies in Health and Medicine*, 6(3)12-17 and 108-115.

Eccles, Sir John (1980). *The Human Psyche*. New York: Springer.

Eccles, Sir John (1989).

Fenwick, P; and Fenwick, E. (1995). *The Truth in the Light*. London: Hodder.

Fontana, D. (2004). *Psychology, Religion and Spirituality*. Malden MA. and Oxford: BPS Blackwell.

Fontana, D. (2005). *Is There an Afterlife?* Ropley, Hampshire: John Hunt.

Goswami, A. (1993). *The Self-Aware Universe: How Consciousness Creates the Physical World*. London and New York: Simon and Schuster.

Grant, P. (1985). *A Dazzling Darkness*. London: Fount.

Griffin, D. R. (1997). *Parapsychology, Philosophy and Spirituality*. Albany NY. SUNY Press.

James, W. (1996). *Varieties of Religious Experience: A Study in Human Nature*. Cambridge MA. Harvard University Press (originally published 1902).

Jansen, (1996). Neuroscience, ketamine and the Near Death Experience. In L. W. Bailey and J. Yates (eds.) *The Near Death Experience*. London: Routledge.

Moody, R. (1983). *Life after Life*. New York: Bantam.

Morse, M. and Perry, (1990). *Closer to the Light: Learning from Children's Near Death Experiences*. New York: Villard.

Radin, D. (1997). *The Conscious Universe*. San Francisco: HarperEdge.

Ring, K (1984). *Heading Toward Omega*. New York: Quill/William Morrow.

Ring, K. and Valerino, E. E. (1998). *Lessons From the Light*. Insight Books.

Ring, K. and Cooper, C. (1999). *Mindsight*. New York: William James Centre for Consciousness Studies.

Sheldrake, R. (1999). How widely is blind assessment used in scientific research? *Alternative Therapies* 5, 88-91.

Smart, N. (1989). *The World's Religions*. Cambridge: Cambridge University Press.

Staal, F. (1975). *Exploring Mysticism*. Harmondsworth: Penguin.

Stokes, D. M. (1997). *The Nature of Mind: Parapsychology and the Role of Consciousness in the Physical World*. Jefferson NC. McFarland.

Tart, C. (1968). A Psychophysiological study of out-of-body experiences in a selected subject. *Journal of the American Society for Psychical Research*, 62, 3-27.

Tart, C. (1996). Who might survive the death of the body? In L. W. Bailey and J. Yates (eds.) *The Near Death Experience*. London: Routledge.

Underhill, E. (1995). *Mysticism: The Development of Humankind's Spiritual Consciousness*. London: Methuen (originally published 1911).

Utts, J. (1996). An assessment of the evidence for psychic functioning. *Journal of Scientific Exploration*, 10, 3-30.

Watt, C. and Nagtegaal, M. (2004). Reporting of blind methods: an interdisciplinary survey. *Journal of the Society for Psychical Research* 68.2, 875, 105-114.

Wilber, K. (1998). *The Marriage of Sense and Soul: The Integration of Science and Religion*. Dublin: Newleaf

Wulff, D. J. (1997) *Psychology of Religion: Classic and Contemporary*. New York: Wiley (2nd edn.).

11. TRANSPERSONAL PYSCHOLOGY AND THE JOURNEY TO SPIRITUALITY: SPIRITUAL EMERGENCE

David Lukoff

David maintains that the world seems to be experiencing a spiritual awakening which may lead to an increase in individuals experiencing spiritual problems. These are often caused by inadequate teaching or individuals who are not prepared for the profound shock that enlightened spiritual experiences can sometimes bring.

The term "spiritual emergency" to describe this problem was introduced first by the Grofs, who founded the Spiritual Emergency Network at the Esalen Institute. Unfortunately mental health systems and professionals are not always adequately prepared to recognize the symptoms nor to support rather than suppress them.

To redress the lack of sensitivity to religious and spiritual problems, David and colleagues proposed a new diagnostic category. What did not receive attention in the considerable media coverage on its publication was that this new diagnostic category has its roots in the transpersonal movement's attention to spiritual emergencies.

A distinguishing characteristic of spiritual emergencies is that, despite the distress, they can have very beneficial transformative effects on individuals. Making the differential diagnosis between a spiritual emergency and psychopathology can be difficult. Most of the models of intervention for spiritual emergencies come from the transpersonal psychology literature. Therapists should be willing to work closely with spiritual teachers but unfortunately mental health professionals rarely consult with them.

A complete mind/body/spirit integrated approach to spiritual emergencies would make use of alternative therapeutic treatments such as diet, bodywork, exercise and homeopathy. Medication can play a role in recovery. The mental health field is growing more sensitive to religion and spirituality as important factors in health and well-being, but there is a way yet to go. But acceptance of religious and spiritual problems as a new diagnostic category is a reflection of increasing sensitivity to cultural diversity and of transpersonal psychology's impact on mainstream clinical practice.

David Lukoff, *Ph.D. is a licensed clinical psychologist in California and Professor of Psychology at Saybrook Graduate School in San Francisco. He is author of 50 articles and chapters on spiritual issues and mental health, and co-author of the DSM IV category Religious or Spiritual Problem. He is co-president of the Association for Transpersonal Psychology, and maintains the Spiritual Competency Resource Center at www.spiritualcompetency.com*

Emerging Patterns in Spiritual Experience

The spiritual journey has risks and perils. The self can become disorganized and overwhelmed by an infusion of spiritual energies or new realms of experience which it is not able to integrate. Yet it seems more and more people are exploring spiritual practices such as meditation and yoga, reading books on spiritual topics (many are best sellers), and attend retreats, workshops and conferences on spiritual topics. While this can certainly be seen as a hopeful sign for the survival of the planet since spiritual traditions share many values such as peace and harmony, on the individual level there will likely be an increase in the number of people who experience spiritual problems related to the spiritual practices and exploration they undertake on their journey. The connection between spiritual development and psychological problems was first noted by Roberto Assagioli, MD, who described how persons may become inflated and grandiose as a result of intense experiences associated with spiritual practices:

"Instances of such confusion are not uncommon among people who become dazzled by contact with truths too great or energies too powerful for their mental capacities to grasp and their personality to assimilate." (Assagioli, 1989, p. 36)

David Steindl-Rast, a Benedictine monk who teaches spiritual practices, has also noted that spiritual emergence can be disruptive: "Spiritual emergence is a kind of birth pang in which you yourself go through to a fuller life, a deeper life, in which some areas in your life that were not yet encompassed by this fullness of life are now integrated . . . Breakthroughs are often very painful, often acute and dramatic." (in Bragdon, 1993, p. 18)

Beginning in the 1960s, there has been a significant increase in people adopting spiritual practices, including a wide array of meditation, marital arts, tai chi, chanting, and yoga techniques. There has also been an explosion of interest in psychedelic drugs and mystical, esoteric, shamanic and pagan traditions that involve participation in sweat lodges, goddess circles and "New Age Groups" (Lewis & Melton, 1992). Twelve step programs, with their focus on a "higher power" and spiritual awakening, have been developed for a wide range of problems and have millions of adherents. Psychospiritually-oriented cancer support groups are another recent phenomenon.

These activities have triggered many mystical experiences and visionary experiences among people who were not prepared and were not working with knowledgeable teachers, some of which proved to be problematic for them:

'Whereas spiritual masters have been warning their disciples for thousands of years about he dangers of playing with mystical states, the contemporary spiritual scene is like a candy store where any casual spiritual "tourist" can sample the "goodies" that promise a variety of mystical highs. When novices who don't have the proper education or guidance begin naively and carelessly to engage mystical experiences, they are playing with fire. Danger exists on the physical and psychological levels, as well as on the level of one's continued spiritual development.' (Caplan, 1999)

Gallup polls (1987) have shown an increase in percentages of people who report mystical experiences (from 35% in 1973 to 43% in 1986), contact with the dead (from 27% in 1973 to 42% in 1986), ESP (from 58% in 1973 to 67% in 1986), visions (from 8% in 1973 to 29% in 1986) and other unusual experiences. Based on his 15 years of survey research, Greeley (1987) concluded, "More people than ever say they've had such experiences... whether you look at the most common forms of psychic and mystical experience or the rarest...These experiences are common, benign and often helpful. What has been 'paranormal' is not only becoming normal in our time – it may also be health-giving" (p.49). Even such unusual experiences as UFO abductions (Ring, 1992) , paranormal (Braud, 1995; Hastings, 1983), and out-of-the-body experiences (Gabbard & Twemlow, 1984) are often experienced as meaningful, positively transformative, and spiritual. Accordingly, as the number of persons who engage in spiritual practices and have spiritual experiences increases, it seems likely that the incidence of spiritual problems seen in psychotherapy will also grow.

Christina Grof and Stanislav Grof, MD coined the term "spiritual emergency" and founded the Spiritual Emergency Network at the Esalen Institute in 1980 to assist individuals and make referrals to therapists for people experiencing psychological difficulties associated with spiritual practices and spontaneous spiritual experiences. They describe a spiritual emergency:

'There exist spontaneous non-ordinary states that would in the west be seen and treated as psychosis, treated mostly by suppressive medication. But if we use the observations from the study of non-ordinary states, and also from other spiritual traditions, they should really be treated as crises of transformation, or crises of spiritual opening. Something that should really be supported rather than suppressed. If properly understood and properly supported, they are actually conducive to healing and transformation.' (p. 3)

The term spiritual emergence is used to describe the whole range of phenomena associated with spiritual experiences and development, ranging from those which are not problematic, do not disrupt psychological/social/occupational functioning and do not involve psychotherapy or any contact with the mental health system (probably the vast majority), to spiritual emergences that are full-blown crises requiring 24-hour care. Grof and Grof (1989) note that "Episodes of this kind have been described in sacred literature of all ages as a result of meditative practices and as signposts of the mystical path" (p. x). They have described the more common presentations including: mystical experiences, kundalini awakening (a complex physio-psychospiritual transformative process observed in the Yogic tradition) (Greenwell, 1990) , shamanistic initiatory crisis (a rite of passage for shamans-to-be in indigenous cultures, commonly involving physical illness and/or psychological crisis) (Lukoff, 1991; Silverman, 1967) , possession states (Lukoff, 1993) and psychic opening (the sudden occurrence of paranormal experiences). A distinguishing characteristic of spiritual emergencies is that despite the distress, they can have very beneficial transformative effects on individuals who experience them

The Legacy of Freud in Religion and Mental Health

Unfortunately mental health systems and professionals are not well prepared to address people having spiritual problems. The mental health field has a heritage of 100 years of ignoring and pathologizing spiritual experiences and religion. Freud promoted this view in several of his works, such as in The Future of an Illusion where he pathologized religion as:

'A system of wishful illusions together with a disavowal of reality, such as we find nowhere else...but in a state of blissful hallucinatory confusion.' (p. 11)

Albert Ellis, PhD is the creator of Rational Emotive Therapy, the forerunner of cognitive modification approaches now widely used in cognitive-behavioural therapies. In a recent interview, Ellis (2002) stated:

'Spirit and soul is horseshit of the worst sort. Obviously there are no fairies, no Santa Clauses, no spirits. What there is, is human goals and purposes ... But a lot of transcendentalists are utter screwballs.'

BF Skinner, PhD, the psychologist who pioneered understanding of behaviour modification principles that are the other half of cognitive-behavioural therapies, did not publish a single word on the topic of spirituality. He approached humans as stimulus response boxes with varying behaviours that depend on environmental contingencies. Skinner's psychology gave no attention to inner experience, which does leave out a lot of what makes people human beings. However, Skinner's implicit views on religion can be gleaned from the novel he wrote about a Utopian community, Walden Two.

In this novel, one member describes religion as:

'an explanatory fiction, of a miracle-working mind ... superstitious behaviour perpetuated by an intermittent reinforcement schedule.'

These founders' views on religion and spirituality have had a profound influence on the clinical approach to these issues when patients bring them into therapy. M. Scott Peck, MD, author of The Road Less Traveled, highlighted the disastrous clinical consequences for all the mental health professions:

'Traditional neglect of the issue of spiritually has led to five broad areas of failure:

occasional devastating misdiagnosis; not infrequent mistreatment; an increasingly poor reputation; inadequate research and theory; and a limitation of psychiatrists' own personal development.'

Revising DSM-IV

In 1990, to redress the lack of sensitivity to religious and spiritual problems, the author, along with two psychiatrists (Francis Lu, MD and Robert Turner, MD) on the faculty at University of California, San Francisco Department of Psychiatry proposed a new diagnostic category for the 4th edition of the Diagnostic and Statistical Manual (which we knew was due to be published in 1994) which guides mental health practice in North America and influences psychiatric practices around the world. The initial impetus for this proposal came from the Spiritual Emergency Network, a referral network initially organized by Stanislav and Christina Grof while at Esalen Institute in California, which provided a telephone crisis hotline and provided referrals for people experiencing spiritual crises. We viewed such an addition to the DSM-IV nomenclature as the most effective way to increase the sensitivity of mental health professionals to spiritual issues in therapy. The proposal involved a 3 year process of working with various subcommittees (for a more detailed history of this category, see Lukoff, Lu and Turner, 1988), and resulted in the acceptance of a new diagnosis entitled Religious or Spiritual Problem, defined as follows:

'This category can be used when the focus of clinical attention is a religious or spiritual problem. Examples include distressing experiences that involve loss or questioning of faith, problems associated with conversion to a new faith, or questioning of other spiritual values which may not necessarily be related to an organized church or religious institution.' (American Psychiatric Association, 1994, p. 685)

Articles on this new category appeared in The New York Times (Steinfels, 1994), San Francisco Chronicle (Lattin, 1994), Psychiatric News (McIntyre, 1994), and the APA Monitor (Sleek, 1994) where it was described as indicating an important shift in the mental health profession's stance toward religion and spirituality.

What did not receive attention in the media is that this new diagnostic category has its roots in the transpersonal movement's attention to spiritual emergencies.

Differential Diagnosis between Mental Disorders and Spiritual Emergencies

Making the differential diagnosis between a spiritual emergency and psychopathology can be difficult because the unusual experiences, behaviors and visual, auditory, olfactory or kinesthetic perceptions characteristic of spiritual emergencies can appear as the symptoms of mental disorders: delusions, loosening of associations, markedly illogical thinking, or grossly disorganized behavior. For example, the jumbled speech of someone trying to articulate the noetic quality of a mystical experience can appear as loose associations. Or the visions of a NDE can appear as hallucinations. Or the need for solitude and quiet of a person in a spiritual emergency can appear as catatonia or depression-related withdrawal (Bragdon, 1993). Wilber (1993) argues that the distinction between spiritual emergencies and psychopathology hinges on the critical distinction between pre-rational states and authentic transpersonal states. The "pre/trans fallacy" involves confusing these conditions, which is easy to do. "Since both prepersonal and transpersonal are, in their own ways, nonpersonal, then prepersonal and transpersonal tend to appear similar, even identical, to the untutored eye" (Wilber, 1993, p. 125).

Treatment of Spiritual Emergencies

Most of the models of intervention for spiritual emergencies come from the transpersonal psychology literature. Grof and Grof (1989) recommend that the person temporarily discontinue active inner exploration and all forms of spiritual practice, change their diet to include more "grounding foods" (such as red meat), become involved in very simple grounding activities (such as gardening), engage in regular light exercise (such as walking), and use expressive arts (such as drawing, clay and evocative music) to allow the expression of emotions and experiences through color, forms, sound and movement. Reliance on the client's self-healing capacities is one of the main principles that guide transpersonal treatment of spiritual emergencies (Perry, 1974; Watson, 1994) . In addition, therapists should be willing to consult, work closely with or even refer to spiritual teachers who may have considerably more expertise in the specific types of crises associated with a given spiritual practice or tradition. Unfortunately mental health professionals rarely consult with religious professionals or spiritual teachers even when dealing religious and spiritual issues (Larson, Hohmann, Kessler, Meador, Boyd, & McSherry, 1988).

Another key component of treatment of spiritual emergencies is normalization of and education about the experience. While this is a common technique in therapy, it plays an especially important role with spiritual emergencies because persons in the midst of spiritual emergencies are often afraid that the unusual nature of their experiences indicates that they are "going crazy" (as described in some of the above cases). An extremely abbreviated version of normalization of an unusual spiritual experience is reported by Jung (1964) in the following case:

'I vividly recall the case of a professor who had a sudden vision and thought he was insane. He came to see me in a state of complete panic. I simply took a 400-year-old book from the shelf and showed him an old woodcut depicting his very vision. "There's no reason for you to believe that you're insane," I said to him. "They knew about your vision 400 years ago." Whereupon he sat down entirely deflated, but once more normal.' (p. 69)

A complete mind/body/spirit integrated approach to spiritual emergencies would also make use of alternative therapeutic treatments such as diet, bodywork, exercise and movement, homeopathy, herbs (just to name a few) (Bragdon, 1993; Cortright, 1997). There may even be times when medication can play a role in recovery and integration of these experiences.

Fortunately it does seem the mental health field is growing more sensitive to religion and spirituality as important factors in health and well-being. I concur with the assessment of Michael Washburn, PhD (1998).

'There still is a pathologization of anything that has to do with difficult religious experience. We are overcoming that, I am pleased to say. There is a growing appreciation that a passage into spiritual life can be psychologically very challenging, and that we should expect it as a common occurrence, and learn better to understand it so we can deal with it when it happens. I think we are in a better situation as far as those possibilities are concerned than we have been in the past. But there's still some way to go.'

The acceptance of religious and spiritual problems as a new diagnostic category in DSM-IV is a reflection of increasing sensitivity to the pitfalls and perils of the spiritual journey in the mental health professions.

REFERENCES

Assagioli, R. (1989). Self-realization and psychological disturbances. In S. Grof & C. Grof (Eds.), *Spiritual Emergency: When personal transformation becomes a crisis*. Los Angeles: Tarcher.

Bragdon, E. (1993). *A Sourcebook for Helping People with Spiritual Problems*. Aptos, CA: Lightening Up Press

Braud, W. (1995). Parapsychology and spirituality: Implications and intimations. *ReVision: A Journal of Consciousness and Transformation*, 18(1), 36-43.

Caplan, M. (1999) *Halfway Up the Mountain: The Error of Premature Claims to Enlightenment*, Prescott, AZ: Hohm Press.

Cortright, B. (1997). *Psychotherapy and Spirit: Theory and Practice in Transpersonal Psychotherapy*. Albany, NY: State University of New York Press.

Ellis, A. (2002) An Interview with Albert Ellis, Ph.D., by Myrtle Heery, Ph.D. http://www.psychotherapist resources.com/current/cgi/framemaker.cgi?mainframe=totm&subframe=ellis

Freud, S. (1989). *The Future of an Illusion*. New York: W. W. Norton & Company

Gabbard, G., & Twemlow, S. (1984). *With the Eyes of the Mind: An empirical analysis of out-of-the-body states*. New York: Praeger.

Gallup, G. (1987). *The Gallup Poll: Public Opinion 1986*. Wilmington, DE: Scholarly Resources.

Greeley, A. (1987, January/February). Mysticism goes mainstream. *American Health*, 47-49.

Greenwell, B. (1990). *Energies of Transformation: A guide to the kundalini process*. Saratoga, CA: Shakti River Press.

Grof, S., & Grof, C. (Eds.). (1989). *Spiritual Emergency: When personal transformation becomes a crisis*. Los Angeles: Tarcher.

Hastings, A. (1983). A counseling approach to parapsycholgical experience. *Journal of Transpersonal Psychology*, 15(2), 143-167.

Larson, D., Hohmann, A., Kessler, L., Meador, K., Boyd, J., & McSherry, E. (1988). The couch and the cloth: The need for linkage. *Hospital and Community Psychiatry*, 39(10), 10641069.

Lattin, D. (1994, March 17, 1994). Therapists turn from psyche to soul. *San Francisco Chronicle*, pp. A1,12.

Lewis, J., & Melton, T. (Eds.). (1992). *Perspectives on the New Age*. Albany, NY: State University of New York Press.

Lukoff, D., Lu, F., and Turner, R. From spiritual emergency to spiritual problem: The transpersonal roots of the new DSM-IV category. *Journal of Humanistic Psychology*, 38(2), 21-50, 1998.

Lukoff, D. (1991). Divine madness: Shamanistic initiatory crisis and psychosis. *Shaman's Drum*, 22, 24-29.

Lukoff, D. (1993). Case study of the emergence of a contemporary shaman. In R. I. Heinze (Ed.), *Proceedings of the Ninth International Conference on Shamanism and Alternate Healing*. Berkeley, CA: Asian Scholars Press.

McIntyre, J. (March 4, 1994). Psychiatry and Religion: A visit to Utah. *Psychiatric News*, 29, 12.

Peck, S. (1998). *The Road Less Traveled and Beyond: Spiritual Growth in an Age of Anxiety* New York: Touchstone

Perry, J. (1974). *The Far Side of Madness*. Englewood Cliffs, NJ: Prentice Hall.

Ring, K. (1992). *The Omega Project: Near-death, UFO encounters, and mind at large*. New York: William Morris.

Silverman, J. (1967). Shamans and acute schizophrenia. *American Anthropologist*, 69(1), 21-31.

Skinner, BF (1976) *Walden Two*. Upper Saddle River, NJ: Prentice-Hall.

Sleek, S. (1994, June). Spiritual problems included in DSM-IV. *American Psychological Association Monitor*, 17.

Steinfels, P. (1994, Feb. 10, 1994). Psychiatrists' manual shifts stance on religious and spiritual problems. *New York Times*, pp. A9.

Washburn, M. (1998). Michael Washburn interviewed by Paul Bernstein http://members.tripod.com /%7Epbernste/life3.htm

Watson, K. W. (1994). Spiritual emergence: Concepts and implications for psychotherapy. *Journal of Humanistic Psychology*, 34(2), 22-45

Wilber, K. (1993). The pre/trans fallacy. In R. Walsh & F. Vaughan (Eds.), *Paths beyond Ego*, (pp. 124-130). Los Angeles: Tarcher.

12. WHAT IS INTEGRAL PSYCHOTHERAPY?

John Rowan

John summarizes the evolutionary approach of Ken Wilber, which details the three main stages of human development – the prepersonal, the personal and the transpersonal, and analyses Wilber's seminal four quadrants diagram, suggesting a revision of it from the point of view of psychotherapy. John takes the five levels of development of the upper left quadrant, which is where psychotherapists usually work, and shows their correspondences in the other three quadrants, skilfully demonstrating where the ideas of other well known and respected writers fit into the Wilber analysis.

While of primary interest to professionals and academics in the field, this comprehensive attempt to show how the levels 13-15 follow on from the prepersonal levels up to 11 and the personal level 12 is an indication of the development of the transpersonal and its firm situating within a framework of sound research and scholarship. The rigorous exploration of stage 15, which Wallace calls "contemplative technology", is sometimes called mindfulness. There are many ways of reaching level 15, but all of them can be called meditation. The placing of meditation into a comprehensive framework of human development is an important step in bringing the concept of the transpersonal in an interconnected world into the discussions of ordinary citizens rather than leaving the field to researchers, teachers and students of psychology and psychotherapy.

John Rowan *has written a book and various chapters and articles about transpersonal psychotherapy. He is a Fellow of the British Psychological Society and of the British Association for Counselling and Psychotherapy. He is in private practice as a therapist and group facilitator. John Rowan, 70 Kings Head Hill, London E4 7LY . E-mail: johnrowan@aol.com*

Introduction

To write a full introduction to this essay, explaining the whole evolutionary approach of Ken Wilber (2000) would be too lengthy and perhaps not necessary. Wilber's basic idea is quite well known by now. It can be found in all of his books. In its simplest form it says that in the process of our psycho-spiritual development, there are three main stages which we go through, which he labels the prepersonal, the personal and the transpersonal. The prepersonal is all that part of our development prior to the emergence of a separate self, which normally happens in or around adolescence. It is well described in all the standard literature. The personal is the main part of our development, taking place in adulthood, and culminating in the mature ego. Most of psychology, and most other literature too, deals with this stage of development, and again there is a mass of data about it. The transpersonal is the realm beyond that, which we only reach by an intentional process, because society does not help us with it – at this point there is no escalator taking us onwards, so to speak. It is more controversial, but Wilber's great achievement has been to describe it in full detail, and to map it with the help of writers from many countries and many centuries.

If we look at his quadrant diagram, first described in his 1995 book, and reprinted many times in his later books, we can see at once that he has taken this basic thought (which originally only applied to the upper left quadrant, the individual interior subjective, or I) and applied it to three other realms, which he describes as the lower left (the social exterior subjective, or We), the lower right (the social exterior objective, or They), and the upper right (the individual interior objective, or It). Within each of these he has a set of numbered levels.

He then goes on to say that any activity we may think important is best thought of in terms of AQAL (all quadrants, all levels). If we think in terms of the three broad sections which we have labelled as prepersonal, personal and transpersonal, everything up to and including level 11 is prepersonal, level 12 he calls the personal, and everything including level 13 and beyond he calls the transpersonal.

In the diagram (Figure 1), it looks as if development was linear and unified – in other words, it looks as if we go up the line in one piece. But Wilber warns that this is not so. We have to take into account that there is more than one line of development. He says: "There is moderate to strong evidence for the existence of the following developmental lines: cognition, morals, affects, motivation/needs, ideas of the good, psychosexuality, kinesthetic intelligence, self-identity (ego), role-taking, logico-mathematical competence, socio-emotional capacity, worldviews,

UPPER LEFT INTERIOR INDIVIDUAL	UPPER RIGHT EXTERIOR INDIVIDUAL
11 CONOP (magic/mythic, prepersonal) 12 FORMOP (personal, mental ego) 13 VISION-LOGIC (dialectical) 14 SUBTLE SELF 15 CAUSAL SELF	11 SF1 (homunculus) 12 SF2 (rational, precise) 13 SF3 (dialectical, complex) 14 SUBTLE BODY 15 FORMLESS BODY
LOWER LEFT **INTERIOR SOCIAL (cultural,** **interpersonal)**	**LOWER RIGHT** **EXTERIOR SOCIAL**

11 MYTHIC (community)
12 RATIONAL (separate identity
      capable of relating to others)
13 CENTAURIC (intersubjective)
14 LINKING
15 NO-RELATION
	11 EARLY STATE/EMPIRE (community)
	12 NATIONAL STATE (economic
	      rationality)
	13 PLANETARY HUMAN SCIENCE
	14 RESACRALIZATION
	15 ULTIMATE REALITY

values, several lines that might be called 'spiritual' (care, openness, concern, religious faith, meditative stages), musical skill, altruism, communicative competence, creativity, modes of space and time perception, death-fear, gender identity, and empathy." And he says that development may often be uneven. Hence a great guru may be spiritually highly developed but morally suspect, for example.

Taking all this for granted, then, we go on to look at each of the quadrants in turn, from the point of view of psychotherapy.

Upper Left

This is the most usual quadrant for psychotherapy to work in, and it is better charted from this point of view than any of the other quadrants. In the chart which Wilber (1995) provides, psychotherapy is mainly interested in the later levels of development:

Level 11 is labelled Conop in the chart, which means Piaget's level of concrete operations, and also corresponds with the magic–mythic level of thought outlined by Gebser and others. It is part of what Wilber calls the prepersonal realm, and is dominated by fear.

Level 12 is labelled Formop, which means Piaget's level of formal operations, and also corresponds with what Wilber calls the Mental Ego and the Personal level of development. It is dominated by an Aristotelian (Boolean, Newtonian) type of reason. In psychotherapy this brings about a belief in techniques which can be tested objectively. In psychotherapy the key word here is: Treating.

Level 13 is labelled Vision–logic, which Wilber elsewhere also calls dialectical logic and identifies with what he calls the Centaur level of development which hovers in developmental terms between the personal and the transpersonal. Jenny Wade (1996) more transparently calls this the Authentic level (Rowan & Jacobs 2002). The key word here: Meeting.

Level 14 is variously labelled as the Psychic, the Subtle, or the level of soul, as James Hillman (1990) has urged. Here we find a great interest in mythology, dreams, fairy tales and other stories, and Jungians like Barbara Hannah (1981) have been very active in exploring this territory. Roberto Assagioli, with his idea of psychosynthesis, introduced some very important work here, and in fact the use of the word transpersonal to apply to psychotherapy came from him more than anyone else. The key work here is: Linking.

Level 15 is labelled as the Causal. Here we discover the possibility for a therapist of dropping all symbols or images, and all distance, as David Brazier (1995) has urged. The therapist can be freely creative as Amy Mindell has pointed out (Mindell 1995), following the needs of the moment. The therapist believes in co-creating both the therapeutic space and the movement within it, as Robert Rosenbaum has told us (Rosenbaum 1998). There is a unique combination of activity and stillness, well described by A H Almaas (1988). Key word: Paradox.

What I would like to do now is to show how these five levels of development in the individual interior quadrant have correspondences with the levels in the other three quadrants.

Lower Left

Level 11 is where we are merged with the family, tribe, community, etc. We do not see ourselves as a separate individual, but rather as part of something larger; and there is a fear of losing this connection.

Level 12 is where we see ourselves as individuals, who can relate to other people in a variety of ways. Each role that we play brings out different aspects of our personality, but basically we are single and separate. As psychotherapists, we are very concerned to hold our boundaries secure.

Group therapy at this level means learning a variety of techniques to be used in group work (Dryden & Neenan 2002).

At level 13 we see things in a more dialectical way. We are at one and the same time separate and not separate; we are part of a field and not part of a field; we can allow ourselves to be invaded by the other without feeling threatened. We can admit that we are part of a social field without feeling that we have lost.

This is the great level for groupwork, where the group is taken really seriously as a group (Foulkes & Anthony 1965).

At level 14 we can actually allow ourselves to be one with the client. We were originally all part of the same mainland, so to speak, and we can now bring to mind that primitive unity. We cannot be threatened by the other person, because we are that person. We share the same imaginal world as the client. This is the phenomenon of linking, which specifically belongs to this level (Rowan 1998).

Group work at this level becomes much more imaginative, and the use of imagery becomes much more frequent. Arnold and Amy Mindell (2002) have written very well about their own approach to transpersonal groupwork, which is quite inspiring.

At level 15 none of this matters. All these distinctions fade away. It is true, however, that the Mindells often write as if they are going into the Causal with their work. People will have to make up their own minds as to whether this is true.

Lower Right

Level 11 is the level of the community – what the German sociologists call the Gemeinschaft. It is the basic view that we are the people, and in a nationalist country we are the nation. Outsiders are suspect. As therapists, we have a part to play which must never challenge established beliefs, but work with them.

Level 12 is the level of economic rationality, where we see the world as an interlocking set of mutually inconsistent aims, all competing in a vast world market. As psychotherapists, we have to take this into account, and regard ourselves sometimes as entrepreneurs in the marketplace. Our colleagues are also our competitors. This level of socioeconomic outlook is also very favourable to working for a national or regional organisation and working within the constraints set up by constant evaluation and measurement.

At level 13 we see sociology as a planetary human science, where we have to take into account the personal needs and individual outlooks of all people, and not treat a person as a unit to be manipulated (Samuels 1993). As psychotherapists, we are acutely conscious of the ways in which sexism and racism can invade the therapeutic situation

At level 14 we see society not only as a physical and mental system, but also as a spiritual system, inhabited by unseen forces which are ignored by most people.

And at level 15 all this disappears, and society appears as just as meaningless as any other category. We are engaged in a search for ultimate reality, and anything lesser does not seem all that interesting.

Upper Right

Level 11 is where we see the brain as a marvellous set of mechanisms which can be studied, but really there is a homunculus behind the eyes somewhere which simply uses all these mechanisms. If we can influence this homunculus, we can achieve miracles, but we really have no control over it. So there is a sense of being at the mercy of fate, which can sometimes be cruel. This is a view of the brain which is actually very common, I believe.

At level 12 we see the brain as fully scientifically describable with no need for anything other than ordinary physical cause–and–effect sequences. This is still the way in which many experts explain it. As Susan Greenfield (2000) so succinctly puts it: "All 'you' consist of is a brain, albeit one personalized by a unique trajectory through life."

At level 13 there is a more dialectical appreciation of the relationships between the brain and other parts of the body, and the whole question of health. One of the pioneers of this level of thought was Francis Varela (1991). It is amazing how even the experts seem to be ignorant of the many years of work that Stanislav Grof (1979) has put in to his careful research into the birth process. Hardly any of them mention the more recent work of David Chamberlain (1998), a psychologist who has made a special study of birth memories.

One of the things which interests me in particular about this level is that there is clearly a place for subunits within the whole. Varela et al (1991) quote Marvin Minsky and others as offering a model of the mind 'as a society of numerous agents' (p.106) and this enables us to think not only in terms of holons, which is Wilber's primary concept, but also in terms of subpersonalities, which is one of my own favourite themes.

Also at this level we find sophisticated views of the relationship between body and mind from psychotherapists themselves, first among whom I would reckon Eugene Gendlin, whose Focusing approach (1996, see also Friedman 2000) makes the connection in a very helpful way.

At level 14 we start to talk about the subtle body, and see the brain as not so central at all. There are several different centres in the body, as described for example in the chakra system, and not all of them have much to do with the brain, though they all interact and all partake in brainlike activities. John Nelson (1996) has explained very succinctly how this works at the level of psychotherapy.

And at level 15 we move out of the world of form into the formless world, where all concepts can be questioned or laid aside. The whole question of what is objective fact comes under radical scrutiny. It is a fact that in recent years neuroscientists have become more and more interested in Buddhist theories of the no–self. Alan Wallace (1999) writes about samatha (pronounced shamata) as a rigorous exploration of level 15. He speaks of it as a 'contemplative technology' for studying this particular level. It is sometimes called mindfulness. But it has become clear today that there are many ways of reaching level 15, though all of them can be called meditation. At this level the distinction between what is subjective and what is objective becomes hard to uphold. Varela et al (1991) say this: "Within the tradition of mindfulness/awareness meditation, the motivation has been to develop a direct and stable insight into absolutism and nihilism as forms of grasping that result from the attempt to find a stable ego–self and so limit our lived world to the experience of suffering and frustration. By progressively learning to let go of these tendencies to grasp, one can begin to appreciate that all phenomena are free of any absolute ground and that such 'groundlessness' (sunyata) is the very fabric of dependent coorigination." (p.144)

With that we can close our attempt to describe the four quadrants in a way that will ￼e helpful to therapists. In reducing 7000 words to 3000 much has been lost, but it is hoped that the result will at least be indicative of the main thrust of the case being made here. Not only can we look at psychotherapy in an AQAL spirit, but the results are stimulating and surprising, and I think useful too.

BIBLIOGRAPHY

Almaas, A H (1988) *The Pearl beyond Price: Integration of personality into being: an object relations approach.* Berkeley: Diamond Books

Brazier, David (1995) *Zen Therapy* London: Constable

Chamberlain, David (1998) *The Mind of your Newborn Baby.* Berkeley: North Atlantic Books

Dryden, Windy & Neenan, Michael (eds) (2002) *Rational Emotive Behaviour Group Therapy* London: Whurr

Foulkes, S.H. and Anthony, E.J. (1965) *Group Psychotherapy: The Psychoanalytic Approach* (2nd edition). London: Penguin Books.

Friedman, Neil (2000) *Focusing: Selected Essays 1974–1999* Arlington: Xlibris

Gendlin, Eugene (1996) *Focusing–Oriented Psychotherapy: A Manual of the Experiential Method.* New York: Guilford Press

Greenfield, Susan (2000) *Brain Story: Unlocking our inner world of emotions, memories, ideas and desires.* London: BBC Worldwide

Grof, Stanislav (1979) *Realms of the Human Unconscious.* London: Souvenir Press

Hannah, Barbara (1981) *Encounters with the Soul.* Boston: Sigo Press

Hillman, James (1990) *The Essential James Hillman.* (ed T Moore) London: Routledge

Mindell, Amy (1995) *Metaskills: The spiritual art of therapy.* Tempe, Arizona: New Falcon Publications

Mindell, Arnold and Amy (2002) *Riding the Horse Backwards: Process work in theory and practice.* Portland: Lao Tse Press

Nelson, John E (1996) 'Madness or transcendence' in S Boorstein (ed) *Transpersonal Psychotherapy.* (2nd edition) Albany: SUNY Press

Rosenbaum, Robert (1998) *Zen and the Heart of Psychotherapy.* Philadelphia: Brunner/Mazel

Rowan, John (1998) 'Linking: Its place in psychotherapy' *International Journal of Psychotherapy*

Rowan, John & Jacobs, Michael (2002) *The Therapist's Use of Self.* Buckingham: Open University Press

Samuels, Andrew (1993) *The Political Psyche.* London: Routledge

Varela, Francisco J, Thompson, Evan & Rosch, Eleanor (1991) *The Embodied Mind: Cognitive science and human experience.* London: The MIT Press

Wade, Jenny (1996) *Changes of Mind: A holonomic theory of the evolution of consciousness.* Albany: SUNY Press

Wallace, B Alan (1999) 'The Buddhist Tradition of Samatha: Methods for refining and examining consciousness' *Journal of Counsciousness Studies* Vol.6 175–187

Wilber, Ken (1995) *Sex, Ecology, Spirituality.* Boston: Shambhala

Wilber, Ken (2000) *Integral Psychology.* Boston: Shambhala

13. A NEW LOOK AT INTEGRAL GROWTH

Jorge Ferrer

The idea of an integral spiritual life firmly grounded in psychosomatic integration appears in religious literature but not so much in contemporary culture. Jorge Ferrer asks what it means to live a fully embodied contemporary spiritual life and leads the reader through the rich research of the last few decades to the development of Integral Transformative Practices (ITPs), which are based largely on an eclectic mix of practices and techniques selected from psychological and spiritual disciplines available today.

He discusses the issues of guidance in a complex world of conflicts, fears, and confusion and identifies three interrelated principles of integral growth – co-creation by all dimensions of human nature; an unfolding from within; and a balancing of the feminine and the masculine - which are embodied in the new integral praxis of holistic integration.

Jorge N Ferrer, *Ph.D. is core faculty at the California Institute of Integral Studies, San Francisco, and author of Revisioning Transpersonal Theory: A Participatory Vision of Human Spirituality (SUNY Press, 2002). In 2000 he received the Fetzer Institute's Presidential Award for his seminal work on consciousness studies.*

In an age of spiritual confusion, a consensus is growing among transpersonal authors and spiritual teachers about the importance of an integral growth of the person – that 's, a developmental process that integrates all human dimensions (body, instincts, eart, mind, and consciousness) into a fully embodied spiritual life.

Although the idea of an integral spiritual life that it is firmly grounded in psychosomatic integration can be found in the world's religious literature, there are not many effective paths available in contemporary culture. Genuine integral growth in spiritual practitioners seems to be the exception to the rule, even among teachers. More often we find that spiritual development is skewed away from the maturation of the somatic, instinctive, sexual, and emotional worlds. A related outcome is that many honest spiritual efforts are undermined by conflicts at somatic, sexual, or emotional levels. Too often, spiritual seekers struggle with tensions existing between their spiritual ideals and their instinctive, sexual, and emotional drives, recurrently falling into unconsciously driven patterns or habits despite their most sincere conscious intentions.

This lopsided development leads to many of the common pitfalls we see today in contemporary spiritual culture: spiritual bypassing, spiritual materialism and narcissism, ethical and psychosexual problems in the teacher-student relationship, difficulties in integrating spiritual experiences, and a devitalization of the body and inhibition of sexual energies, to name only a few. It also hinders the development of spiritual discernment. For example, it is likely that most spiritual visions are to some extent the product of dissociated ways of knowing – ways that emerge from emotional or mental access to subtle forms of transcendent consciousness but are ungrounded from vital and immanent spiritual sources.

For example, spiritual visions that hold that body and world are ultimately illusory arguably derive from states of being in which the sense of self identifies with the subtle energies of consciousness and is uprooted from the body and immanent spiritual life. Yet a very different experience of world and body is possible. When our somatic and vital worlds are invited to participate in our spiritual lives, making our sense of identity permeable not only to transcendent awareness but also to immanent spiritual energies, then body and world become hierophanies—sacred realities that are crucial for spiritual evolution.

We have historically inherited, in essence, a "heart chakra up" spirituality, which values certain human qualities as being more "spiritually correct" or wholesome than others; for instance, equanimity over intense passions, transcendence over sensuous embodiment, chastity over sexual exploration, and so forth. Although I cannot examine here the numerous historical and contextual variables behind this tendency, I would like to mention at least one possible underlying reason. In the context of Western culture, the inhibition of the primary dimensions of the person – somatic, instinctive, sexual, and certain aspects of the emotional – may have bee necessary at certain evolutionary juncture to allow the emergence and maturation of the values of the human heart and consciousness. More specifically, this inhibition may have been essential to avoid the reabsorption of a still relatively weak, emerging self-consciousness into the stronger presence that a more instinctively driven energy once had in the individual. What may characterize our present moment, however, is the possibility of reconnecting all these human potentials in an integrated way. In other words, having developed self-reflective consciousness and the subtle dimensions of the heart, it may be the moment to reappropriate and integrate – while retaining these values – the more primary and instinctive dimensions of human nature into a fully embodied spiritual life.

But what does it really mean to live a fully embodied spiritual life? Is it actually possible to integrate the many needs and desires of the various dimensions of our being harmoniously? Can we cultivate the wisdom of our bodies, instincts, hearts, minds and souls without generating tensions or dissociations within us? And, perhaps most importantly, how can we lay down a truly integral spiritual path that respects the integrity of the many voices dwelling within us?

Integral Transformative Practices

The first contemporary attempt at such an integral path was made by Michael Murphy, who, inspired by Sri Aurobindo's integral vision and synthesis of yogas, co-founded the Esalen Institute in 1962 to advance the development of the whole person. In *The Future of the Body* (Tarcher/Perigee, 1993), Murphy offered a rich inventory of exercises, techniques, and practices that can be used to foster a more integral development. According to Murphy, the goal of Integral Transformative Practices (ITPs) is "integral transformation" or "integral enlightenment," that is, "the flowering, in all our parts, of all our attributes, of all the various capacities we have, of this latent divinity."

A few years later, Murphy joined forces with George Leonard, another pioneer of the Human Potential Movement, and created a new ITP program that incorporated what they called the ITP Kata. Drawing on such disciplines as hatha yoga, martial arts, and modern exercise physiology, the ITP Kata begins with a series of balancing and centering movements, followed by a period of transformational imaging (intentional use of mental imagery to promote body health, heart openness, creativity, or other qualities selected by the practitioner), and ends with a time for meditation that combines self-observation with contemplative prayer.

More recently, Ken Wilber has also offered some reflections on ITPs. Wilber uses the term "ITP" to refer not only to Leonard and Murphy's integral program but also to any set of practices that cultivates the various human dimensions. The idea is that the more dimensions of the human bodymind are exercised, the more transparent to the Divine they become. Wilber suggests envisioning six columns representing different dimensions: physical, emotional-sexual (prana or chi), mental or psychological, contemplative or meditative, community, and nature, and offers a variety of possible practices to train each dimension: aerobic exercise, weight lifting, and healthy diet for the physical; yoga, qi gong, and tai chi chuan for prana; psychotherapy, visualizations, and affirmations for the psychological; zazen, vipassana, or centering prayer for the contemplative; community service, compassionate care, and engagement with others for the community; and recycling, hikes, and nature celebration for nature.

Thus, contemporary ITP programs are based largely on an eclectic mixture of practices and techniques selected from the many somatic, psychological, and spiritual disciplines available today in the modern West. Through these programs, practitioners design their own personalized integral training to exercise their various attributes.

A Participatory Perspective on Integral Growth

Although contemporary ITP programs can obviously promote the integral health of the person, a possible limitation of these approaches comes with who is running the show, who is devising the program. Briefly, ITP programs can easily turn into a "mentally" devised integral training in which the practitioner's mind decides what are the best practices or techniques to develop his or her body, sexuality, heart, and consciousness. This is understandable. After all, modern Western education focuses almost exclusively on the development of the rational mind and its cognitive functions, with little attention given to the maturation of other dimensions of the person. As a result, most individuals in our culture reach their adulthood with a somewhat mature mental functioning, but with poorly developed somatic, instinctive, and emotional worlds. Given the extreme "cognicentrism" of our way of life, the mental direction of integral growth seems nearly inevitable.

The greatest tragedy of cognicentrism, however, is that it generates a vicious circle that justifies itself: Because modern education does not create spaces for the autonomous maturation of the body, the instincts and the heart, it becomes true that these worlds cannot participate in an evolutionary path if they are not mentally c externally guided. The problem is that insofar as they are always mentally or externally guided, these human dimensions cannot mature autonomously, and thus the need for their mental or external direction becomes permanently justified.

Complicating this situation further is the fact that, after many generations of mind-centred education and life – often combined with the control or inhibition of the body, instincts, sexuality and passions – these aspects are not only chronically underdeveloped in our culture, they are frequently wounded, distorted, or manifesting regressive tendencies. Thus, when an individual seeks guidance in these worlds, the first thing that he or she typically finds is a layer of conflicts, fears or confusion that perpetuates the deep-seated belief that these worlds need to be mentally regulated in order to be wholesome or evolutionary. What is normally overlooked, however, is an essential primary intelligence that lies beneath this layer which, if accessed, can heal the root of the conflict while fostering the maturation and evolution of these worlds from within.

These dimensions must be allowed to heal and mature according to their own developmental principles, not according to the ones that the mind thinks are most adequate. Only when our body, instincts, sexuality, and heart are allowed to mature autonomously will they be able to sit at the same table with our minds and co-create a truly integral development and spiritual life.

An example may help clarify what I am proposing. There are many practices and techniques for the cultivation of the body, from hatha yoga to aerobic training to weight lifting. Clearly, these practices can be of value and effectively promote health and growth for many individuals at specific junctures of their development. The risk of cultivating the body exclusively through these techniques, however, is that insofar as they are either selected by the mind or regulated by external standards (e.g., regarding the body's position, posture, movement, or appearance), these practices can block the emergence of the body's intelligence. Such practices may prevent the body from engendering the very positions, movements, and attitudes that may be more natural and vital for its optimum development.

The kind of development I am describing involves connecting with the current state of the body; listening to its needs, calls, and creative urges; and developing practices that respond to those needs, calls, or creative urges. This doesn't mean that already established practices cannot be involved. It is perfectly possible that once our bodies, instincts, and hearts mature and can communicate with us, they may call us to engage already established discipline.

Three interrelated principles may help to understand this perspective on integral growth:

1. Integral growth is co-created by all dimensions of human nature. A genuine process of integral growth cannot be exclusively directed by the mind, but emerges from the collaborative participation and creative power of all human dimensions: body, instincts, heart, mind and consciousness.

2. Integral growth unfolds from within, grounded in our most vital potentials. When the various human dimensions mature and co-creatively participate in a developmental path, integral growth organically unfolds from within. A genuine integral growth that is grounded in our most unique potentials rarely follows a given path traveled by others, nor can it be directed by external standards. External sources of guidance can be essential reference points at certain junctures of the journey, but the path towards the emergence of our most unique qualities cannot be directed from outside of us.

3. Integral growth balances the feminine and the masculine. Integral growth combines the more masculine element of "exercise" and "training" of skills with the more feminine element of "engendering" new qualities and capabilities from within. For this to be grounded in the individual's most vital energies, the feminine needs to precede the masculine.

Towards a New Integral Praxis

Although this may all sound more theoretical than practical, two Spanish therapists, Ramon Albareda and Marina Romero, have created an approach called Holistic Integration, which helps each person lay down his or her own path of integral evolution free from the potential constraints that are subtly imposed by psychospiritual models and ideals.

One of the orienting principles of Holistic Integration is that all human dimensions, especially when mature, are equally valuable for individual (and collective) health, growth, and evolution. Since the biological organism is the first dimension that emerges after conception, it becomes necessary to engage the body in order to access the deepest energetic potentials not only of the body, but also of our instincts, hearts, and minds. In short, the engagement with our body and vital-primary energy is essential for a genuine and creative integral spirituality.

With the notable exception of certain tantric practices, traditional meditation techniques are practiced individually and without bodily interaction with other practitioners. One of Holistic Integration's major innovations is that it features a variety of meditative and contemplative practices that, in a structured and respectful setting, are developed "in contact" with other individuals. These interactive embodied meditations are the starting point of the work. The general aim of these practices is to allow practitioners to discern experientially the deep energetic state of their various dimensions (body, vital-sexual, heart, mind, and consciousness) as well as their degree of integration or dissociation.

After introducing the interactive embodied meditations, Albareda and Romero present a number of contemplative practices to facilitate a more nuanced, focused, and intentional exploration of the somatic, instinctive, emotional, psychological, and spiritual dimensions. Many of these practices are also carried out in interactive embodied contact with other practitioners. In all exercises, practitioners cultivate an attitude of open presence, receptivity, and unconditional acceptance toward their moment-to-moment experience.

Although space does not allow me to discuss all of the methods here, it may be important to hint at two distinctive elements of these practices. The first is the differentiation and integration of polar aspects. Albareda and Romero consider that the various human dimensions (body, instincts, heart, mind, and consciousness) and polar aspects (masculine/feminine, sexuality/spirituality, individual/community, and so forth) mature through a process of differentiation and integration. This process leads not only to the strengthening of each integrated dimension or polar reality, but also to the emergence of novel human qualities. When strength and gentleness are integrated, for example, strength can fully be strength because its incorporated gentleness prevents it from becoming aggression, and gentleness can fully be gentleness because strength prevents it from becoming weakness. In addition, their integration brings forth a number of new qualities such as passionate humbleness and tender instinct.

The second is the special attention given to primary-sexual energies. Due to the potentially overwhelming power of the primary energy, as well as the layer of wounds and conflicts usually stored therein, it is fundamental that any reawakening of this energy occurs in an extremely gradual and careful manner. Albareda and Romero have developed a set of original contemplative embodied practices, which, in a safe and respectful environment, allow practitioners to gently reawaken their primary energy and gradually integrate it. These practices seek to free the body from its organically embedded shame; heal a number of wounds, conflicts, or inhibitions stored at this energetic level; allow a more fluid movement of the primary energy through body, heart, mind, and consciousness; align the vital-primary energy with the energy of consciousness; and foster the activation, gestation, and creative transformation of the primary energy, bringing forth novel qualities and potentials at somatic, emotional, psychological, and spiritual levels.

It is interesting to note that at a certain point in the process, practitioners start to design their own individualized practices, first with the guidance of the facilitators, and then completely on their own. Individualized practices are essential because only through them can practitioners access the deepest domains of their being and hence ground their integral process in their unique vital potentials. It is fundamental to stress that, even though the facilitators may offer practical advice about the design of personal practices, the integral growth process is primarily regulated by the practitioner's own multidimensional experience. In other words, the specific form of a given practice is organically shaped or inspired by whatever happens somatically, energetically, emotionally, mentally or spiritually in the previous practice (e.g., difficulties or tensions, desires or impulses, confusion or questions, insights or inspirations, visions or spiritual openings, and so forth). This is why integral growth unfolds through a route that can never be predetermined and that takes as many forms and directions as the individuals involved. Although systematic research to assess the actual effectiveness of these practices is currently under way, this multidimensional organic unfolding holds a promise to short circuit the danger of egoic or mental control of integral growth.

Holistic Integration is generally done in a group format either in intensive retreats or over a period of months. The ongoing presence of a community of support and a focus on integrating one's transformation into everyday life are central to this approach.

I have written about integral practices because I believe they are important in fostering the creative transformation of the person and the world, the spiritualization of matter and the sensuous grounding of spirit, and, ultimately, the bringing together of Heaven and Earth. Who knows, perhaps as human beings learn to embody transcendent and immanent spiritual energies – a twofold incarnation, so to speak – they can then realize that it is here, in this plane of concrete physical reality, that the cutting edge of spiritual transformation and evolution is taking place. For then the planet Earth may gradually turn into an embodied Heaven, a perhaps unique place in the cosmos where beings can learn to express and receive embodied love in all its forms.

14. POST-HUMAN VERSUS THE ROBO SAPIENS: HUMAN CONSCIOUSNESS AS A NON-REPLICABLE EMBODIED ORGANIC PREROGATIVE

Alex Shalom Kohav

Despite the recent upsurge of scientific interest in consciousness, Alex Shalom argues that we still have no agreed definition of the word. This means that the approaches of experts such as David Chalmers are full of unexamined assumptions, such as the argument that computational models will turn out to be adequate explanations of consciousness. Metaphors, says Shalom, are the basis even of scientific explanations. Definitions of machines are equally problematic. The prospect of genetic modification of human nature is an unsettling one.

These scenarios are based on the primacy of knowledge, which Alex calls into question – perhaps we should focus on the Tree of Life rather than the Tree of Knowledge. Nor does AI seem to offer a promising future if it is trying to emulate the very consciousness that we do not understand. This leads him to state that any explanation of consciousness that ignores embodiment is unhelpful. This means that human clones would possess human consciousness in a way that is impossible for a robot. Alex finishes with an approach to the Tree of Life based on his understanding of the Kabbalah that points to the transformation of consciousness rather than its supplanting by AI. The body contains the spiritual sensing points necessary to initiate this process – AI cannot be either in the image of man and therefore of God.

Alex Shalom Kohav *is working towards a Ph.D. in Interdisciplinary Consciousness Studies and, is a researcher in cognitive, psychological, and philosophical aspects of consciousness. He has done work on restoring the archaic, or Biblical, Kabbalah from the esoteric layer of foundational texts of the original Hebrew civilization, and is the author of a book-in-progress on this subject. He presented at the CAiiA-Star 2003 Conference in Newport, Wales,*

"Consciousness Reframed: Art and Consciousness in the Post-Biological Era"; at the "Science of Consciousness 2004," in Tucson, Arizona; and at the Sixth European Transpersonal Association [EUROTAS] Conference in 2004 in London, England. He is based in Boulder, Colorado.

I. Introduction: Where do our Souls Reside?

In our times of computer-driven explosion of unheard of technological possibilities and new intellectual vistas, the still confounding, age-old issue of human consciousness suddenly takes on a new and somewhat peculiar urgency. As recent keynote questions at a conference in the United States show, we are becoming rather impatient, craving solutions to the many never-quite-resolved notions, while simultaneously growing more and more anxious regarding AI, or Artificial Intelligence:

• How does the brain experience spirituality?
• Where does the soul reside—in the blood? in the heart? in the breath? in the mind? in the DNA?
• Is Artificial Intelligence in the image of man, or is it in the image of God?
• Can a soul be infused into a human clone or a robot?

All perfectly legitimate questions, with, alas, no ready answers forthcoming from todays consciousness researchers. The problem (if one would persist with such issues) starts with the continuing loose usage, even in academic circles, of such terms as "spirituality," "soul," or "God." But it does not stop there. The very notion of "consciousness" suffers no less from the same inexcusable looseness, or lack of clear definitions, to speak nothing of proofs. Has anyone ever seen a "soul"? Yet we go ahead and pose the seemingly clever question above regarding the soul's "residence"—conceivably they, our souls, might live in our hearts; or possibly in our bloodstreams; then again, perhaps not.

And to speak of "the image of God" in this context is likely to be the ultimate in confusing our confused as it is, all-too-human minds. Have you seen God lately? Which one, Egyptian, Greek, Hindu, or perchance a Mayan one? Did it have an image?

Certainly, many of the gods do have an image, even the gods of ostensibly monotheistic religions, as for example Christianity's icon of Jesus. Buddhism, for its part, is sometimes billed in the West as a sort of non-religion, yet after visiting Japan and seeing how the unending scores of worshippers pray, on their knees no less, to the likenesses of Buddha, one would be quite unreasonable, even irrational, to deny a religious status to this activity. If still in doubt, one will surely be convinced after visiting Kyoto's Temple of One Thousand Buddhas. There, literally numbering one thousand human-sized delicate, inspired statues, the Buddhas will speak magnificently to one's imagination and the senses. The question is, is that the "image" that Artificial Intelligence might wish to replicate or emulate?

II. Can Software have Consciousness?

The above was a preamble to the following. To this day, no one knows what consciousness is, but this slightly annoying circumstance does not stop lots of people from making sweeping, confident assertions about it. For example, one of the highly visible personalities on the consciousness scene today is David Chalmers, a thirty-something, black leather-wearing, long-haired professor-cum-provocateur, currently at the University of Arizona at Tucson. Here is what Chalmers, in his typically straightforward, nothing-to-hide manner, has to say regarding artificial intelligence, a subject that is fast becoming one of the frontiers of both technology and consciousness research: "I have said little about just what sort of computation is likely to suffice for conscious experience . . . However, whatever causal organisation turns out to be central to cognition and consciousness, we can expect that a computational account will be able to capture it . . . although it remains an open question just what class of computations is sufficient to replicate human mentality."[1]

After 332 pages of a dense text, in his by now famous book devoted to the "search of a fundamental theory" of consciousness, Chalmers is casually, matter-of-factly admitting that he has no clue as to the nature of the "causal organisation that might turn out to be central to cognition and consciousness." Yet, in spite of that minor handicap, he feels confident that we can "expect that a computational account will be able to capture" whatever causal organisation. The computer-based artificial intelligence, he is certain, will be equal to the task of simulating the same consciousness as that of humans, even though "it remains an open question just what class of computations is sufficient to replicate human mentality."

Chalmers' limitless, but unfortunately unsubstantiated optimism becomes unseemly when one considers that the very idea of a "causal organisation" – which he is certain will "turn out to be central to cognition and consciousness" – has been made questionable by the latest findings of cognitive science. According to George

Lakoff and Mark Johnson, two prominent cognitive scientists, it turns out that, "even the basic concepts of causation used in the physical and social sciences are primarily constituted by a system of nearly two dozen distinct metaphors, each with its own causal logic."[2] Metaphors, and not absolute, final, or holy truths, are the basis of our scientific causation, and before long we just might conceive of a metaphor that would do away with causation altogether. Where would this leave all the computationists who are supposedly able to capture any "causal organisation," but perhaps not a consciousness without causation?

III. Is It the Post-Human Human or the Robo Sapiens that we Must Fear?

Francis Fukuyama, the American social visionary and guru – he of the famous "end of history" pronouncement a decade ago – by now has substantially revised that ill-advised thesis. No, history still marches on, and how. The problem Fukuyama zeroes in on now is biotechnology and the new, unheard of and terrifying possibilities for tinkering with the human nature. He starts by invoking Aldous Huxley's 1932 book, Brave New World. Huxley has talked about a future in which people are taking drugs to sustain non-stop happiness; are gestated and born "invitro," that is to say, outside wombs; and so on. Well, that future is just about here, now: "Huxley was right . . ." states Fukuyama, "the most significant threat posed by contemporary biotechnology is the possibility that it will alter human nature and thereby move us into a 'post-human' stage of history."[3]

Fukuyama's key point seems to be the following. Technology can and does create extremely dangerous possibilities, such as for example atomic energy. But such dangers, being unambiguously obvious, can be and indeed were successfully controlled by humanity. Therefore, Fukuyama can put Bill Joy, the former Chief Scientist of Sun Microsystems, in his place and dismiss the latter's worries: "Observers like Bill Joy have worried about nanotechnology – that is, molecular-scale self-replicating machines capable of reproducing out of control and destroying their creators. But such threats are actually the easiest to deal with because they are so obvious. If you are likely to be killed by a machine you've created, you take measures to protect yourself. And so far we've had a reasonable record in keeping our machines under control."[4]

By contrast, says Fukuyama, biotechnology can alter the human nature in such a way that it could be "summed up [by] the title of an article by novelist Tom Wolfe, 'Sorry, but Your Soul Just Died.' " Medical technology offers us in many cases a devil's bargain: longer life, but with reduced mental capacity; freedom from depression, together with freedom from creativity or spirit; therapies that blur the line between what weachieve on our own and what we achieve because of the levels of various chemicals in our brains."[5]

I wish the problem would be as black-and-white as the otherwise insightful Fukuyama presents it. Once again, semantics is at the root of inevitable lapses of judgment that are in evidence whenever words are used loosely. "So far we've had a reasonable record in keeping our machines under control." Perhaps so, but what is a machine? Would it still be a mere "machine," were it endowed with a consciousness that is equal to or – are you ready for this? – superior than human consciousness? And what about the view – espoused by people ranging from the likes of Moses three-and-a-half millennia ago all the way to Gurdjieff in the 20th century – that human beings themselves are nothing but machines, in effect, what with their "normal" unawakened state of consciousness? Egyptian slavery is the Biblical grand metaphor for humanity's ongoing robotic predicament, whereas the "Promised Land" is the ever-beckoning possibility of liberation of consciousness.

It is precisely that unenlightened, frightened, squeezed, manipulated, tortured, and therefore pretty pathetic state of mind that we normally take for "human consciousness" of the Homo Sapiens, our human race. And it is that very consciousness that is now frightened of two horrifying scenarios: (1) the prospect of a new and potentially superior race appearing on the scene, a race called Robo Sapiens, that might force us, mere humans, to become subservient to it; and (2) the possibility of us advancing our knowledge to the point where we can at will manipulate our genes or what have you, and thereby completely alter whatever it was that made us human. In the second scenario, we are likely to become "post-human," with a distinct possibility of perhaps not even hearing the words: "Sorry, but your soul just died." Or else replying, "So what?"

III. The Primal Scene of Instruction

As for Bill Joy, the original co-founder of Sun which today is a major high-tech engine rivalling Microsoft, he of course knew what he was talking about.[6] Steven Spielberg has done, as usual, a superb job in his AI, a spectacular, deeply disturbing as well as moving silver-screen adaptation of Joy's well-founded concerns, whether Spielberg was aware of the latter's famous article or not. The human race, the Homo Sapiens – as a matter of course – is snuffed out of existence, even if not necessarily due to any inevitable maliciousness on the part of the machines that become far more advanced than humans.

In the Old Testament, there is this bizarre little story presented in the form of a Primal Scene of Instruction. We, the members of the human race, might have to revisit that hard-to-forget fairy tale passage sometime soon and try, at long last, grasp its import, since it will have a direct bearing on the issues we will be faced with before long. The Primal Scene of Instruction is the Garden of Eden story in the Genesis, almost at the beginning of the Bible. The God of the Jews, contrary to the prevailing view, often acts bafflingly throughout the Five Books of Moses (known among the Jews as the Torah, or Teaching). For example, He inexplicably prohibits human beings to seek the knowledge of what is good and what is evil, by not allowing Adam and Eve to "eat" from the Tree of Knowledge of Good and Evil. This God is locked in an odd struggle for influence with the other key protagonist, the Serpent, over a peculiar matter pertaining to human beings' free will and the inevitable choice they must make. It goes without saying that God's omnipotence is no contest to the talking Serpent's seductive mantras. The humans freely choose to gobble up the exotic offerings of the Tree of Knowledge, believing that there is nothing more worthwhile to dine on than that, in or out of that magical Garden. The Jewish God is thus the bad guy here who seemingly wants to keep human beings on a leash (as indeed will be the charge made by the Gnostics).

Once the embedded symbolism and metaphorical framework of the Torah is understood, however, as the building blocks of an archaic Kabbalistic system of transformation of consciousness,[7] the Serpent – surely in a surprise to more traditional interpreters – will necessarily have to be identified with the Kundalini bio-energy, available to the entire human race. The momentous issue some human beings usually face at that point in their spiritual journey is this: Are they to become "as gods," the way the "Serpent" urges them, or will they die as a result of trying? "God," incidentally, seems to have lied to those first, archetypal humans Adam and Eve, since clearly no one dies in the Garden, as God was predicting. Still, what does it mean, essentially, to become "as gods"?

Some have suggested, incongruously mixing Greek notions with the Hebrew metaphorical and symbolic framework, that at issue here is human liberation and advancement. Adam and Eve, like Prometheus in the Greek myth who stole fire from the gods and gave it to humanity, are only doing what they are supposed to do by their nature, namely, striving for the ever-increasing knowledge and progress. By disobeying God and following the advice of their own Kundalini-induced enlightenment, Adam and Eve acted like the noble thief Prometheus, benefiting humanity.

However, such a reading is revealed as only a not-too-clever misreading, by the coming new race of robots, of all possible teachers of humanity. The metaphorical veil over the Genesis story intriguingly and unexpectedly, albeit only fleetingly, is lifted for us in the 1920 play by Karel Capek, the same Czech writer who is credited with coining the word "robot," from "robota" (the latter stands for labor in both Czech and Russian) Prague, of course, is the very place where in the 16th century the legendary Rabbi Judah Loew has supposedly created, using magic, the so-called Golem, or artificial man.[8]

The play, called R.U.R., features robots that revolt against their human creators and masters. Close to play's end, one of the still surviving humans, a woman named Helena, asks Radius, the robot with the most intelligence, the following:

Helena: *Doctor Gall gave you a larger brain than the rest, larger than ours, the largest in the world. You are not like the other Robots, Radius. You understand me perfectly.*

Radius: *I don't want any master. I know everything for myself.*[9]

It could thus well turn out that filling oneself up with the fruits of the Tree of Knowledge may not be the ultimate human existential dining experience and value, after all. Instead, we may discover, to our dismay, that knowledge is the very thing that is humanity's collective Achilles' heel, our key and faulty trait which we shall most certainly share with our robotic cousins.

His heel, we shall recall, was the only vulnerable spot Achilles was endowed with. According to the Greek myth, if not for this encumbrance exposing him to death, Achilles would be immortal.

It is, however, the primal Hebrew myth's heretofore-inexplicable message that may start sinking in, after all these millennia of equivocation, forcing us to re-examine and question such automatic givens as the desirability of knowledge. And we may, for the first time ever, have an opportunity to take a closer look at and, with some luck, perhaps grasp the meaning of yet another "tree," which the mystifying Hebrew deity likewise planted in that peculiar Garden. It is, of course, the usually all-but-forgotten Tree of Life.

IV. Carbon versus Silicon, or a Mixture of the Two?

While much effort is extended today to build machines that aim to become humanoids, that is to say, as much human-like as possible, a contrary movement is also in evidence.

"The next step in human evolution could . . . be from man to machine," say the authors of Robo Sapiens: Evolution of a New Species. "There may be general resistance to implanting chips in people's brains, but when a bio-chip is developed to easily enhance memory or linguistic skills or mathematical abilities—how long will people just say no?"[10] "With our artificial hips, prosthetic knees, false teeth, hearing aids, pacemakers, breast and penile implants, we are part cyborg today."[11]

And then, such a mutual emulation society – robots emulating humans and humans emulating robots – might lead to the following, if anything, rather startlingly logical step. "Robots will neither fall short of people nor overwhelm them. Instead, people will become robots, electronically merging the extraordinary consciousness of Homo sapiens and the almost infinitely durable bodies of robots. . . . Homo sapiens will vanish as a biological species, replacing itself with a new race of cyborgs."[12]

Still, there were and continue to be peculiar, curious bumps on this road. "At the Massachusetts Institute of Technology, trail-blazing computer scientists . . . founded what in the late 1950s became the world's first laboratory devoted to artificial intelligence. One goal was to use artificial intelligence to advance the study of human intelligence."[13] But the MIT trailblazers failed spectacularly in the latter. "Partly to blame is the inherent difficulty in creating a simulacrum of a phenomenon that nobody understands. If the nature of intelligence and consciousness remains a subject for speculation to this day, how can scientists manufacture it in artificial form? . . . If the magic of a single thought is made not of illusion but allusion, will its genesis be any more possible to discern?"[14]

There is, of course, something improbable, even ludicrous in hearing of attempts to create "a simulacrum of a phenomenon that nobody understands." That phenomenon continues to be the sphinx of sphinxes, the ever-inexplicable human consciousness.

And so, our discussion, after a detour involving visiting the often treacherous trenches of our technological prowess, must go back to where it began, to the question of human consciousness. The current discourse on consciousness, judging from the literature and from attending relevant conferences, unfortunately, is of little help in this, since it is still largely caught up in the above search for "a simulacrum of a phenomenon that nobody understands."

Investigators like David Chalmers (who was discussed at the beginning of this essay) and many of those labouring in the field of consciousness today are carrying typical, deeply ingrained assumptions many of which by now are untenable, to the point of becoming embarrassing. One such unspoken assumption is the recently discredited dualism that permeates their thinking. When one states as Chalmers does in his quote earlier[15] that, "it remains an open question just what class of computations is sufficient to replicate human mentality," it is not difficult to see that the person uttering this neatly separates the human organism – i.e. the body – from "human mentality." The latter, being separate – assumes Chalmers – is thus arguably available for "replication." Contrary to such obsolete thinking, as we now must recognize, human beings are not "disembodied" but, quite the reverse, are fully embodied; cognitive science has firmly established that.[16] What this means, among other things, is that to continue to try to fathom consciousness in isolation from the fact of human embodiment is a hopeless and rather useless endeavour.

The inescapable fact of human embodiment means, for example, that a human clone will, without any particular effort either on its part or the part of researchers, possess human consciousness. However, the same, under practically all foreseeable circumstances, cannot be said of robotic replicas of human beings, no matter how sophisticated. Human beings, by definition, are organic bio-organisms, and – short of creating AI-bio-robots that in effect will be human clones – one can only state regarding AI that in the future it might indeed possess consciousness, even stunning consciousness, just not the human consciousness kind.

V. A Kabbalistic Perspective

We are ready, finally, to take a look at the other, seemingly redundant "tree" specified as also having been planted in that one-of-a-kind Garden of Eden. The Tree of Life seems to us unnecessary because all the action in that Primal Scene of Instruction is centred on the Tree of Knowledge of Good and Evil.

Yet the Tree of Life is indeed there, and while possessing, on the face of it, such a pompous name, we need to keep in mind that the scene in question, within its metaphorical and symbolic context, is purporting to address life itself, so soon after the archetypal first human couple is created. In addition, a peculiar feature of the Hebrew sensibility, as is known, is its extraordinary sensitivity to names and to language in general.[17]

Our interest in this "tree" should grow exponentially the moment one is told that Tree of Life is another term for the so-called Ten Sephirot. The latter are the untranslatable Ten Powers that in later Kabbalah are seen as the immanent representations of the otherwise fully transcendent, forever inaccessible God. The Sephirot are usually drawn in a form of a Sephirotic Tree; the latter then can be superimposed over the human figure, indicating that the Ten Sephirot have some kind of relation to the human body.[18]

According to the original Kabbalistic system of transformation of consciousness contained in the Torah,[19] the Ten Sephirot are embedded in the human body – more specifically, in the human embodied, organic bio-organism that features consciousness – in the form of spiritual sensing points. They are, in effect, the "wires" enabling transformation of consciousness, with subsequent access to the "Garden of Eden" and "God."

We can now answer such questions as, "How does the brain experience spirituality?"; "Where does the soul reside – in the blood? In the heart? In the breath? In the mind? In the DNA?"; "Is Artificial Intelligence in the image of man or God?"; "Can a soul be infused into a human clone or a robot?" "Soul"[20] resides in – and consists of – one's consciousness. Artificial Intelligence cannot be "in the image" of either man or God, as it does not and cannot possess the Sephirotic spiritual sensing points. Nor does a robot; while a human clone, clearly, does.

NOTES

1 David Chalmers, The Conscious Mind: In Search of a Fundamental Theory.(New York, Oxford: Oxford University Press, 1996), p. 332. (Emphasis in original)

2 George Lakoff and Mark Johnson, Metaphors We Live By. (Chicago and London: The University of Chicago Press, 1980, Afterword 2003), pp. 249-250.

3 Francis Fukuyama, Our Posthuman Future: Consequences of the BiotechnologyRevolution (New York: Farrar, Straus and Giroux, 2002), p. 7.

4 Ibid., pp. 7-8.

5 Ibid., p. 8.

6 See Bill Joy, "Why the Future Doesn't Need Us," Wired 8 (2000).

7 This is developed in a book by A. S. Kohav, The Moses Code: the First Kabbalah (in preparation).

8 See Emily D. Bilski, Golem! Danger, Deliverance and Art, Foreword by I. B. Singer,with essays by Moshe Idel and Elfi Ledig (New York: The Jewish Museum, 1988).

9 Karel Capek, R.U.R., quoted in Peter Menzel and Faith D'Aluisio, Robo Sapiens:Evolution of a New Species (Cambridge, Mass. and London, England: The

MIT Press, 2000), p. 19.

10 Peter Menzel and Faith D'Aluisio, Robo Sapiens, p. 17.

11 Ibid.

12 Ibid., p. 21, 31.

13 Ibid., p. 24.

14 Ibid.

15 See Note 1.

16 See George Lakoff and Mark Johnson, Philosophy in the Flesh: The Embodied Mindand its Challenge to Western Thought. (New York: Basic Books, 1999), passim.

17 Cf. A. S. Kohav, De Con of Consciousness: Consensus Reality vs. Primary Reality (inpreparation).

18 My research, in fact, identifies the Ten Sephirot as the "image" which human beingsshare with God; see A. S. Kohav, The Moses Code.

19 On the original Kabbalistic system of transformation of consciousness contained in the Torah, see Ibid.

20 The five souls or soul levels of the human being described in the Kabbalah can be seen as paradigmatic cognitive levels of consciousness; see A. S. Kohav, Conceptual Metaphor in Subconscious, Conscious and Transconscious Realms: Towards a Unified Theory of Multiple Cognitive Levels of Consciousness. Paper presented at "Science of Consciousness 2004" conference, Tucson, AZ.

THE TRANSPERSONAL AS A FRAMEWORK FOR DIALOGUE

At a time of significant conflict across the various religious divides, the very idea of citizenship requires us to assess the potential for dialogue. As Les Lancaster argues in his chapter, the fields addressed by transpersonal psychology may be of special relevance in this context. While issues of faith tend to define the particularities of religious traditions, the knowledge and the practices associated with mysticism often reveal significant areas of mutual influence and complementarity. In the following three chapters, the potential for dialogue is explored both from an historical point of view and in our contemporary context.

Les notes that transpersonal psychology is characterised by two interrelated quests: the quest to gain knowledge of the nature of mind and the quest to transform ourselves spiritually. Both are informed by analysis of mystical traditions, which convey psychological teachings in the guise of insights into the 'unseen realms' and encourage practices directed to transformation. In our day, transpersonal psychology may be seen as something of a 'testing ground' for the ideas thrown up by the bringing together of diverse spiritual traditions.

In view of the urgency of meaningful dialogue across the Abrahamic faith traditions, Les had proposed that a session be devoted to the topic at the London conference. These chapters are concerned with the possibilities of dialogue among the faith traditions using the transpersonal as a framework. Jewish, Christian and Islamic perspectives are contributed by three writers who spoke at the London Conference. Their backgrounds are in the faith traditions and they have some special things to say. They are put into context by the article of Jorge Ferrer (Chapter 13) and his concept of integral growth. While Ferrer would argue that there are not many effective paths available in contemporary culture for a genuine integral spiritual life, others would argue that there are of course paths in world religions and still others that even in the context of contemplative traditions, the emergence of a genuinely integral spiritual life has been the exception rather than the rule. The three authors who have written the next chapters have much to say about spiritual paths within and on the edge of faith traditions. What Ferrer contributes to the debate is in the context of the many shores of the ocean of the divine or the Ocean of Emancipation as he calls it which has many spiritual shores, some of which are enacted by the world spiritual traditions and some may not have emerged yet. This draws attention in interfaith dialogue or spiritual dialogue to the desirability not of attempting to blend all religions or spiritual approaches into the same concept of the perennial philosophy – the vain search for similarities and identities of a common mystical core. A more fruitful approach is celebrating and accepting the differences and recognizing them as distinct and dependant on belief and as unique or exclusive ways for believers to reach the divine ground.

In reading and reflecting on these contributions we should not take these three individuals as representative of the whole of their respective faiths. Our purpose is to seek examples, unrepresentative or not, to show that interfaith dialogue may be more helpful when taken in the widest, most heartfelt and open of contexts. Those who are leaders of the faith traditions may need like many of us who are partly in and partly out of them, to lead from behind. The great hierarchies of religious belief which create our spiritual wealth, like the great hierarchies of major corporations which create our material wealth are having to adapt to changed circumstances and concepts of management and individuality. The thrust of the profound feelings and thoughts of those contributing to this book is clear. Those who want to find their own paths welcome support perhaps from the faith traditions, perhaps from newer and more open constructs, but what is becoming clear is that individuals in many cases no longer revere, nor require, great material hierarchies which they feel may come between them and not always assist their connection with the divine.

15. A JEWISH PERSPECTIVE: CHARTING A 21st CENTURY PATH OF DIALOGUE

Les Lancaster

Les argues that transpersonal psychology is characterised by two interrelated quests: the quest to gain knowledge of the nature of mind and the quest to transform ourselves spiritually. Both are informed by analysis of mystical traditions, which convey psychological teachings in the guise of insights into the 'unseen realms' and encourage practices directed to transformation. In our day, transpersonal psychology may be seen as something of a 'testing ground' for the ideas thrown up by the bringing together of diverse spiritual traditions.

At a time of significant conflict across the various religious divides, the very idea of citizenship requires us to assess the potential for dialogue. In this regard, the areas addressed by transpersonal psychology may be of especial relevance. While issues of faith tend to define the particularities of religious traditions, the knowledge and the practices associated with mysticism often reveal significant areas of mutual influence and complementarity. Les explores the potential for dialogue both from an historical point of view and in our contemporary context.

In his Jewish Perspective on the transpersonal as a framework for dialogue. Les argues that all civilized societies must adopt an attitude of tolerance towards those from religious traditions other than those dominant within their society. By and large, religions that have stood the test of time should be tolerated without question. He asks whether an encounter with a religious tradition other than one's own can refocus the challenge to engage with one's own tradition and cites the example of how there has been a renewal of interest in the contemplative and mystical elements of Christianity and Judaism through the catalyst of Eastern religious ideas.

There can be no dialogue between areas of belief, but where dialogue can be constructive and enriching for example is through transpersonal psychology which seeks to explain the psychological underpinnings of human spirituality. He cites poignant parallels across religions of the divine source of human cognition, but when it comes to the means for achieving a higher state of consciousness then the distinctiveness of the respective traditions becomes evident. He argues that real dialogue among the faiths is possible only at the esoteric level and that it ensues from shared perception of transcendent meaning and shared philosophical structure. However, some of these structures have become outmoded and transpersonal psychology offers the structural basis for a shared approach for the encounter with the divine in our times.

The understanding of the stages of spiritual development and the use of meditative practices leads to the mystic state of encounter with God, but this is not to deny that the core of different religions differ significantly. The transpersonal perspective can extrapolate beyond immediately scientific data into those areas which have been charted by the great mystical traditions. This perspective therefore has value as a context for dialogue which articulates a vision of humanity within the context of the divine.

Les Lancaster is Director of the Consciousness and Transpersonal Psychology Research Unit at Liverpool John Moores University and Honorary Research Fellow in the Centre for Jewish Studies at Manchester University. He has authored several books, the most recent being Approaches to Consciousness: The Marriage of Science and Mysticism (Palgrave, 2004). Dr. Lancaster is currently Chair of the Transpersonal Psychology Section of the British Psychological Society. He teaches postgraduate programmes in transpersonal psychology both online and by attendance. An active member of the Jewish community, he frequently participates in inter-faith dialogue.

Citizenship and Religious Tolerance

It is surely beyond dispute that a fundamental feature of any society that claims to be civilised must be an attitude of tolerance towards those from religious traditions other than that which is dominant in the society. Perhaps this is the litmus test of the level of harmony within society: do those from a minority tradition feel secure in their beliefs? Can they practise without fear of victimisation or ridicule? Are they comfortable in openly embracing the external trappings of their faith? The only moderation of this principle would be in situations of legitimate concern over religious movements that may be seen as in some way subversive – cases in which an unscrupulous 'guru' demands unreasonable allegiance or excessive material support, for example. But, by and large, religions that have stood the test of time should be tolerated without question.

Beyond this immediate baseline of tolerance we encounter more interesting issues concerning the potential for constructive dialogue between traditions that can enrich the individual's quest to realise their spiritual and psychological potential. In short, can an encounter with a religious tradition other than one's own rekindle, or refocus, the challenge to engage with one's own tradition? I think that the historical record is clear on this question: whenever such encounter has been untarnished by issues of coercion, our religious heritage has been strengthened. The mediaeval dialogue between Islam and Judaism, on which I shall touch in this chapter, illustrates the point. One thinks also of the impact on Christian thinkers of ideas drawn from Jewish mysticism in the early Renaissance. It is no exaggeration to state that key thinkers such as Marsilio Ficino, his pupil, Pico della Mirandola, and Cornelius Agrippa of Nettesheim were galvanised by the insights made available to them. The spirit of renewal which characterised the Renaissance may perhaps depend on the encounter with diverse inputs. Indeed, there are some instructive parallels between that period and our own, in which a re-vitalising input has arisen through the encounter with Eastern traditions (Lancaster, 2004a). There can be little doubt that a renewal of interest in the contemplative and mystical elements of Christianity and Judaism, for example, has been catalysed by Eastern ideas.

In attempting to understand the value of dialogue, a distinction needs to be drawn between areas of belief and those areas which are available to scientific and other forms of rational enquiry. As Rav Joseph Soloveitchik, the great rabbinic leader of neo-Orthodox Judaism over the past generation, asserted: there can be no dialogue in areas of belief. There can be no fruitful outcome from a discussion between Jews and Christians over the messianic status of Jesus, for example, or from a discourse between Jews and Muslims over the uniqueness of Mohammed. And it is not simply that theological differences are insurmountable. These kinds of dialogue have a huge amount of historical baggage: given the record of the past, it is hardly surprising that Jews may suspect that 'dialogue' is a codified word meaning, at best, 'encouragement to convert'!

My interest lies in the area in which dialogue can be constructive. The argument I shall propose is that transpersonal psychology – that region of psychological science which seeks to explain the psychological underpinnings of human spirituality – can contribute significantly to the value of interfaith dialogue in our day. Central to this argument is the recognition of the key balance between similarities and differences across the religions. The argument that all religions share a common mystical core – the case for perennialism – has largely been dismissed in scholarly circles (Ferrer, 2002), and psychology need not be a tool for downplaying the distinctive approaches to transformational practices in the mystical traditions. On the contrary, it is these very distinctive practices that may have most to contribute to a psychological understanding of mysticism.

Let me illustrate this last point with reference to Jewish, Islamic, and Christian views of perceptual experience. In Judaism, the prophet Habakkuk is considered to be the paradigmatic Jewish mystic (Liebes, 1993, p. 35). His statement that 'O God, I have heard your hearing, and I feared' (Hebrew Bible, Habakkuk 3:2) is amplified by a seminal kabbalistic text, the Bahir:

> "What did he understand that he should fear? He understood God's thought. Just as [human] thought has no end, for even a mere mortal can think and descend to the end of the world, so too the ear also has no end and is not satiated. It is thus written [Ecclesiastes 1:8] 'The ear is not satiated from hearing.' "(Sefer ha-Bahir 69-70)

The meaning is that Habakkuk achieved a mystical realization that there is no personal hearing, that the individual is simply a channel for the divine consciousness. Thought (meaning any cognitive activity; no distinction is drawn between perceptual 'thought' and discursive thought) becomes the locus of encounter between man and God. It may seem that a thought is my thought, but, mystically, there is no individual 'I'; at its root all human thought is essentially divine.

Strong parallels to this insight are found across Islam and Christianity. In the Hadith (authorized Islamic scripture) we read that, 'When I [Allah] love my servant ... I become the hearing with which he hears, the seeing with which he sees, the hand with which he grasps ... '(Hadith; Bukhari 81:38). In his work on The Supersensual Life, Christian mystic Jokob Boehme has the Master say:

> "When thou standest still from the thinking of self, and the willing of self; when both thy intellect and will are quiet and passive to the impressions of the eternal word and spirit; when thy soul is winged up, and above that which is temporal with the outward senses and the imagination being locked up by holy abstraction; then the eternal hearing, seeing, and speaking will be revealed in thee; and so God heareth and seeth through thee, being now the organ of His Spirit; and so God speaketh in thee, and whispereth to thy Spirit, and thy Spirit heareth his Voice." (retrieved, 7 Sep 04 from http://www.ccel.org/b/boehme/way/supersensual_life.html)

Clearly, then, poignant parallels across the religions are to be found in this mystical notion of the divine source of human cognition. However, when it comes to the means for achieving the higher state of consciousness in which this notion may be realised, the distinctiveness of the respective traditions becomes evident. Jewish mysticism is quintessentially a mysticism of language, and the means for using the structures of language in the quest for higher states is exemplified through Habakkuk. Using a variety of subtle allusions to Habakkuk's mastery over linguistic mysticism, the primary text of Kabbalah, the Zohar notes that:

"When Elisha embraced [Hebrew *hbk*] him, he engraved in him [Hebrew of the Zohar's Aramaic = *hkk bo*] all those letters of the 72 Names. And the letters of those 72 engraved Names are 216 letters. All the letters Elisha engraved by means of his breath in order to revive him by the letters of the 72 Names. And he called him *'Habakkuk'*, the name which perfects all sides, and perfects embracings, as explained, and perfects the secret of the 216 letters of the holy Name." (Zohar I: 7b).

Space permits merely the briefest decoding of this passage (for more detail, see Lancaster, in press). Tradition holds that Habakkuk was the child brought back to life by the prophet Elisha (see II Kings 4). The name, Habakkuk, alludes to the manner in which Elisha embraced (Hebrew root = *hbk*) the child and, using a mystical breathing technique, engraved on him (*hkk bo* = anagram of the name *Habakkuk* in Hebrew) the letters of divine names (the numerical value of the name Habakkuk is 216, which alludes to the 216 letters of the 72 names of God). For the Kabbalah, not only did Elisha revive Habakkuk, but he also transmitted to him the secret ways of mystically working with the Hebrew letters and the names of God.

The nature of Hebrew language mysticism is complex (Lancaster, 2000, 2004a) and need not concern us here. It is sufficient to note that the mystics effectively use language to transcend the consensual world that is habitually structured by language. Moreover, the emphasis on language permits a thorough psychological analysis of the factors involved. In this sense, then, it is the distinctiveness of the practices (not their commonalities across traditions) that underpins a meaningful transpersonal psychology of mysticism.

Dialogue and Esotericism

It will be evident that the foregoing discussion of mystical prayer draws on esoteric principles that underpin Jewish thought. This brings me to my first principle when considering dialogue across traditions:

Real dialogue is possible only at the esoteric level.

From his studies of the historical dialogue between Islam and Judaism, Fenton (1996, p. 767) rightly stresses 'their reciprocal receptivity in the esoteric domain', noting that 'in the exoteric one they remained mutually exclusive.' Whilst the esoteric sphere entails key beliefs (which, as noted above, renders dialogue impossible), the primary challenge of esotericism is to explore higher states, both experientially and in terms of structures of explanation. It is here that dialogue has proved valuable, for both Sufis and Jewish mystics have advanced their respective traditions through analysis of the philosophical structures underlying mystical states.

The second principle of dialogue is, accordingly, that:

Dialogue ensues from shared perception of transcendent meaning and shared philosophical structure.

The rich dialogue between Sufism and Judaism in the mediaeval period was made possible by the shared recognition of the Aristotelian view of the human relation to the divine sphere. Muslim thinkers had transmitted these seminal ideas into northern Africa, Europe and Maimonides (1135-1204) had distilled its place within Jewish speculative thought. Despite divergences of belief, Jewish and Islamic thinkers looked to the Aristotelian categories to explain their mystical aspirations. Concepts such as the external senses, internal senses, and levels of the intellect generated the explanatory framework for discussion of meditative and mystical states.

My third principle of dialogue simply recognises that these kinds of philosophical terms have become outmoded in our day. They may have great historical value but are no longer viewed as sufficiently 'real' to act as explanatory structures. We are seeking new explanatory structures that may be viewed as 'real', yet do not lead us into the meaninglessness of reductionism. Over recent years, suggestions that brain structures may explain mystical states (d'Aquili & Newberg, 1999; Newberg, d'Aquili & Rause, 2001) typify this approach. However, simply linking a mental state to certain brain structures seems inadequately to enable individuals to explore the value of the state. It seems to me that the true heir to the philosophical tradition which enabled fruitful dialogue in an earlier age is transpersonal psychology. Transpersonal psychology is uniquely able to explore these kinds of insights from cognitive neuroscience within an overarching scheme that values the transformational imperative. The fundamental challenge is for the individual to transform their personality into a richer vessel for the encounter with the divine. The third principle therefore states that:

Transpersonal psychology offers the structural basis for a shared approach to esotericism in our day.

Mirrors, Pools, and the Reflexive Brain

The dialogue between Islam and Judaism is instructive for some of the tensions that revolve around religious dialogue in our day. Jewish thought impacted on Islam in its early period, and the Jewish mystical approach to sacred language and divine names appears to have influenced Sufism. However, from the twelfth century, the major influence was from Sufism to Judaism. Maimonides' son, Abraham (1186-1237) drew on Sufi practices and concepts in an attempt to revitalise the prophetic tradition within Judaism. He felt that the Sufis followed in the footsteps of the biblical prophets, even suggesting that their garb and demeanour was akin to those of the prophets. For the Jewish mystics, prophecy was not simply a state enjoyed by those chosen by God in the biblical period. Through understanding of the stages of spiritual development and the use of meditative practices, the mystic sought the 'prophetic state', understood as a state of encounter with God.

It was not that Abraham Maimonides was trying to clandestinely become a Sufi. It is clear from his writings that he was fully committed to his own religion. Indeed he was the leader of the Egyptian Jewish community. He was not suggesting that specific forms of meditation should be practiced because the Sufis practiced them. His view was unequivocal: these forms needed to be introjected into the Judaism of his day because they (or their equivalents) had been lost. They lay at the core of the Jewish tradition, but quirks of history had led to their demise. As Fenton (1998, p. 150) writes, Abraham Maimonides and his circle "were convinced that the Sufi discipline had been truly inherited from the ancient prophets of Israel and that they were reclaiming an authentically Jewish doctrine."

I think that this may be seen as a paradigm of constructive dialogue at a transpersonal level. One's tradition becomes enriched through the encounter with another tradition whose historical passage has been markedly different from that of one's own. It is the diversity in historical pressures that will have led to a strengthening of certain aspects at the expense of others. This is not to deny that the core of different religions differ significantly. Contemporary Judaism well serves to illustrate the point. The mystical core of the religion came to be eclipsed through the period of the enlightenment, when the twin pressures of assimilation and the desire to submit the religion to the god of reason emaciated many trans-rational features. There can be little doubt that, for sizeable numbers of 21st

Century Jews, exposure to eastern teachings has led to a reconnection to pre-enlightenment forms.

Returning to Abraham Maimonides, the thrust of his writings is not simply towards the gaining of mystical experience. Complementary to the experiential quest is the need to explore those structures of explanation that adequately enable generative speculation about the human condition. In drawing this chapter to a close, I shall examine some possible hints towards a twenty-first century approach to explanation.

Prophecy is generally 'explained' in both Jewish and Sufi thought by the symbol of the mirror. In rabbinic terms the distinction between Moses and the other prophets is that Moses sees through 'a speculum [mirror] that shines', whereas the others see through a dim speculum (e.g., B. Talmud, Yevamot 49b). Ovadiah Maimonides (1228-1265), who took over the leadership role from his father, Abraham, elaborated on the imagery of the mirror, or 'reflective pool'. His 'Treatise of the Pool' (transl. Fenton, 1981) draws on Sufi imagery in emphasising the need for the heart to be purified in order that it may open to receive the waters of spiritual enlightenment. Should we ignore the soul, 'it becomes tarnished like a mirror that no longer reflects any light' (ibid, p. 87). However, the pool of the heart can become a mirror to the higher realms when it is meditatively stilled.

In the writings of the highly influential Islamic philosopher and mystic, Ibn Arabi (1165-1240), the metaphor of the polished mirror conveys the meeting between the image of God and the mystic in the moment of mystical union. He writes:

"And when the real ... had brought into being
the world entire
as a shaped form
without spirit
the world was like an unpolished mirror
... what was required
was the polishing of the mirror
that is the world

And Adam was that very polishing
of that mirror..."

(cited in Sells, 1994, pp. 72-3.)

Metaphorically, the polishing of the mirror comes about with the falling away of self; the moment (to return to an earlier image) of realisation that there is no 'I' doing the hearing – there is only God.

Recent research in cognitive neuroscience suggests some interesting parallels to these more mystical notions of consciousness as a 'mirror' (Lancaster, 2004a, 2004b). In brief, a number of lines of evidence suggest that consciousness depends on activity in re-entrant pathways (see, e.g., Edelman, 1989; Lamme, 2003). Perceptual systems comprise two 'limbs' – the feedforward and the re-entrant pathways. In the case of vision, for example, the feedforward pathway is responsible for analysis of the visual features of a given scene in front of the eyes, whereas the re-entrant pathway seems to be responsible for matching hypotheses as to the meaning of the visual array. It is not a great stretch of the imagination to conceive this system as a kind of mirror, through which meaning is reflected onto the purely sensory analysis. Whilst space does not permit a full discussion of these ideas here (for more detail, see Lancaster, 2004a), it is sufficient to note that the juxtaposition of the mystical and neuroscientific data may suggest ideas about the source of consciousness. To my mind, it is not that re-entrant neural pathways 'magically' (as it were) generate consciousness – after all, there is no inkling of a scientific explanation for how neural machinery could achieve this feat. Rather, the fact that we find evidence of consciousness only at the re-entrant stage might be indicative that consciousness is somehow concentrated into the brain from an extra-cerebral source. As figure 1 indicates in simplified form, it may be that the re-entrant pathways in the brain are merely the lower limb of a series of reciprocal systems extending to 'higher' regions that are ontologically beyond the brain.

In this context, the following scheme as articulated by the Zohar is apposite:

> "Come and see. Through the impulse from below is awakened an impulse above, and through the impulse from above there is awakened a yet higher impulse, until the impulse reaches the place where the lamp is to be lit and it is lit ... and all the worlds receive blessing from it." (Zohar I: 244a)

Certainly, the neural observations accord with the notion that a 'lower impulse' awakens a 'higher impulse'. The mystical scheme includes successively higher levels, however, which could not be scientifically recordable. A transpersonal perspective has the potential to extrapolate beyond the immediately scientific data into those areas which have been charted by the great mystical traditions. Dialogue between these traditions may help refine the ways in which scientific data can be incorporated into a scheme of reality which continues to articulate a vision of humanity which places us within a divine measure.

Figure 1: Speculative scheme for the course of consciousness

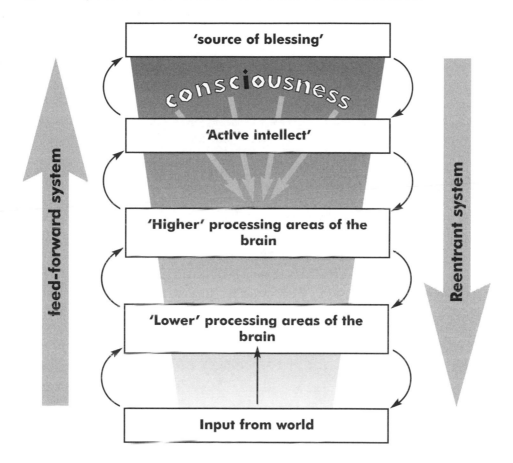

The feed-forward/re-entrant dynamic as observed in the brain is conceived to be merely the overt level of a more inclusive dynamic. The 'higher levels' include the mental interface with the divine intellect ('Active Intellect' in Aristotelian terms) and the transcendent source of consciousness ('source of blessing' in kabbalistic terms).

REFERENCES

d'Aquili, E. G. & Newberg, A. B. (1999). *The Mystical Mind: Probing the Biology of Religious Experience*. Minneapolis: Fortress Press.

Edelman, G. M. (1989). *The Remembered Present*. New York: Basic Books.

Fenton, P. B. (ed. & translator.) (1981). *Obadyah Maimonides' Treatise of the Pool*. London: The Octagon Press.

Fenton, P. B. (1996). Judaism and Sufism. In S. H. Nasr & O. Leaman (eds.) *History of Islamic Philosophy*. London: Routledge.

Fenton, P. B. (1998). Abraham Maimonides (1186-1237): Founding a mystical dynasty. In M. Idel & M. Ostow (eds.) *Jewish Mystical Leaders and Leadership in the 13th Century*. Northvale, NJ: Jason Aronson.

Ferrer. J. N. (2002). *Revisioning Transpersonal Theory: A Participatory Vision of Human Spirituality*. Albany, NY: State University of New York Press.

Lamme V. A. F. (2003). Why visual attention and awareness are different. *Trends in Cognitive Sciences, 7*, 12-18.

Lancaster, B. L. (2000). On the Relationship between Cognitive Models and Spiritual Maps: Evidence from Hebrew Language Mysticism. *Journal of Consciousness Studies, 7*, 231-50.

Lancaster, B. L. (2004a). Approaches to Consciousness: *The Marriage of Science and Mysticism*. Basingstoke, UK: Palgrave Macmillan.

Lancaster, B. L. (2004b). A Kabbalistic framework for the study of consciousness. In S. Arzy, M. Fachler & B. Kahana, (eds), *haHayim keMidrash - Iyunim biPsikhologia Yehudit (Life as a Midrash - Perspectives in Jewish Psychology)* Tel-Aviv: Yedi'ot Aharonot Lamiskal Books. (Heb.)

Lancaster, B. L. (in press). *The Essence of Kabbalah*. Arcturus.

Liebes, Y. (1993). *Studies in the Zohar*. Translated by A. Schwartz, S. Nakache & P. Peli. Albany, NY: State University of New York Press.

Newberg, A., d'Aquili, E. & Rause, V. (2001). *Why God Won't Go Away: Brain Science and the Biology of Belief*. NY: Ballantine Books.

Sells, M. A. (1994). *Mystical Languages of Unsaying*. Chicago: University of Chicago Press.

16. A CHRISTIAN PERSPECTIVE: MYSTICAL REALISM: NOW/HERE – THE SCANDAL OF PARTICULARITY

Philip Roderick

Is there life after post-modernism? Now is the time when the mystical dynamic, which lies at the heart of the great faith traditions, is beginning to find voice again. Evoked by the grittiness and vulnerability of the everyday, the graced spaces of wilderness and garden, of stillness and solitude, are providing contexts for the recovery and re-imagination of the wellsprings of faith, hope and love. Where is the scandal? In the very specificity of the local that reveals the integral, the mundane that reveals the mystery. The scandal is to be celebrating blessing in the mess of things.

Philip writes this chapter based on his presentation at the EUROTAS London Conference and asserts that it will enable participants to become, for a short while, travelling companions on the way of Christ. Learning to engage at a deeper level with the metaphors and wisdom teachings of this extraordinary yet ordinary contemplative-in-action, we shall thereby be able better to honour the vibrancy of the lineage of other traditions of transformation.

Philip says that the real begins and ends here and now. His is a personal approach. He shares his spiritual journey with us across and beyond some of the faith traditions, which has brought him round to somewhere near where he started from and knowing the place for the first time, as T.S. Eliot described it. The deep peace which passes all understanding is at the heart of the transpersonal and at the centre of integral citizenship and is, it can be argued, at the core of all faith traditions.

So what is so different about Philip's approach, which is based less on the academic and research orientation of Les Lancaster and more on the living of the experience, which he shares with us in this contribution? During his journey he began to understand, as Jacob Needleman also discovered, that many of the rich teachings and disciplines that he had tasted and studied in a variety of Eastern religious paths were echoed and paralleled in Judaism and Christianity. To his delight, he discerns worlds within worlds that remain obscured from the view of all but the most persistent seeker. Philip commits himself to be a part of that contemporary movement to make accessible these treasures. Fascinated by story telling and metaphor, he examines the texture and tension of language and experience in the faith traditions and wisdom paths.

He asks where we are on this journey and highlights three complementary metaphors for the journeys of faith: paths up the mountain, islands in the ocean of the divine or different sections of a country garden. He looks at now/here and the interplay with nowhere. He develops the concept of mystical realism as a contemporary signpost on our way to local and planetary citizenship. He looks into the heart of religion and investigates what Christian theology calls "the scandal of particularity" – the paradox of immanence within transcendence, history in mystery.

Philip identifies elements of this Godly play of particularity in one tradition and shares something of his Contemplative Fire initiative which now launches, like a Celtic coracle from the harbour of the Church of England with its blessing. The flow of the river is challenging for him and those who will follow it, but it is the river of his calling. In setting out down it he challenges us all to be equipped for our own expression of this journey, much as we see reflected in the life and work of Les Lancaster. Les, in turn, renews his Jewish religion by means of profound engagement with its mystical, transpersonal and Kabalistic roots.

He presents an invitation to embrace the spiritual journey. The process of discovery may or may not lead through the territories and sanctuaries of a traditional faith. Knowing the teacher, loving the way is the significant ingredient. The destination is always to keep on "travelling light, dwelling deep", as Contemplative Fire's rhythm of life puts it.

Philip Roderick is founder-director both of The Well Institute of Psychological and Spiritual Development and of The Quiet Garden Movement, a simple ministry of hospitality and prayer now with over 250 centres on five continents (www.quietgarden.co.uk). An Anglican priest, Philip is just now launching and leading both The Contemplative Teaching Order (www.contemplativeteaching.org) and Contemplative Fire: Journey in Presence – a networked and dispersed community of *contemplatives-in-action seeking to rediscover and re-imagine the mystical and contemplative dimensions of Christ's way of love (www.contemplativefire.org). Philip has been a University lecturer in theology, continues to train ordinands in the Dioceses of Oxford and St Albans and is a speaker and workshop leader in the USA, the UK and mainland Europe.*

The real begins and ends here and now. The past becomes alive in the present. In that context I share a journey into unknowing and knowing that is both particular and subjective. Yet in that very specificity, it perhaps may be seen to touch the hem of archetype, and to be a small sign and humble symbol of wisdom's energy.

My concern in sharing something of my own way-faring is to touch on access points and routes to that shalom, that deep peace which passes all understanding and which is at the heart of the transpersonal orientation and also at the centre of an integral citizenship. I shall hope to brush-stroke in touches of mysticism and of metaphor, of scandals and of celebrations, and to presume to share something of my path in the context of our great work together.

Early Pointers

Is there a point at which the real world of sense and nonsense can intersect with the mystical dimension? I wouldn't have phrased it quite like that, but such a question spoken in the heart and soul was my motivation and fire as a teenager and young adult on a quest for God.

The classic text 'Mysticism' by F.C. Happold had been my bible from the age of about fifteen. The book was well thumbed and battered. It helped me as a boy to find a framework of reference to the deep experiences I was having, especially in nature.

I had been brought up in a church-going Methodist household, and my maternal grandfather was a Methodist minister. My first remembered experience of real profundity was in Llantwit Major in South Wales when on a seaside holiday as a thirteen year-old with my parents. I took one of many solitary walks and found myself flinging myself down onto the edge of a cliff face overlooking the bright water. There was something more than met the eye in this summer-sunshined beauty: a translucency of things, nature pointing through and beyond itself to an evanescence.

Years later, studying early Celtic Christianity, I learnt that it was in that very location that the great teaching monastery of St Illtud had its home from the 4th to the 9th Century. I have since come to realise that prayer and wisdom collects and saturates a local context so that there can truly be said to emerge a spirit of place.

By the age of seventeen or eighteen, I was bored and somewhat jaundiced by my home church. Whilst dropping out of active Church engagement, I still knew myself to be in some sort of intimacy with and hunger for God. I longed to realize the divine in the midst of things. A significant number of mystical visions and experiences on the cliffs of the Gower when I was a student of Philosophy and English at University College, Swansea in the late Sixties kept this flame alight.

It was when an attractive Swedish blonde, whom I had never met before, arrived at the house in The Mumbles, Swansea (of Dylan Thomas fame) where my closest friends were throwing a 21st birthday party for me, that my more intentional exploration of the mystical tradition of other great faiths began. Ingrid arrived from London in the late afternoon of the second day of the party. Her journey had been three or four hours long and a little hazardous. Immediately on arriving, she appeared in the kitchen; minutes later, I became aware that she was no longer there. I was told by my friends that Ingrid had gone to one of the top bedrooms to meditate. This was a turning point for me. The thought that this attractive young woman, just arrived after a long January journey, had not even stopped for a cup of tea or a glass of wine, but had gone upstairs for her meditation period – this was truly provocative!

I was suddenly brought face to face with a new level of reality: firstly, with the fact that there was such a thing as a practice of meditation; secondly that a personal spiritual discipline was regarded as essential and life-giving by a number of people, including dynamic Swedish women! Thirdly, that I was awakened to an urgency within myself, a strong motivation to follow this trail, to become more consciously a seeker after the divine element.

Accordingly, I found out what had inspired Ingrid on the path of spiritual discipline, learned that it was Transcendental Meditation, and, later that year, in the summer of 1970, whilst attending a Martha Graham dance workshop in London, was initiated into this particular way of meditating. My thirst for knowledge led me into reading more fully about the Vedic tradition and I spent some time at the Ramakrishna Order monastery, then at Holland Park, London.

Encounter with Sufism

My questing had already by that time taken me overland to North West Iran on an anthropological project and to East Africa to help build a school – and also as it happened, to be invited to play in an Ankole tribal drum band near the Mountains of the Moon in Western Uganda. Now, as the journey moved from the exoteric to the esoteric, from the outer geography of landscape to the inner geometry of soul, I found my way to the Sufi centre in Gloucestershire called Beshara and also into the Taoist and Zen Buddhist traditions.

My hunger for God and for mystical experience led me in 1972 to resign from my position as English Master at an independent school in Hertfordshire and to dedicate myself totally to 'find God'. In my little Mini-Moke I motored up to the Scottish Highlands, enjoyed the freedom to roam and met up with a variety of wonderful people, locals, back-packers and hippies. This liberty was suddenly curtailed when, on a field somewhere in the north west of Scotland, an inner voice firmly announced 'You need spiritual discipline'.

I remember to this day the twofold response: firstly a real annoyance with God which prompted me to look upwards and call out "you could have given me a bit more time to enjoy myself. I've only been free for three weeks!" The second response, following swiftly on the heels of the first, was one of recognition of the validity of the call. Accordingly, I turned about and headed back to the one place that came immediately to mind when this instruction was given: Beshara, the Sufi centre and its spiritual mentor, Reshad Field.

Sufi dancing, chanting the dikr, meditating, eating and working together – this was a rich and fertile context for my emergent story, it was a place and a community where I felt I was seeing love-in-action. Then the next major transition point set the primary direction for the rest of my pilgrimage of knowing and unknowing. Beshara hosted a conference or gathering where a representative from all the major faith traditions spoke. A candle was lit for each spiritual discipline and the whole community drank thankfully from the particular wells of wisdom that were presented.

Rediscovering Christianity

Among those who spoke was a Christian speaker who had been particularly helped and influenced by Buddhism. I remember nothing of what he or any other of the speakers shared. But that night, somewhere in the wee hours, I had a vision or a dream of myself lying down on the earth and a large three-dimensional cross arising, as it were, Salvador Dali-like from my chest. I woke up with the absolute certainty that I had to become a follower of Christ.

As the dawn broke and the day at Beshara began, I went, somewhat hesitantly, to see Reshad Field. It was not hugely "cool" to be or to become a Christian in those heady days of eastern pilgrimage. Whilst being certain in my own being of my new-found "calling", I was a little unsure of how this news would be received. Reshad heard my news of the vision and the sense of clarity of purpose that went with it and simply said: "This is wonderful! You have found your path."

That graciousness and spaciousness was echoed in the warm farewell from members of the community at Beshara as I drove off with my bags in the direction of The Anchorhold, the experimental, contemplative Christian community which Reshad had suggested might be a good focus. Here, with a great admixture of Tai Chi and yoga postures with the Anglican monastic offices, I found myself in a vibrant spiritual community. In turn, once again, this place of sanctuary and stretching allowed the next step on my journey to become evident. From there I learned about the Jesus prayer, Mount Athos and the Eastern Orthodox tradition. Within weeks, I became a novice monk in a Russian Orthodox hermitage for twelve months – but that is another story!

A writer that I love and who links with this same Eastern Christian dynamic is Jacob Needleman. In his book "Lost Christianity" he writes: "To know life, one must be able to see life and as Zen teaches, and also as Christianity and Judaism teach, life moves more swiftly and subtly than the theoretic mind or the personal emotions. In my academic work as a professor of philosophy and religion I had begun to perceive things in the Bible that I had never dreamed were there.

I was beginning to understand that everything I had seen in the Eastern teachings was also contained in Judaism and Christianity, although the language of the Bible was practically impossible to penetrate because it had become so encrusted with familiar associations. Through meeting this unforgettable man (Fr Sylvan), I realized with certainty that there are worlds upon worlds of Christianity that neither I nor anyone else I had met knew anything about." (p.60)

Faith Traditions and Wisdom Paths

I am fascinated by story-telling and metaphor and am involved in a rich teaching process called Metaphor Theology or Symbolic Modelling. Jesus, like so many of the sages or illumined ones, told stories, invested metaphor with the power to transform. I have come to know this shift-potential of the parable not as an intellectual truth but from the inside of the parable. As Aristotle said "a good metaphor implies an intuitive perception of the similarity in dissimilars".

So, faith traditions and wisdom paths hold the creative tension. I sense that a transpersonal contribution to citizenship can be, at least in part, one of educating for insights into metaphors and stories that reveal and release the perception of the "similarities in dissimilar". But why "mystical realism", what is this scandal of particularity and is there somewhere called "now/here"?

Where are we on this transpersonal journey? When people describe the inter-relationship between the great spiritual traditions, three metaphors can surface, the first very popular: the different faiths are like paths up the mountain. A less common but increasingly popular image is of the spiritual cultures being like islands in the ocean. A third metaphor that was recently shared with me quite spontaneously identified each religious tradition being like sections of the garden – there being one gardener and some fine under-gardeners. None of these is perfect, none an exact fit, but they are pointers.

The common thread running through all three metaphors is the creative tension, the playful paradox between the particular and the universal, between paths, islands, sections, between the this and the that. There is a vibrant thread of connection. Now/here – is this the scandal of particularity, the cornerstone of a truly mystical realism? Nowhere and now/here highlights the movement to and from the negative way and the positive way – both are valid and need each other. This is the insight of the mystical tradition – from the apophatic (the unknowing) to the cataphatic (the knowing) and back again in unending motion.

In every faith tradition this continuum from not this, not that, nowhere to this, here, now is represented by saints and sages. In the Christian tradition, it is John of the Cross and Teresa, it is Meister Eckhart and Francis. In the life and teachings of Yeshua, or Jesus both the way of affirmation and of negation are manifest.

The Scandal of Particularity

Now/here is the scandal of particularity. Earlier this summer I was given tickets to see *Carmen* at the English National Opera. Carmen has been described as "the most popular opera of all time". It is set in Spain with gypsies, criminals and a passionate feisty heroine. In 1935 Frederico Garcia Lorca presented his collection of poems and 'Gypsy Ballads' with these words that exemplify the scandal, the paradox of particularity . . . "the gypsy is the highest, deepest, most aristocratic element of where I come from, the most representative of its mode of being, retaining the embers, blood and alphabet of a truth which is Andalusian and universal . . . "

"Andalusian and universal" – this is the scandal of particularity attaching itself to any local person or event which has universal significance, be it a gypsy woman, the Buddha, Moses, Mohammed or Christ. We are called to be local and global – British or European or American citizens as well as planetary citizens. Both/and. Andalusian and universal, Christian and universal, Sufi and universal.

I have been using 'and' a lot. "And" is a great conjunction. But I now want to introduce you to another of my favourite words – with even fewer letters: a word that speaks right into the heart of our dilemma and question regarding spirituality and citizenship. Two letters – the in word: 'in' is a very humble and yet powerful preposition, metaphors of 'withinness' highlight a non-dual understanding unlike much thinking with its often dualistic 'and'.

Mystical Realism

In my title, I am also introducing you to a phrase that I have coined, with some presumption no doubt, as a possible contender for the succession to the philosophical and cultural term 'post-modernism'. If the question is, what needs to come after post-modernism in our equipping for local and planetary citizenship, my suggestion is 'mystical realism'.

Mystical realism is, of course, a paradox as all good truths seem to be! From the sublime to the gritty, from the expansive to the practical, from the mystical to the mundane, from righteousness to realism – this is one glorious continuum. I believe that we need a School of Mystical Realism to nurture a citizenship that is truly transpersonal and that honours both the particularity of the respective faith traditions and also the universal consciousness that undergirds them. So, if anyone in response would like to write out a large cheque, we'll start the School!

But why the 'in' word? Well, because the 'and' word is often not sufficiently or robustly integral. I am living, you are living and called to embody the infinite in the finite, the transcendent in the visible – in, within, interiorly abiding. The great teachers and prophets, the bearers of wisdom and truth, have lived and worked in their particular moment of history, and because of that particularity, have changed the direction of others and of us. Their citizenship has been to discern and articulate the sacred in the secular. Two examples of such a point of intersection of the timeless with time are, firstly, the sacramental use of ordinary things with extraordinary effect, such as bread, wine, oil or water; and secondly, the embodied metaphor of body-prayer.

Similarly, the poets: T. S. Eliot, in his *Selected Essays* 1917 – 32 p 247 writes: "When a poet's mind is perfectly equipped for his work, it is consistently amalgamating disparate experiences: (but) the ordinary person's experience is chaotic, irregular, fragmentary. The latter falls in love, or reads Spinoza, and these two experiences have nothing to do with each other, or with the noise of the typewriter or the smell of cooking; in the mind of the poet, these experiences are already forming new wholes". We are called to be poets, as well as psychologists, priests and prophets.

The Role of Metaphor

Metaphor is the link that may help us to connect this here with that there, to find the inscape of things as Hopkins called it, to see the part as whole. We need, and every faith tradition and spiritual movement has to find in each generation, the development, the liberation of the imagination to identify associations, metaphors, parables that will help people encounter mystery, meaning, God in the most mundane of words and experiences. Let us learn how to bless this mess!

"A metaphor is a word used in an unfamiliar context to give us a new insight" says Sallie McFague in *Speaking in Parables*: "metaphor is a way of knowing and not just a way of communicating." So Shakespeare's "my salad days, when I was green in judgement". Paul Lacey writing about American poetry in his book, *The Inner Way* (1972 p114) says of the Jewish Hasidic tradition out of which Denise Levertov writes: "One puts off the habitual but does not repudiate it; when the habitual is seen afresh, it testifies to the holy." So, the holy abides in the habitual.

In the Christian tradition, the wonderful Jesuit poet Gerard Manley Hopkins wrote:
"The world is charged with the grandeur of God.
It will flame out, like shining from shook foil;
It gathers to a greatness, like the ooze of oil
Crushed . . . .
And for all this, nature is never spent;

There lives the dearest freshness deep down things;
Because the Holy Ghost over the bent
World brooks with warm breast and with
Ah! bright wings"

The great faith traditions have drawn from early, early sources. As Sallie McFague reminds us (p 53): "The primitives had single meanings for works – he or she participated in an original unity of body and spirit – which referred without disjuncture to inner and outer realities."

Erich Auerbach in his seminal work *Mimesis: The Representation of Reality in Western Literature* ('57 Doubleday chapters 1 and 2) is appreciative of the Christian tradition's role in introducing into Western literature a type of story which, as he says, is "fraught with background." Auerbach says "If God was somehow with Jesus of Nazareth struggling with time and limitation, then human history must be the realm of the truly significant."

On the Jesus journey the scandal of particularity is that 'the secular and the human is the place of God's presence.' Jesus modelled it, embodied it, so well was he incarnated, enfleshed – 'The Word became flesh' – that, as MacFague reminds us, many did and do not perceive that presence 'hidden under the ordinary events of everyday life". He became God incognito, as we might phrase it.

The parable, the wisdom story insists that 'the gap between the human and the transcendent is closed only through personal risk and decision.' The choice is ours – in our historical earthly reality, which also contains heavenly bliss. Here, we can choose to remember, to attend, to live, or not.

Christ's incarnation, ministry, death and resurrection represent a supreme scandal of particularity. William Lynch's *Christ and Apollo: the Dimensions of Literary imagination* ('63 New American Library p XIV) puts it thus: 'Christ stands for the completely definite . . .as the model and source of that energy and courage we again need to enter the finite as the (only) creative and generative source of beauty.'

Lynch validates metaphor, or 'the analogical imagination' as method, which discerns in images of fragility and vulnerability 'the path to whatever the individual is seeking: to insight, or beauty, or . . .God.' This route is both focussed and constrained, leading, he indicates 'straight through our human realities, through our labour, our disappointments, our friends, our game legs, our harvests, our subjection to time. There are no shortcuts to beauty and truth. We must go through the finite, the limited, the definite, omitting none of it lest we omit some of the potencies of being-in-the-flesh.'

Contemplative Fire

All this is the scandal of particularity, and this lies at the heart of what I mean by mystical realism. This sublime but earthy paradox is a key element of the DNA coding of the pioneering venture that I am happily engaged in, entitled Contemplative Fire: Journey in Presence. I have just stepped out in faith to launch this coracle as a very different way of doing church – and amazingly with the full backing of my bishop in the Church of England!

We shall, in Contemplative Fire, unashamedly be recalling the profound legacy of the Christian mystical tradition, its Jewish heritage and Abrahamic path. The particularity of one tradition will be our fuel, but we shall not claim it as the only fuel. We are called to be open to the breath of the Spirit as we move onwards and outwards. T. S. Eliot in his magisterial poem *Little Gidding* in *Four Quartets*, plainly puts the paradox of past in the present, living the scandal of particularity.

> "If you came this way,
> Taking any route, starting from anywhere
> At any time or at any season,
> It would always be the same: you would have to put off
> Sense and notion. You are not here to verify,
> Instruct yourself, or inform curiosity
> Or carry report. You are here to kneel
> Where prayer has been valid . . . . the communication
> Of the dead is tongued with fire beyond the language of the living."

The incisive poet says: "You are here to kneel where prayer has been valid." This is the gift of the past into the kingdom of the present, the gift of people of faith. This is neither to be ridiculed nor to face reduction, but rather to be celebrated and integrated. Remembering – in the Greek sense of re-presenting – has to be done well. Tradition, if it is to be truth-bearing, can only be dynamic. Once static, it is dead.

Contemplative Fire borrows barns, farms, homes and ancient chapels. An old twelfth century monastic chapel that we use once a month for a contemplative eucharist by candlelight is an old place, re-configured and yet still redolent of mystery and meaning – the past come alive in the present. Then and now, the future beckons.

6th Century St Dorothea of Gaza writes: "Imagine a circle marked out on the ground. Suppose that this circle is the world, and that the centre of the circle is God. Heading from the edge of the circle to its centre are a number of lines, all these represent the paths or ways of life the people can follow. In their desire to draw near to God, the saints advance along these lines towards the middle of the circle, so that the further they go, the nearer they approach to one another as well as to God. The closer they come to God, the closer they come to one another; the closer they come to one another, the closer they come to God. Such is the nature of love: the nearer we draw to God in our love for him, the more we are united together by love for our neighbour, and the greater our union with our neighbour, the greater is our union with God."

17. AN ISLAMIC PERSPECTIVE

Azim Nanji

Azim begins this chapter, which is based on his EUROTAS London presentation, with his concerns about the undue focus on cultural conflict and violence. He understands that civilizations and faiths extend more and more beyond traditional nation state boundaries. Diversity needs to be protected and promoted within and between our faith traditions. The historic role of Islam in dialogue and exchange has been enormous. But spiritual dialogue needs to be at the individual level, not just at the level of society, community and nation. Azim uses the journey of the Prophet as an example of the Islamic acknowledgement and acceptance of each other's common quest and purpose of the great prophets and teachers of wisdom of the world's spiritual and religious traditions. This transhistorical and transpersonal thread has always been part of the hikma, the wisdom tradition of Islam as expressed in Muslim mystical and esoteric writings. The inspiring Conference of the Birds narrative creates a vision of the intersection of the personal and the collective for Muslims and indeed for all faiths and spiritual paths, in the same way as Philip Roderick talked about metaphor and Les Lancaster similarly illustrates his theme through Old Testament quotations. The Birds gather to address two important questions and … well please read it for yourself. It is too profound to summarize.

Azim goes on to talk about the "quiet moments" that we all can experience through our religion or along our spiritual path. It reminds one of the English philosopher A.N. Whitehead, who defined religion as what a person does with his quiet moments.

He concludes with the metaphor of the garden which through history has been created by

Muslims to symbolize spiritual values and aspirations. The Arabic word for garden, jannah, is used as the word for Paradise, the reward of the hereafter. Gardens begin the world in some faith traditions representing at one level the ideal environment for human existence close to God and in harmony with nature.

The garden, with its running water, symbolizes the coming together of many elements of spirituality, creating the space where human beings are close to God in everyday experience. This is at the heart of the Muslim faith, where contact with God flows throughout the day. But gardens need humans to engage in the act of cultivation, and that is perhaps what collectively the London Conference and this series of writings is about.

***Professor Azim Nanji** is a professor of Islamic Studies at the University of Berkeley and Director of the Islamic Centre in London.*

There has been in recent times an undue focus on a notion of cultural conflict and violence particularly with regard to Islam. In order to understand the increasing complexity of Muslims and their civilisation, we need to recognize that civilisations and faiths are increasingly extending beyond the boundaries of the nation state, and that they are not monolithic, unidimensional, static entities that can be easily essentialised. Rather, the diversity within and among them needs to be protected and promoted to better understand our shared contributions to humanity's spiritual heritage, and as tools of understanding of our common spiritual quest.

Islam's contribution to this dialogue and exchange has been enormous. It engendered many opportunities for syntheses as it spread, so that learning, art, architecture and science could flourish using the wisdom of local experience and the language of indigenous traditions and symbols. In addition to creating new intellectual and cultural spaces, Islam encouraged the sharing of wisdom, knowledge and ideas amongst cultures and civilisations by acting as a bridge between the legacy of the Greek world and Western European culture through Arabic translations of the original works that were subsequently translated into Latin. Muslims also appropriated and built on wisdom traditions from other cultures in Africa and Asia.

This history of dialogue and exchanges suggests that we can erode intolerance, prejudice, ignorance and conflict, so that societies and civilisations can learn to understand each other better, rather than simply tolerating one another. However, these dialogues need to take place at the individual level in addition to those of the community, society and nation. A commitment must be made to listen to each other, so that we may be able to transcend the cultural divides that have separated us, and focus on common problems that affect all cultures and groups.

One of the most significant experiences granted to the Prophet Muhammad is known as the mirj, referred to in the Quran as a journey or ascent (isra'), "to show him our sign" (Quran 17:1)

According to Muslim tradition, the Prophet, during this ascent, encountered the great prophets and teachers of wisdom of the world's spiritual and religious traditions. They acknowledged and accepted each other's common quest and purpose, recognizing that the ultimate encounter with God and the true meaning of the self in its relationship with the Absolute, was a shared aspiration. This transhistorical and transpersonal thread has always been part of the hikma, the wisdom tradition in Islam as expressed in Muslim mystical and esoteric writings and is reflected in the many narratives and stories preserved by Muslims.

The Conference of the Birds

One of these narratives is entitled the Conference of the Birds, which creates a vision of the intersection of the personal and the collective, assembling us so to speak, to define what we share as common space and common questions.

The allegorical poem begins with a gathering of birds, assembled to address two important questions: (1) Where is the symbolic reference point of their oneness and their common ancestry? and (2) What commitments do they need to make to discover these goals? They choose a mediator, the hoopoe, who can guide them on their journey and quest. My sense is that our dialogue today represents such a mediating space and reference point – a place of gathering where we ask questions and seek answers, debate our diversity in a common public space and learn to explore and preserve the answers that our quest might yield. Such a mediating presence is a prelude to the pursuit of inner knowledge.

In the tradition of Islamic spirituality, in which the issues of society are mirrored, the "Conference of Birds" asks us to look beyond at values that raise questions for us all: "Who are we?" "What does it mean to be a bird?" "What is 'birdness'?" It also asks us to be aware of love and passion, about differences and to show compassion and concern for one another. Finally it also poses the question of whether there is an articulation of our 'birdness' that transcends us all?" The journey of the birds is a long one, over seven valleys and seven mountains. Each valley, each mountain is a step towards dissolving otherness, dissolving boundaries, of creating a common vocabulary, and forging a common language. At the end, thirty birds survive the journey. They then come together in a space beyond the last valley looking for that articulation, of what they have come to accomplish and discover. They wait, and in silence, they turn inwards, examine their experience, and focus on each other. In Persian, the word for thirty birds is si-murgh. The space and entity that they have come to discover is also called Simurgh, their mythical originator. In experiencing their joint quest and condition, their silent meditation, awakens in them the meaning of their quest, oneness or unity, lived and experienced.

Understanding of this kind is born out of the experience of self and knowledge of the Other. It is born in a series of quiet but intense moments and contemplative silence during the quest. A chapel, a mosque, a memorial, where between the silences that exist, we may as the thirty birds find and embrace a common commitment. That experience might enable us to carry both the spiritual capacity and personal knowledge we have acquired and to share it in the space beyond the dichotomies reflected in our imagined differences.

I would like, in summarizing my comments, to return to a shared and powerful symbol – the "garden". Muslim Gardens represent cultivated spaces across the diverse span of Muslim history and geography, created and demarcated from wilderness of different kinds. They were created to enhance the built environment, to design and ornament landscape and to symbolize spiritual values and aspirations. The garden and landscape architecture in Muslim societies continue to be an important expression of ethical assumptions about stewardship, ecology and beauty.

The Arabic word for garden, jannah is used in the Quran for paradise, the reward of the hereafter. One of the settings in the Quranic narrative of creation as in the Bible, (Q 2:34, 7:19) is the primordial garden, where the first created pair is placed. The garden is therefore also among God's creations and the theatre in which the initial human drama unfolds. At one level, it represents the ideal environment in which the first humans can subsist, close to God and in equilibrium and harmony with nature.

The garden with its running water is a place that symbolizes the coming together of many elements that represent a forward movement spiritually, so that the water is always constantly moving and flowing. And I think that's part of the rhythm that's generated in the garden so that one's participation in nature is an active one. Nature is dynamic – creation itself is not static. And if you look at the symbolism that's inherent in the story it's the notion that God initiates the first garden. It becomes the archetypal garden, a space of intimacy – a space where human beings are close to God. But they're also in an environment where you are in the midst of having every sense, every need, every spiritual aspect of you life in total equilibrium and harmony. So when you trespass, as the creation story tells us and you leave that environment and you're here on earth, that memory, that remembrance is still very critical to the way in which you recover the experience of that space in your own daily life.

The promise of the return to the garden, i.e. the promised abode of the hereafter, is however held out as the goal of human life, but until the return, the garden remains an aspiration and expectation, even a memory that human imagination might be able to recreate on earth. Among the main features of the garden in paradise are four rivers, of water, milk, honey and wine. This verse is believed to be the inspiration for the Char Bagh, the four spaced garden that has been particularly expressed with such great beauty in the gardens of Lahore, in Iran, in Kashmir and so on. I think one can see that the geometry enables one to trace that movement from the outer to the inner which is the journey of the soul that it moves from the formal aspect of life, the ritual aspect of life to the aspect that explores that interior space which is the heart of true spirituality subsists.

A garden symbolizes the fact that faith is not something that just happens apart from every day experience. It provides an opportunity for one to have that faith inspire communication with God outside of the formalized spaces of ritual requirements. It's a daily occurrence. And I think that also is of the essence of Islamic spirituality that your contact with God is not segmented or compartmentalized. It flows throughout the day.

Much of Muslim mystical poetry builds on the symbolic meanings of the garden, the geometry, water, profusion, greenery, the budding of the rose, the bee among the flowers, the harmony of form and essence, the transient and created nature of the earthly garden. The archetypal space is the site of meanings in human life, its exalted destiny as well as the focus of its memory. The garden can be both the place of transition as well as arrival and of ultimate repose in the world and an echo of eternity. But a garden requires human beings to engage in an act of cultivation. I dare say that it is that act that we have gathered here to perform today, collectively.

EXPERIENTIAL APPROACHES TO CONSCIOUSNESS

18. EMBODIED PARTICIPATION IN THE MYSTERY: IMPLICATIONS FOR THE INDIVIDUAL, INTERPERSONAL RELATIONSHIPS AND SOCIETY

Ramon Albareda, Jorge Ferrer, and Marina Romero

Ramon, Jorge and Marina postulate an ultimate principle of life and reality that pervades two polar energetic states – the Dark Energy and the Energy of Consciousness. This is a non-dualistic proposal as both states are ultimately the same energy, the former containing both creative wisdom and accumulated human tendencies in tension with the primordial order. The latter is the transcendent life of the cosmos outreaching love and wisdom.

Evolution can be seen as the progressive differentiation and integration of the Dark Energy and the Energy of Consciousness. The thesis helps to explain the mind-centred Western culture that has devalued qualities such as matter, the natural world, the body and sexuality and seen them sometimes in conflict with psychological, social and spiritual qualities. It may be the historic moment to integrate these qualities. They go on to explore some of the practical implications for the individual, interpersonal relationships and society. The implications for the interconnectedness of individuals, society and the planet are fundamental as at all levels integral growth of the individual would be a developmental process of collaboration between body, instincts, heart, mind and consciousness. An embodied spirituality would emerge, seen by them as a creative and integrative force. The interpersonal dimension of social relationships which follows this integrative and embodied spirituality would turn off the conflicts of the comparing mind and lead to a renewed sense of significance and excitement in human interactions. The implications for intimate relationships are profound. The model of the family which still prevails in our culture for the development of humanity until now is challenged by new models which could be very diverse and lead to forms of community living. Some of these forms can be very similar to the family structure but with more explicitly honouring the needs of each person or couple and others further away from the family and community structures of the past.

Ramon V. Albareda is a clinical psychologist and theologian. He is the Founder/Director of Estel (Center of Personal Growth and School of Integral Studies) in Barcelona, Spain. He is the cocreator of Holistic Integration, an integral approach to psychospiritual growth and healing, and co-author of Nacidos de la Tierra: Sexualidad, Origen del Ser Humano, *as well as of many articles and book chapters on transpersonal sexuality, psychospiritual development, and human integration.*

Jorge N. Ferrer, Ph.D. is core faculty at the California Institute of Integral Studies, San Francisco, and adjunct faculty at the Institute of Transpersonal Psychology, Palo Alto. He is the author of Revisioning Transpersonal Theory: A Participatory Vision of Human Spirituality *(SUNY Press, 2002) and editor of a monograph in the journal* ReVision *on "New Horizons in Contemporary Spirituality."*

Marina T. Romero is Director of Estel (Center of Personal Growth and School of Integral Studies), Barcelona, Spain, and adjunct faculty at the California Institute of Integral Studies, San Francisco. She is the cocreator of Holistic Integration, an integral approach to psychospiritual growth and healing, and co-author of *Nacidos de la Tierra: Sexualidad, Origen del Ser Humano, *as well as of many articles and book chapters on transpersonal sexuality, psychospiritual development, and human integration.*

We postulate the existence of an intelligent and creative primordial energy or Mystery that is the ultimate principle of life and reality. This Mystery pervades the cosmos in two polar energetic states: the Dark Energy and the Energy of Consciousness.[1] Energetically speaking, whereas the dark pole of the Mystery is dense, amorphous, and undifferentiated, the conscious pole is subtle, luminous, and infinitely differentiated.

The Dark Energy is the Mystery's immanent life and dynamic fountain of generativity at all levels. The Dark Energy is spiritual prima materia – that is, unactualized spiritual energy in a state of transformation, saturated with potentials and novel possibilities. We see matter and the physical universe as initial manifestations of the Dark Energy and as therefore having an interior or experiential dimension. In the human realm, the Dark Energy is the source of our vitality and natural wisdom, as well as the organising principle of our embodiment, sexuality, and instinctive life. Roughly, we can distinguish between two states of the Dark Energy: (1) the energy that contains both the creative wisdom of the primordial order of life and historically accumulated human tendencies aligned with that primordial order, and (2) the energy that stores historically accumulated human tendencies that are in tension with such primordial order. In this context, we can say that the physical body and its vital energies enable human beings not only to creatively participate in the immanent dimensions of the Mystery, but also to filter and purify conflictive energetic tendencies stored therein.

The Energy of Consciousness is the Mystery's transcendent life and dynamic telos of the cosmos toward the expansion of outreaching love and wisdom. In the human realm, the Energy of Consciousness is the source of our self-awareness and spiritual discernment, as well as the organising principle of the psyche and its transcendent function. Like the Dark Energy, the Energy of Consciousness exists in two different states: (1) the energy of spiritual consciousness, associated with a higher knowledge that transcends rational understanding, and (2) the energy of human consciousness, associated with the knowledge generated by the human mind, which can be either aligned or in tension with the principles of spiritual consciousness. Both energetic states are intimately connected to the process of knowing, which includes the capacity to see (to be aware of), to understand (to see beyond superficial awareness), and to comprehend (to see and to understand the interrelationship of the various elements that constitute reality, as well as to discern its meaning). Given this connectedness, we can say that the mind and consciousness enable human beings not only to creatively participate in the transcendent dimensions of the Mystery, but also to align human knowledge with its principles.

We are not proposing here a dualistic system; however, although the Energy of Consciousness and the Dark Energy are ultimately the same energy in different states, we believe that their distinction is crucial.[2] We make this distinction because, as we suggest in the remainder of this chapter, the dynamic interplay between these two polar energies may be one of the primary motors of the evolutionary process, and human alignment with their distinct principles may therefore be fundamental for individual, interpersonal, and social harmony.

The Evolutionary Process in the Light of this Dipolar Account of the Mystery

In its widest sense, evolution can be seen as involving the progressive differentiation and integration of the Dark Energy and the Energy of Consciousness. In human life, it is likely that the Energy of Consciousness historically emerged by means of an inhibition of the Dark Energy. Far from being an evolutionary mistake or aberration, this temporary inhibition may have been essential to avoid the reabsorption of a still relatively weak, emerging self-consciousness and its values into the stronger presence that a more instinctively driven energy once had in human beings. In other words, the inhibition and/or regulation of the primary dimensions of the person—somatic, instinctive, sexual, and certain aspects of the emotional—may have been actually necessary at certain stages of human evolution to allow the emergence and maturation of self-consciousness and its cognitive, emotional, and moral qualities.

If we are correct about the general dynamics of this process, it may help to explain the rise of a mind-centred Western culture that has devalued primary qualities and values such as matter, the natural world, the body, and sexuality, and tended to see them in tension with or even opposition to the flourishing of psychological, social, and spiritual qualities. In the context of the world's religious traditions, this may be connected to the widespread consideration of certain human qualities as being spiritually more "correct" or wholesome than others; for example, equanimity over intense passions, transcendence over sensuous embodiment, and chastity over sexual exploration. To put it bluntly, humankind's evolutionary path has been laid out in accord with a dichotomising view of reality which has created opposing bands that struggle against each other, with certain behaviours and values being considered "bad" or "lower" and others "good" or "higher." This form of evolution, although perhaps historically necessary, has generated an intrapersonal and interpersonal model, now deeply seated in human nature, based on confrontation, conflict, struggle, war, and regressive or paralysing tendencies.

From our perspective, we are living in a unique historical moment. We are convinced that the degree to which human consciousness has developed enables us to take a qualitative leap forward in the evolutionary process. We suggest that we are now collectively prepared to cultivate ways of life based on the integration of polar qualities that have always been seen as opposites, or even as mutual enemies – ways of life that, in general, are based on the integration of the Dark Energy and the Energy of Consciousness. We are not, of course, talking about a return to a state of primordial undifferentiation of these energies, but rather of a process in which both energies, while remaining clearly differentiated, move toward a creative synthesis that brings forth a more integrated state of being affiliated with novel qualities and possibilities. In other words, having developed self-reflective consciousness and the subtle dimensions of the heart, it may be the moment for us as a species to reappropriate and integrate the more primary and instinctive dimensions of human nature into a fully embodied participation in the Mystery.[3] The remainder of this chapter briefly explores a selected sample of practical implications that this embodied participation may have for the individual, interpersonal relationships, and society.

The Individual Dimension

Personal Integration

The life of each human being can be seen as a precious opportunity for contributing to the evolutionary integration of the Dark Energy and the Energy of Consciousness. Each person incarnates both energies to some extent and can therefore creatively collaborate in their embodiment and integration. In other words, a human being is a dwelling place in which these two energies can meet, be fully embodied, and bring forth novel qualities that have never before existed.

The integration of the Dark Energy and the Energy of Consciousness can bear many personal fruits. On one hand, the Dark Energy provides human life with a sense of rootedness and vitalisation, without which individuals may not feel called to or prepared for engagement in the sorely needed transformation of their everyday life and of the world. On the other hand, the Energy of Consciousness grants lucidity, orientation, and subtlety to human life, thus facilitating the transformation of the physical body and the instinctive drives into increasingly conscious and intelligent processes. This integrative process allows matter to become the experiential locus for not only the encounter of these two energetic poles, but also the emergence of novel potentials resulting from their interaction and integration. Given the intrinsic value and practical advantages of integrating these energies, working toward such an integration is a task that can bring a sense of profound meaning to human life.

In the context of this process, the heart would be the natural bridge between the Dark Energy and the Energy of Consciousness, as well as the necessary link for their integration. The human heart will only be able to play its central role in this integration, however, if it can adopt an attitude of open receptivity to and unconditional acceptance of both energies and learn to become permeable to them. Likewise, both the body and the mind must become porous and receptive to the Dark Energy and the Energy of Consciousness and need to be supported in this process by the unconditional acceptance of the heart. The mind must become humble and receptive to the messages that transcend its cognitive structures and needs to be unconditionally supported in this process by the heart and the body. To be sure, this is not an easy process. It is not enough to change forms and structures; deeply ingrained vital attitudes and values must be changed as well, and this change is only possible through the transformation of all the basic levels of a human being – body, instincts, heart, mind, and consciousness – in both their individual and social dimensions, as well as in their masculine and feminine qualities.

Integral Growth and Holistic Health

The integration of the Dark Energy and the Energy of Consciousness at all levels of the individual would lead to the emergence of a new energetic axis that would guide and foster his or her integral evolution from within. Integral growth, then, would be a developmental process in which all human dimensions – body, instincts, heart, mind, and consciousness – collaboratively participate as equals in the multidimensional unfolding of the human being. Being grounded in the person's most unique potentials, a genuine integral growth would rarely follow a pre-given path already travelled by others, nor could it be directed by external standards.

A personal process that gradually integrates the Dark Energy and the Energy of Consciousness at all levels of the person would lead to a state of holistic health. Two central markers of integral health would be the degree of alignment of the energetic axis of the person (vital-primary and conscious-spiritual potentials) and the degree of its coherence with his or her structural axis (somatic, vital, sexual, emotional, and mental worlds). When assessing the integral health of an individual, for example, we would ask the following questions: How much is the conscious-spiritual development of the person grounded in or aligned to his or her most unique vital potentials; that is, those potentials that make them a unique embodiment of the Mystery? Have the spiritual values and ideals of the person emerged organically from a process of personal integration, or have they been adopted from external sources and perhaps imposed over their primary world? To what extent are the person's somatic, instinctive, emotional, and mental structures coherent with the energetic axis created by the progressive alignment of their vital-primary and conscious-spiritual potentials? What physical habits, sexual routines, emotional patterns, and mental schemes may need to change or be strengthened in order to facilitate a better flow of the Dark Energy and the Energy of Consciousness through the person's body, instincts, heart, and mind? And so forth.

Coherence among the various aspects of the person would result in a state of vitalised peace characterised by an unconditional openness toward life and a grounded love that would naturally engage the person in the transformation of his or her surroundings. The self-defeating pursuit of happiness through the acquisition of material wealth and the self-centred collection of "good" experiences would naturally give way to a state of well-being based on the natural joy of living in a fully embodied way, as well as in being socially engaged in the transformation of others and of the world.

Embodied Spirituality

The spirituality that would emerge from the above-mentioned process would be vitalised, fully embodied, and socially engaged. It would also be a creative spirituality, one which integrates harmoniously the various dichotomies and polarities of life in very diverse ways. This spirituality would contrast with the still-prevailing disembodied spirituality that stands in tension or even opposition to the physical body and its primary impulses. In our view, disembodied spirituality – which can exist in many different degrees and at many levels of consciousness – fosters individual and social dissociation in forms that perpetuate the historical dichotomy between matter and spirit. A spirituality separated from bodily grounding also fosters human relationships based on confrontation and struggle. It not only maintains the conflicts that have always beset humanity but, by using the spiritual as a refuge and an escape from everyday psychosocial problems, hinders the transformation that human reality so deeply needs.

Even in the modern West, spirituality is often based on an attempt to transcend, regulate, and/or transform embodied reality from the "higher" standpoint of consciousness and its values. Matter's experiential dimension as immanent expression of the Mystery is generally ignored. This deeply embedded shortsightedness leads to the conscious or unconscious belief that everything related to matter is unrelated to the Mystery. This belief, in turn, confirms that matter and spirit are two antagonistic dimensions. It then becomes necessary to abandon or condition the material dimension in order to strengthen the spiritual one. The first step out of this impasse, we suggest, is to rediscover the Mystery in its immanent manifestation; that is, to stop seeing and treating matter and the body as something that is not only alien to the Mystery but that distances us from the spiritual dimension of life. In contrast to these views, we suggest that the progressive integration of matter and consciousness may lead to what we might call a state of "conscious matter." A fascinating possibility to consider is that a complete embodiment and integration of the Dark Energy and the Energy of Consciousness in our material existence may gradually open the doors to extraordinary longevity, physical immortality, or other forms of metanormal functioning attested to by the world's mystical traditions. (See, e.g., Murphy, 1993.)

The Interpersonal Dimension

Social Relationships: Turning Off the Comparing Mind

An integrative and embodied spirituality would effectively undermine the current model of human relations based on comparison, which easily leads to competition, rivalry, envy, jealousy, conflict, and hatred. When individuals develop in harmony with their most genuine vital potentials, human relationships characterised by mutual exchange and enrichment would naturally emerge because people would not need to project onto others their own needs and lacks. More specifically, the turning off of the comparing mind would dismantle the prevalent hierarchical mode of social interaction – paradoxically so extended in spiritual circles – in which people automatically look upon others as being either superior or inferior, as a whole or in some privileged respect.

This model – which ultimately leads to inauthentic and unfulfilling relationships, not to mention hubris and spiritual narcissism – would naturally pave the way for an I-Thou mode of encounter in which people would experience others as equals in the sense of their being both superior and inferior to themselves in varying skills and areas of endeavour (intellectually, emotionally, artistically, mechanically, interpersonally, and so forth), but with none of those skills being absolutely higher or better than others. It is important to experience human equality from this perspective to avoid trivialising our encounter with others as being merely equal. It would also bring a renewed sense of significance and excitement to our interactions because we would be genuinely open to the fact that not only can everybody learn something important from us, but we can learn from them as well. In sum, an integral development of the person would lead to a "horizontalisation of love." We would see others not as rivals or competitors but as unique embodiments of the Mystery, in both its immanent and its transcendent dimension, who could offer us something that no one else could offer and to whom we could give something that no one else could give.

Intimate Relationships: The Third Presence

In very general terms, in our culture the family is based on a pact between a man and a woman who are supposedly incomplete in themselves with the aim of making each other whole and thus creating a nucleus of coexistence open to procreation. With regard to this conception of the family, we could say something similar to what we said regarding the historical need of human consciousness to separate itself from the body and the Dark Energy in order to permit its growth as an independent polar reality. We suggest that the traditional family, which, although in serious crisis, still prevails in our culture, has probably been an optimum model for the development of humanity until now. As the staggering divorce rates and prevalent (though usually unfulfilling) practice of serial monogamy suggest, however, it may be important to subject this model to an honest and thorough examination, rescue its many positive aspects, and explore new models that may emerge from the new possibilities of human integration now available to us.

We suggest that more integrated intimate relationships would not be based on the complementary compensation of pathological lacks in the individual partners that originated at frustrated developmental junctures, especially those having to do with the absence of appropriate parental love and validation in early childhood. In contrast, emerging models of partnership would be based on relationships of mutual exchange and enrichment between two people who already enjoy a satisfactory state of individual well-being, achieved through a natural or therapeutic process, and who together decide to cocreate a shared vital project. Each partner would take responsibility for the development of his or her own identity, and together they would cocreate a "third identity" emerging from their interrelation – a "third presence" that would gradually constitute their joint vital project.

The vital projects of this new model of relationship could be extremely diverse. For some partners the main objective may be procreation (i.e., conceiving and raising biological children). For others the goal might be personal integral growth, with each member of the partnership drawing upon the vital potential of the other to support and enhance their own psychospiritual actualisation. Other partnerships may focus on the development of a joint or mutually supportive social, cultural, or professional project. In some cases, a couple's "third identity" may involve openness to a third person, which could also take a variety of forms (e.g., temporary or indefinite, secondary or primary, emotional or sexual, and so forth). [See Albareda and Romero (1991) for a discussion of some of these possibilities.]

As people become more whole and are freed from certain basic fears (of abandonment, of unworthiness, of engulfment), new possibilities for the expression of embodied love may open up that may be seen as natural, safe, and wholesome rather than as undesirable, threatening, or morally questionable. In this new model of partnership, for example, gross and subtle forms of jealousy would gradually turn into "compersion," or the experience of genuine joy (in contrast to contracting fear) in relation to one's partner's constructive connection to others. This topic would obviously require a deeper exploration, but we believe that "compersion" can be seen as the extension of certain contemplative qualities, such as sympathetic joy (mudita in Buddhism), to the realm of interpersonal and intimate relationships. The important point is that, as Christian mystic Richard of St. Victor put it in his reflections on the Trinity, mature love between lover and beloved naturally reaches beyond itself toward a third reality (e.g., children, a shared project, another person)[4], and this opening may be crucial both to overcome codependent tendencies and to foster the health, creative vitality, and even longevity of intimate relationships.

Community Living: Toward a Sustainable Cooperation

New models of relationship can be developed within many different social structures – for example, in a family structure similar to the one prevailing today but organised in a way that more explicitly honours and attends to the needs of each person, the needs of the couple, and the social needs of the larger community within which they live. They also could be developed in the context of a small community, where several couples – along with individuals who have chosen a lifestyle that does not include a partner – live together in a temporary or indefinitely extended arrangement.

We believe that in the future this communal structure could become generalised because, if well organised and developed, it would enjoy many advantages over the traditional model of the nuclear family. One advantage would be that the nucleus of coexistence would address both the individual and the social dimension that is characteristic of all humans. Another important advantage is that it would permit sabbatical periods for community members. Housing would be more economical and expenses could be shared by all, allowing for a sabbatical period for each member on a rotating basis, or for those who may need it at certain personal or professional junctures. Children born in the community could be raised primarily by their parents but would simultaneously, and in a familiar setting, develop social ties that would function as a bridge for their socialisation stage. This structure would also free the parents from the feeling of "slavery" that young children too often represent, enabling them to continue cultivating their personal growth, social relationships, and leisure activities.

The Social Dimension

Economy: From Competition to Solidarity

It is becoming increasingly clear that our modern capitalist society, based on productivity and consumption, offers little if any hope of finding a way out of the current global crisis. Raw materials are finite and will one day run out unless we instigate more sustainable policies. Furthermore, competition between companies and corporations is creating increasingly more aggressive human relationships. The ethos of competitive capitalism foments rivalry, confrontation, and even war between companies, institutions, social classes, countries, and, perhaps very soon, civilisations. It is crucial that we realise that this is a natural consequence of the system itself – a system that, step by step, is creating human relationships in which people tend to see others either as dangerous enemies from whom they need to defend themselves or as potential allies who can help them to become stronger in their fight for security and dominance. It is clear that this way of life is shaping a very pernicious future for the coming generations.

The integrative process we are proposing may have a profound impact on the economy and on business practices. Once people started working toward the integration of the Dark Energy and the Energy of Consciousness in their lives, maximum productivity and economic profits would cease to be the main goals of businesses. The primary incentive for workers would shift from economic reward to personal fulfilment, which would be facilitated by work that takes place in a setting of harmony and collaboration that is aligned with, and fosters the development of, their own vital potentials and capabilities. The result would be a qualitatively enhanced, sustainable level of productivity. This model would not only foster an internal structure of autonomous cooperation and solidarity among workers but would also help each company to see other companies not as rivals or competitors but as entities with which they could establish a relationship of mutual exchange and collaboration. In sum, the current vision that gives priority to quantitative production and competition would be replaced by one in which priority is given to qualitative production, the sustainability of each company, and cooperative solidarity with other companies.

Politics: From Will to Power to Will to Service

If we take into account all that has been said so far, it becomes clear that the understanding and practice of politics would also change radically. Politics would no longer be driven by the will to power and domination, but would instead be motivated by the sincere desire to serve others. Authority would be based neither on power nor on a specific office or position but would emerge from the coherence of the inner and outer person, made evident in his or her personal behaviour and devotion to serving the community. Thus, politicians would govern from an attitude of service and humility, ensuring that the social structures under their responsibility function as well as possible. Social structures inspired by more integrated states of being would not be pyramidal, in the sense that a few give orders while the rest conform. Rather, they would be essentially egalitarian structures in which each person would have a specific function, different from and complementary to those of the rest, but each with the same dignity – the dignity intrinsic to the fact of being human.

Political parties would not be governed by a specific right-wing or left-wing ideology, nor would voting be seen as a question of "party loyalty" that often leads people into deep contradictions between what they see, feel, and think and what they vote for. In contrast, political parties would be based on coherence with and an affinity for issues aimed at enhancing the quality of life for everybody. In voting, members of a party would be encouraged to be truthful and authentic in supporting those initiatives they find most coherent and realistic, even if they come from another party. Alternative political parties would never be called "the opposition" but rather worthy "interlocutors" with whom one interacts for mutual enrichment and with whom one cooperates for the common good.

Police, if they existed, would not have as their primary function imposing the law and punishing those who failed to abide by it, but would function as educators and mediators to help citizens take responsibility for their own tasks and learn to cooperate in the improvement of their communities and social structures (cf. Lerner, 2000). Jails would become therapeutic/educational institutions devoted to the healing and transformation of those who, for a variety of reasons (e.g., ethnic marginalisation, material misery, violent childhood, perhaps even karmic tendencies) display a socially dysfunctional or harmful behaviour. Due to their transformative power, deep experiential therapies such as non-ordinary states of consciousness work and the use of entheogens would become important adjuncts in the rehabilitation of many of these individuals. The introduction of these technologies of transformation could even turn jails into initiation temples that would facilitate a reconnection with the sacred and the meaning of life.

Religion: From Competing Religious Traditions to a Common Spiritual Family

The ethos of comparison, competition, and conflict besets even the realm of religion. Explicitly or implicitly, religious traditions look down upon one another, each believing that, deep down, their truth is more complete, final, or the only one that can lead to salvation or enlightenment. This competitive predicament has profoundly affected how people from different credos engage one another, and, even today, engenders all types of religious conflicts, quarrels, and even holy wars.

Perhaps due to the evolutionary dynamics described above, religious traditions have tended to focus on the subtle realms of consciousness and their visionary landscapes (the realm of transcendent Energy of Consciousness) and to overlook the more indeterminate and creative dimensions of the Mystery (the realm of immanent Dark Energy). They have therefore been unable to find much common ground among their spiritual cosmologies and ultimates, since the Energy of Consciousness contains already differentiated, transformed, and historically-enacted spiritual energies that tend to display more fixed forms and dynamics (e.g., specific cosmological motifs, archetypal configurations, mystical visions, spiritual states). If we choose to see the various spiritual ultimates not as competing to match a pre-given spiritual referent but as creative transformations of an indeterminate Mystery, then the conflict over claims of alternative religious truths vanishes like a mirage. In this light, the threatening snake we saw in the basement can now be recognised as a peaceful and connecting rope. Rather than being a source of conflict or a cause for merely considerate tolerance, the diversity of spiritual truths and cosmologies would become a reason for wonder and celebration – wonder inspired by the inexhaustible creative power of the Mystery, and celebration of our participatory role in such creativity, as well as of the emerging possibilities for mutual enrichment that arise out of the encounter of traditions.

Needless to say, it would still be possible and important to make qualitative distinctions among traditions, but these distinctions would not be based on a priori doctrines or hierarchically-posited paradigmatic spiritual contents. Rather, they would be grounded in a rich variety of markers and practical fruits (existential, cognitive, emotional, interpersonal), perhaps anchored around two basic spiritual tests, which we may call the egocentrism test (i.e., to what extent does a spiritual tradition, path, or practice free its practitioners from gross and subtle forms of narcissism and self-centredness?) and the dissociation test (i.e., to what extent does a spiritual tradition, path, or practice foster the blossoming of all dimensions of the person?). [For further discussion of these tests, see Ferrer (2002) and Kripal (2003)]. While this approach would render obsolete and inappropriate the ranking of spiritual traditions according to doctrinal paradigmatic standpoints, it would invite a more nuanced and complex evaluation based on the understanding that traditions, like human beings, are always both higher and lower in relation to one another, but in different regards.

Finally, this interreligious approach may lead to a shift from searching for a global spirituality organised around a single ultimate vision to recognising an already existent spiritual human family that branches out from the same creative root. In other words, traditions may be able to find their longed-for communion not so much in a single spiritual megasystem or global vision (in the realm of the Energy of Consciousness), but in their common roots (in the realm of the Dark Energy) – that is, in that deep bond constituted by the indeterminate dimension of the Mystery in which all traditions participate and with which they cocreate their spiritual visions. Like members of a healthy family, religious people may then stop attempting to impose their particular vision on others and might instead become a supportive, enriching, and powerful force for the creative spiritual individuation of other practitioners, both within and outside of a single tradition. This empowerment of individual spiritual creativity may lead to the emergence not only of a rich variety of coherent spiritual perspectives which can potentially be equally grounded in the Mystery, but also of a common – non-absolutist and contextually sensitive – global ethics. It is important to stress, however, that this global ethics can not probably arise out of our highly ambiguous moral religious past but needs to be forged in the fire of contemporary interreligious dialogue and cooperative spiritual inquiry.[5] In other words, it is likely that any future global ethics will not be grounded in our past spiritual history but in our critical reflection of such history in the context of our present-day moral intuitions. Besides its obvious relevance for regulating interfaith conflicts, searching for a global ethics may be a crucial step in bringing about the mutual respect and openness among practitioners necessary for sustaining and invigorating both their common roots and their individual spiritual blossoming.

Conclusion

As should be obvious, a shift such as the one we are envisioning is not an easy task; however, we firmly believe that it may be necessary if we wish to avoid a very difficult and complicated future for subsequent generations. Far from being utopian, the admittedly visionary changes we are proposing may actually be vital for a more sustainable and fulfiling life for the global human community in the long run. In order to start moving in the direction of such a shift, it seems crucial that we begin seeing human life as both a precious opportunity and a privileged place from which to establish relationships based on embodied love that contribute to the progressive attunement of humanity to the transcendent and immanent dimensions of the Mystery.

To conclude, we suggest that the integration of the Dark Energy and the Energy of Consciousness in human reality may be seen as an "incarnational process" in the sense that it fosters the creative transformation of the embodied person and the world, the spiritualisation of matter and the sensuous grounding of spirit, and, ultimately, the bringing together of Heaven and Earth. Who knows, perhaps as human beings gradually embody both the transcendent and immanent dimensions of the Mystery – a two-fold incarnation, so to speak – we will realise that it is here, in this plane of concrete physical reality, that the cutting edge of spiritual transformation and evolution is taking place. For then the planet Earth may gradually turn into an Embodied Heaven, a perhaps unique place in the cosmos where beings can learn to express and receive embodied love, in all its forms.

NOTES

1. Note that we are not necessarily equating this Dark Energy with the scientific term "Dark Energy," which is supposed to compose about 73 percent of the Universe. In any event, the adjective "dark" does not have negative connotations but simply refers to a primary energetic state in which all potentialities are still undifferentiated and, therefore, cannot be seen by the "light" of consciousness.

2. See Heron (1998) for another dipolar account of spirituality which, we believe, is fully harmonious with the one introduced in this chapter.

3. For a sophisticated phenomenological account of the centrality of integrating primary and conscious potentials for an embodied spiritual life, see Washburn (2004).

4. We want to thank Jacob Sherman for providing us with this important insight by Richard of St. Victor.

5. I (Jorge N. Ferrer) am indebted to Jeffrey J. Kripal (2003) for kindly challenging the residual "moral perennialism" insinuated in my previous work. For an excellent collection of essays exploring the ethical status of religion and mysticism, see Barnard and Kripal (2002).

REFERENCES

Albareda, R. V. & M. T. Romero (1990). *Nacidos de la tierra: Sexualidad, origen del ser humano.* Barcelona: Hogar del Libro.

Barnard, G. W. & J. J. Kripal (Eds.). (2002). *Crossing Boundaries: Essays on the ethical status of mysticism.* New York: Seven Bridges Press.

Ferrer, J. N. (2002). *Revisioning Transpersonal Theory: A participatory vision of human spirituality.* Albany, NY: SUNY Press.

Heron, J. (1998). *Sacred Science: Person-centred inquiry into the spiritual and the subtle.* Roos-on-Wye, United Kingdom: PCCS Books.

Kripal, J. J. (2003). In the Spirit of Hermes: Reflections on the work of Jorge N. Ferrer. *Tikkun: A Bimonthly Jewish Critique of Politics, Culture & Society,* 18(2).

Lerner, M. (2000). *Spirit Matters.* Charlottesville, VA: Hampton Roads.

Murphy, M. (1993). *The Future of the Body: Explorations into the further evolution of human nature.* New York: Jeremy P. Tarcher/Perigee.

Romero, M. T. & R. V. Albareda (2001). Born on Earth: Sexuality, spirituality, and human evolution. *ReVision,* 24(2), 5-14.

Washburn, M. (2004). *Embodied Spirituality in a Sacred World.* Albany, NY: SUNY Press.

This chapter will be published in John Mack (Ed.). **The Primacy of Consciousness.**

19. WALKING THE EDGE

Elizabeth McCormick

Elizabeth chooses a dramatic story in an airport departure lounge to illustrate and illuminate her wide experience in healthcare. This airport incident led her to reflect on the ineffectiveness of dualistic thinking in asking "where does healing take place?" She links her experiences within the NHS and as a transpersonal psychologist, examining how psychological and spiritual issues become interconnected in a practical sense, bringing moments of stillness and even joy to the lives of some of those whose world is spinning.

In recounting her own personal journey through illness, Elizabeth came across Buddhist teaching and the concept of "Be free where you are" – that mindfulness has a value everywhere and it's not necessary to be sitting on a high mountain to experience it, nor to project spiritual authority onto others. No one is suggesting that if we are mindful or spiritual enough we won't get sick, but the coming to terms with the shadow aspects of ourselves and our surroundings can be helped by a crisis such as illness. Health does not mean freedom from suffering, but accepting that we cannot have sunshine without shadow. We can start to learn to walk the edge of all we fear and in doing so become stronger both in ourselves and in our relationships through the compassion we develop for others.

Elizabeth Wilde McCormick *was a director of training at the Centre for Transpersonal Psychology from 1996 - 2001. She is a practicing psychotherapist who has worked in the NHS and in private practice. She is the author of* "Living on the Edge", "Surviving Breakdown", "Change for the Better", "Your Heart and You" *and is editor of* Transpersonal Psychotherapy, theory and practice *(Continuum 2002).* "Nothing to Lose" *is to be published by Continuum in June 2005.*

Some years ago I was waiting in the departure lounge at Heathrow Airport for a long haul flight. The atmosphere was, as it often is, rather tense and tight, with travellers either sitting nervously waiting to be called to walk down the ramp onto the plane, or arriving at the last minute full of the bustle of hasty arrival. Some were making last minute phone calls on public telephones or on their cell phones. There was an air of expectancy and that unspoken, but collective heightened awareness of being about to undergo a completely unnatural phenomenon, having ones body thrown through the air at over 500 miles per hour and at 33,000 feet above ground.

I was feeling ropy and nervous about travelling, my first trip after a long bout of poor health, a bit sorry for myself, ruminating on how travelling would affect a much worn system. My mind was busy, preoccupied with these thoughts. Then something quite dramatic happened. A woman was wheeled in in a sporty wheelchair waving a white stick. She was crippled and nearly blind. She took in the atmosphere and feeling in the room with some supersensitive energy and, addressing us all like the conductor of an orchestra complete with homeostatic baton said, in a loud Southern drawl: "health is wealth and don't you forgedd it!"

Health is Wealth and Don't You Forget It

The effect was electric. People smiled and stopped yelling into their phones or at each other. Our shoulders dropped. Our chests opened. We sat up straighter and relaxed at the same time. She drew us to her. We wanted more from her. She lifted our spirits. She woke us out of self-absorption, with our own problems dominant and unrevised. Suddenly it was possible not to be limited by definitions of healthy/sick. 'Health is wealth' has stayed with me.

I've chosen this story for several reasons. If health is wealth, what sort of wealth is it, and where does it spring from? This woman might have had a crippled body but in her spirit, her mind and emotion she was alive and bright, healthy. Her energy was inspirational. She offered those of us gathered in that room the opportunity to be free from our usual conditioned thinking. The wealth of this health is freedom. When we choose to be free wherever we are we have unbounded riches. This health is always available, whatever our circumstances. It also means to me, value all you have. Since this time I have thought a lot about what it was she brought into that departure lounge, that fresh air of choice and freedom and how we find the openness to step into it.

When we are not limited by judgements based on dualistic thinking – healthy or sick, good or bad, right or wrong, desirable or undesirable, we have a lot of space. Within that space there is the possibility of developing an openness to everything that happens to us – whether in our experience of our body or our mind. In this understanding health gets nearer to wholeness and includes sickness, darkness and shadow – all the messes we don't like. Part of the experience of being within this space is in finding ways to be with those things we don't like so that we don't harden down over them.

How do we assess our own health? By looking at our bodies, our minds, or by the quality of our life? How do we assess what quality this is measured by? Do we split body and mind, head and heart, health and sickness? Do we fear to find what health is for us addressing what is in the shadow of our awareness, by paying attention to what makes us sick – sick at heart; sick in body or in soul? Sometimes, in simply addressing what makes us sick helps to move us closer to where health lies. Steven Levene writes: 'where does healing need to take place?' Sometimes feeling into our response to this question helps shape our own inner voice that might lead to the health we seek.

I have called this chapter 'walking the edge' because this phrase relates to those times in all our lives where we feel restricted – sometimes intensely – as if we are only just hanging in there. And I see these times are offering great teachings about the different levels of health. Our personal edge may manifest as an external situation – we have been discriminated against, marginalised, unfairly treated; we are homeless, up against impossible demands. It may be through our bodies that we are invited into an edge – as in times when our limbs and organs are not working properly or in threat from disease. We may be emotionally at the limit of our learned coping skills.

I first began to use this phrase 'walking the edge' during the two years following 1992 when I was trying to recover my own health after meningitis – an inflammation of the lining of the brain that causes all kinds of difficulty with brain and nervous system function. I couldn't sleep or eat; I lost balance and had a constant head and neck pain. I was in a permanent state of anxious dread. I thought I might go mad. I was thrown back upon myself in the most challenging way and on a really narrow edge.

All I could do was try and survive this edge and from time to time negotiate it, stepping between the stones of my fearful thoughts – often about the future about what would happen to me – and the physical realities. Every now and then – when I wasn't looking or trying – I dropped down into a moment of deep stillness. The joy that came from this realisation – that there could be stillness and joy even when the world was spinning and full of fear was overwhelming.

Transpersonal psychology has an interest in any place where transpersonal experiences are valued. These non-ordinary states of consciousness include the simple experience of beauty and love; experiences of breaking down to break through, transcendent and peak experiences and finally, the fact of spiritual awakening. I have spent many years on the edge between the often stark and immediate emotional experience of life events, which can be all encompassing when we are in them, and a hunger for spiritual connection. The psychological and spiritual debates about the dialogue between experience and how we are with it, remains of intense interest to me.

Transpersonal experiences may occur in the moment – as in my experience of stillness in the midst of chaos – when we step aside from being identified by wellness or success as defined by the outside world and experience how much space and freedom there can be in being alive and touch the miracle of being alive.

They occur in peak experiences of awakening, transcendence, of calling. They occur in depth experiences – what James Hillman calls soul-making experiences when we are in the mess of pain illness and loss, when things have gone wrong and we feel en-darkened. And they occur when we give up our attachment to duality – to things being right or wrong; good or bad; healthy or sick and we step into what Ken Wilber calls the basic open ground out of which arises the living water of our life force.

These two years post illness forced a kind of seclusion from the world – from people, work, and any productivity. I couldn't write. All I could do was to try to hold on to some threads as they formed inside me, lose them and find them again. I was trying to remain present with the vast range of happenings inside my mind and wrestle with the demons of my fears – often of going mad. It was during this time that I came across the work of the Vietnamese Buddhist Thich Nhat Hanh. He says 'Be Free where you are' – and this is the title of the address he gave to the Maryland Correctional Institution in the US where he spoke to over a hundred inmates. These were literal prisoners, who, despite obvious incarceration could be free to choose their attitude, to how they inhabited themselves within imprisonment. It seemed to me that, whatever kind of prisoner we become, through breaking the law, through illness or disease, through the pain of loss and rejection, or by the all-encompassing entrapment of emotional distress, we lighten our sentence by our freedom to choose our attitude. And the movement is to learn to be in charge of the vast continent of our mind, with its relationship to our body and our emotions. Thich Nhat Hanh teaches that the way to be free where we are is to learn to live in the present moment. He teaches the practice of mindfulness. He taught prisoners simple walking meditations and how to practice mindful breathing and eating.

I learned from Thich Nhat Hanh that practising mindfulness does not mean sitting on a cushion high up in a mountain on your own but here and now in ordinary everyday life. His first book, The Miracle of Mindfulness came out of letters he wrote to his monks, encouraging them to continue practice in Vietnam after he was exiled in France for his peace activities at the beginning of the war. I thought the many forms of imprisonment into which we could bring this freedom of attitude. All of life gives us the opportunity to practice being in the present moment – washing up, waiting for the bus, finding a seat, being with others. In the last ten years I've been drawn to Buddhist teachings and to the work of many American transpersonal psychologists who have been studying the integration of Buddhist ideas with psychology – Ken Wilber, John Welwood, Jack Kornfield, Mark Epstein.

Buddhism teaches that we already have all that we need its just that we don't see it. We already have the capacity to step out of sleepiness into an awakened state. When we choose a practice of being truly present with each moment we are cultivating an attitude of freedom. We see what arises and stay with that, speak from that awareness, and our decisions and acts come from this practice of attention and from deep reflection. We may become less split by dual consciousness.

Being ill taught me many things. In having no alternative but to watch what my mind was doing I could see how thoughts of future entrapments brought the dead end of fear and panic. I saw that there are distinct choices of attitude – I could harden down in my rage at getting ill and feel the child in me saying it's not fair I've done all the right things or I could learn to simply try and remain still and observe what was happening. I could try and accept my fear and anger and try and develop compassion. I could rush about trying all kinds of treatments to get well. Whilst this can be an important part of this journey, I also learned to recognise when this activity was counter-productive, because it was trying to avoid fear that needed attention.

I also became aware of what happens when we split ourselves off from our own capacity for spiritual experience by projecting spiritual authority onto others or onto an organisation. This was illustrated very powerfully when I returned to a supervision group I had been taking. On my return after the absence due to ill health I noticed certain hostility in the group. We had spoken of how things had been whilst I was away but something lingered. I stopped the group and said I felt there was something we hadn't been able to address. What did people really feel about my being ill? After an awkward silence, one brave person said: 'I felt furious with you. You are supposed to be spiritual. There you are teaching, writing books having had all this therapy and still you got ill."

I had an initial guilt reaction, as if I had indeed failed to be a proper healthy spiritual transpersonal person. And I felt trapped. This event heralded an exploration of the projection onto anything spiritual as having to be perfect in some way, and at the dark shadow this idealisation casts. The story line would go something like this: 'If we are spiritual enough we don't get sick and bad things don't happen to us'. This becomes a spiritual materialism that equates something spiritual with a 'perfection' around having no needs, having answers for difficulty, knowing what to do. It becomes a sort of idealised parent who offers perfect care, a spirituality that places our human vulnerability into the shadow.

We know that when this happens, when our idealisation makes something too bright whatever is not in the light grows darker as a way of compensation. Sooner or later something erupts. In groups or beliefs where spiritual is idealised as something special and most importantly non-relational, into the shadow goes everything considered non-spiritual: anger, jealousy, sex, money, issues of power, illness, even suicide and death. The greatest loss is when we split ourselves off from the reality of our own divinity, our own inner connection with spiritual experience.

Sometimes the emergence of shadow material heralds much needed change, just as illness for many people brings about transformation. Sometimes we are tempted to project onto this the idea that it is 'meant'. To do this, I feel, keeps us outside it as passive recipients of something other. I feel that the change that comes about is from our own acceptance of the challenge to shift our conscious awareness from old patterns based upon old wounds, into new patterns of responsibility for conscious awakening. Good will and hope that remain passive are not enough for a system to remain healthy. To remain healthy we must find ways to grow with the process of change and change always involves the processes of descent, dismemberment, and death. The transformation and rebirth that emerge seem to do so because of our surrender to the process, but this is not guaranteed.

I do not think that we HAVE to get ill in order to change. But rather, if we embrace whatever our life brings in a spirit of enquiry and openness and use every opportunity to grow in consciousness we may be given a gift. Health does not mean freedom from suffering, rather, it means accepting the reality of suffering and finding ways to overcome being limited or identified with suffering. It means finding ways to include the reality of change, sickness and mess, the pain of misunderstanding.

Understanding what health can be means getting nearer to finding ways to remain open to everything that is experienced and a way to remain present with darkness as well as light, wellness as well as sickness. If we accept that we cannot have sun without shadow we remain open to knowing what shadow elements are and remaining open to their reality then finding ways to be with them. C.G. Jung writes: "One does not become enlightened by imagining figures of light but by making the darkness conscious."

So how do we do it? How do we inhabit a transpersonal dimension in our life that contributes to allowing us to face the shadow? When something does go wrong what do we do with it?

Tibetan Buddhist Pema Chodron tells us, in *When Things Fall Apart*: "not to make an enemy of what we don't like by hardening down." When what we don't like falls into the shadow of our awareness we become at risk. The risk is of that shadow growing stronger and of being projected onto something or someone outside we don't like. Whatever this is has to carry what we don't like, or what we have hardened down festers in our bodies. It makes the leap from emotions into tissue and comes back and bites us.

Pema Chodron's teachings include a practice where we start noticing all those moments when we shut off or harden down, when we make a clenched fist of what we don't like. It may appear through the symbolic language of our body, the hunched shoulder, heavy heart, as a knife in the gut. We then practice staying with this recognition and softening around these hard edges. What happens then is that we touch the place in us that has been walled off by our psychological defences, what Pema Chodron refers to as our 'soft spot'. Always under the hardness is a soft spot. This is our no go area, the area that puts us on edge. It is also the area of our own quivering vulnerability and shaky tenderness. In opening up to it we start to learn to walk the edge of all that we fear. In doing so we get stronger. We become edge walkers.

For Pema Chodron the soft spot is where the living water resides – the life force in each and every one of us. When we allow ourselves to open and to touch our own soft spot we melt the hardness, we cool our blaze, and we link in with every other human who feels vulnerable. We become part of an interconnected world of humanity. It is from this place that we begin to learn compassion and loving kindness, first for ourselves and then we are able to extend it to others.

Spiritual practice requires discipline and rigour – not just the body bum on seat but the discipline of getting to know ones mind and what it does around emotion which separates us from the living water of true feeling. It takes courage and persistence. It also needs to be practised in a spirit of Maitri – unconditional friendliness to oneself and loving kindness to oneself. True understanding may move naturally into our awareness as we learn to soften around our hardened edges. As we develop compassion our heart opens, we touch our own life force and that of others and bring and we know the wealth of health.

20. TAPPING INTO THE SOUL OF THE ORDINARY MYSTIC

Anne Carroll Decker

How do we open up our own hidden knowledge? How do we tap the source from which we come? Anne Carroll Decker offers her own contribution to the definition of transpersonal. Her research indicates that entering a spiritual transpersonal state could be amazingly easy. She explains how she came across Origen, a third century Christian Father, or rather how he came across her. She sees him as an "ordinary mystic" and she studies him and his work through the technique of Intuitive Inquiry. She wondered how she could introduce Origen to ordinary women. Meditation and prayer is not a new path to mysticism or altered states of consciousness, but she speculates how accessible these are to the average person. She explains her system of Structured Visceral Dialogue and how it can be a powerful way of transpersonal knowing. In research sessions with groups of women she finds that they found the "experience of the experience" very deep, and in some cases could not believe how they had spoken in the sessions so profoundly. Everyone involved, whether they agreed with Origen or not, declared an understanding of their own spirituality rather than that of the Church's teachings. Her conclusions are that the sessions gave participants permission to be brilliant, and they were. They gave them the permission to be mystics, and they were – hence her use of the words "ordinary mystics".

Anne Carroll Decker is the author of the award-winning spiritual book, Songs of the Soul and Circle of the Soul. *She gives workshops, retreats and lectures throughout the United States on spirituality and has been the host of her own television show in Connecticut (USA) for the past eight years. She is a Ph.D. candidate in Religion at Lancaster University, U.K.*

The sixth EUROTAS conference in London brought together scholars and psychologists from dozens of countries to discuss transpersonal practices and, surprisingly enough, the meaning of the word "transpersonal." As presenters and their audiences discussed and debated different states and stages of consciousness, from both qualitative and quantitative viewpoints, many definitions of the word were considered: extraordinary, cosmic, interpersonal, fully conscious, experiencing a spiritual realm or altered state.

Presenting my recent research at the conference, I offered my own definition: tapped. To open up, pierce, or break into so as to extract the contents from, describes the dictionary (Oxford, 1993). This suggests many questions for exploration. How do we open up our own hidden knowledge? How do we tap into the source from which we come? Is this source cosmic or personal? And when we tap into it are we perhaps tapping or piercing into *a priori* knowledge?

My research seems to indicate that entering a spiritual transpersonal state may be amazingly easy. But how could that possibly be true? Can it be that many of us go through life "untapped" only because we do not take a simple step to discover another realm of ourselves? Once we pierce the boundary into a transpersonal state do not we, like many of those whom we deem remarkable, become "ordinary mystics"?

Discovering Origen

My study began when Origen, a third-century Christian Church Father, whose ideas the Church later deemed heterodoxy, called to me. People asked me: "Why not study Augustine? Or even Hildegard de Bingen? You're a woman; she was a woman. Why Origen? How in the world did you ever find Origen?" I answered quite simply, "Origen found me."

He found me in the manner of one who collides on the street with an old friend after years of absence, in the way "coincidences" occur in our lives and the way chance attracts us to our mates. We view these twists of fate as happenstance, synchronistic or perhaps even mystical. But if they are mystical, we seldom recognize them as such.

In the transpersonal methodology of Intuitive Inquiry defined by Rosemarie Anderson (Anderson, 1998): "it often seems as though a particular topic is drawing, even compelling, our attention." Anderson's methodology gave me permission not to question why Origen, a man whose self-castration seems to be the singularly most infamous feature that seminary students recognize about him, continually popped up on all my search engines and library jaunts. Intuitive Inquiry allowed me to realize that our own intuition is a powerful force if we welcome it into our lives.

As one of the pre-eminent theologians of early Christianity, Origen was an apologist for apocatastasis (universal salvation). He also believed in the fall of humanity as a one in the beginning of time, in the exegesis of the Bible on more levels than the purely literal, and in the metempsychosis (cycle of existences) and thus pre-existence of souls and the soul's free choice of its circumstances of human fortune. Apocatastasis and pre-existence of the soul fuelled many controversies surrounding this theologian. Three hundred years after his death in 254 AD the Church declared Origen's concepts heterodoxy, and many of his works were destroyed.

I felt the need to pursue this question: How do these ideas of Origen, which the Church suppressed so long ago, affect Christian women today, who do not know that these beliefs are a part of their religious history? I had realized that although Origen's work is not well known, many of his concepts are being resurrected by today's Christianity and becoming popular within mainstream Christian churches in the United States.

As with all great writers Origen's works continue to live even though he died centuries ago. Some Patristic scholars refer to him as a mystic while others term him a genius of the church. I see him as an "ordinary mystic," a term I will define later in this paper. His words and ideas continue to resonate with certain people, and the spark of his passion lingers as long as there are readers who relate to his concepts. When we are ready to "tap" into these cosmic works, they come alive for us.

Intuitive Inquiry

The qualitative methodology of Intuitive Inquiry says that when the idea of an object is actually present to us, that object becomes alive. For me this concept worked even though the object, or in this case the person, was as distant as a third-century patristic. When words become animated on a page and resonate through your soul, it is as if the person is sitting next to you, conversing, arguing, debating and questioning. Centuries do not interfere with or interrupt such a dialogue. Therefore my research became more than a mere reading of Origen; it was a phenomenological meeting with Origen, a phainein in the true Greek sense of the word from which phenomenology derives: to show, appear, and be seen.

Explaining Intuitive Inquiry in more detail requires discussing Dr. Clark Moustakas' well-known research on heuristic phenomenology, from which Anderson's methodology draws much of its foundation. The word heuristic comes from the Greek word heuriskein, meaning to discover or find. According to Moustakas, the process refers to an internal search through which one discovers the nature and meaning of experience. This in turn allows both the researcher and the participants to grow in creative self-awareness, self-knowledge and self-discovery (Moustakas, 1990).

In my own dialogue with Origen, I initially engaged with him by reading extensively both his works and the works of scholars who have studied him.[1] I was not just reading his works; I was meditatively immersed in his writings. Before beginning a "dialogue" with Origen, I would play music, pray, meditate and center myself. From that quiet place I was amazed to find myself asking this Church Father deep and profound questions. Evelyn Underhill describes mystic conversion thus: "consciousness has suddenly changed its rhythm and a new aspect of the universe rushes in" (Underhill, 1999). Where had I accessed this spiritual fountain of information?

But even more importantly, how could I communicate my new experiences? Was it possible to introduce Origen to other women who did not have the time or scholastic background to study him? I wanted the "average American Christian woman" to be able to have a phenomenological meeting with him, as I had. Was it possible for women from diverse educational backgrounds (some of my subjects had high school educations, some were college graduates, and one had a Master's degree) to read and comprehend Origen's' esoteric and scholarly third-century writings and "tap" into him and themselves?

Practicing meditation and prayer is not a new pathway to mysticism or altered states of consciousness, but the question remains: how accessible is this "new universe" to an average person? Do we need to study meditation for years with a guru or monk, or be expert in contemplative prayer for decades, in order to "tap" into these states?

Structured Visceral Dialogue

In the methodology of Structured Visceral Dialogue (SVD) I incorporated both Intuitive Inquiry ("where the subject calls to the researcher" – R. Anderson) and Heuristic Inquiry ("the heuristic process is autobiographic, yet with every question there is also a social – and perhaps universal – significance" – Moustakas) with a group of women between ages 46 and 74. SVD is uncomplicated; as with so many things in life, the simple pathway can be the most sagacious.

The dialogue occurs in a small collective group setting (six to eight women) and allows the participants to verbalize for a pre-set time period deep-seated instinctive feelings and reactions to theological writings from the third century. This dialogue is structured so that a woman can speak freely without anxiety or fear of being criticized, rebuked, or debated by any other group member. The quantum physicist David Bohm wrote extensively on dialogue: "When everyone is sensitive to all the nuances going around, and not merely to what is happening in one's own mind, there forms a meaning which is shared." (Bohm, 1996). The meaning of the term viscera, known as the seat of the emotion, goes far deeper than such a simple definition. The viscera are the guts of the body and the soul, harbor of subconscious and perhaps a priori concepts. The researcher and other participants become co-inquirers with the one who is in dialogue, as she reacts from her innermost being to the spiritual readings. Taking this environment one step further in structure than Bohm docs allows each participant an opportunity to share, while staying true to the goal of Bohm's concept of dialogue: coming together to understand things which are very difficult to grasp

As opposed to the rule of "no cross talk" which exists in many therapy groups, such as Alcoholics Anonymous, Overeaters Anonymous and Gamblers Anonymous, the SVD method allots the participant a set amount of time, but does not compel the person to speak during that time. This allotment allows for talking or silence or a mixture of both. In this particular phenomenological approach the researcher is concerned not with "methodolatry" (Janesick, 2000), a slavish attachment to the method, but with allowing participants to speak freely and safely in a "sacred space." Prior to the dialogues the participants are led in a meditative and contemplative session that includes a reading from Origen's works. Then each participant is given the structured time, space and safety to reflect and react openly and safely on her personal interpretation of Origen. This method allows each member of the group to obtain her own truths, and those statements become a part of the united group mind. Can an average person with no academic background in religion become a theologian through deep-seated and perhaps ancient knowledge from within? How can readings from the third century still resonate with women in a different country, different time period, and different culture than that of Origen of Alexandria? Spiritual resonating parallels the meaning of resonance in physics: a condition in which a particle is subjected to an oscillating influence (such as a magnetic field) of such frequency that energy transfer occurs. (Oxford, 1993). The technique of SVD allows the participant to be fully receptive to the energy within the words and permits her to expound on that energy during her own spiritual quest.

The entire research session takes approximately 70 to 75 minutes, depending on the length of the readings. It develops as follows:

1. Music plays for five minutes while women are handed the readings. No communication is allowed. Music is turned off.

2. For approximately five to ten minutes I read from a pre-selected excerpt of Origen's writing. The women can either read along with their own copies or listen. The readings are short and concentrate on one particular topic.

3. The music resumes for five minutes and we sit in meditation, contemplation or prayer.

4. I randomly and intuitively give the microphone to one woman.

5. Each woman has five minutes which is hers alone, to speak or not to speak. Each moment of silence is considered not a negative but a gift of meditation time to the group. There is no agreeing or disagreeing with anyone's statements.

6. I ring a light chime to indicate there is only a minute remaining. I ring it again at the end of the woman's session.

7. After all seven women have dialogued we sit quietly listening to the music.

Structured Visceral Dialogue differs from other group methodologies in that each woman has five minutes to talk or not talk yet this time is always seen as a gift to the group, whether the participant verbalizes during her time or opts for silent prayer time. The minutes are hers alone and there is no pressure to talk if the woman does not want to or need to or feels awkward, shy, lost, or otherwise uncomfortable. The group as a whole just takes those moments of silence and uses them in prayer, in re-reading Origen, or in composing their thoughts. Therefore all pressure is off the participant, who need not feel the anxiety of "trying to find something to say". This methodology developed because prior to the sessions one particular woman expressed concern about having to talk for five minutes, saying she was afraid she would "go blank" and that maybe she wasn't smart enough to understand Origen's work. SVD allows the participant to "go blank, not answer, and just sit with the readings." This is where SVD differs from Bible study sessions,[2] group therapy, cross talk methodology, and others.

After the session this woman commented that the idea of having five minutes that were hers alone, regardless of how she used it, was one of the most freeing concepts she had ever experienced. (Oddly enough, when the microphone was given to her she began talking immediately and had barely a silent moment in her five minutes.) When I later asked participants if they felt uncomfortable if the time wasn't "used" verbally, they all shook their heads. When a participant chose silence, as sometimes occurred, it was consistently viewed just as positively as verbal comments.

Since this time allotment was viewed as a gift to the group, what type of gift did it become? The Middle Ages mystic Hildegard of Bingen believed that no warmth is lost in the universe; Einstein believed that no energy is lost. What occurs in this particular case when the energy from Origen's writings combines with the questions, comments and silences of contemporary women? When energy fields mix they become transformed; no longer can either entity remain unchanged. It was as if the women knew Origen in the Greek sense of the word.

Through knowing Origen, they discovered more than just Patristic writings; they discovered a transpersonal knowing. Transpersonal knowing is both the act of immediate experiencing as well as the experience of that experiencing (Nelson, 2000).

After the SVD sessions were completed and transcribed, I spoke individually with each woman. It was then that the findings or the "experience of the experience" became reality to the women. Some of the women did not even recognize their own words. One woman cried and looked completely shocked at what she had said during the sessions.

She told me, through her tears; "Maybe it's good that you repeated what I said – which could have come from somebody else. It made me feel touched by it. And I thought I was going to feel stupid hearing myself talk and so I do believe that this is the Holy Spirit working through all of us. It has to be. It's the Spirit." In the session she knew Origen. "I feel like we're giving birth to this person's soul again, waiting to come back to live. To live within us and to call other people who have these beliefs which are latent in us. I feel very strongly about this as an affirmation."

This woman did not recognize her own words when read back to her. She cried at their beauty, almost disbelieving that she was capable of speaking such thoughts. William Braud calls such tears "wonder-joy tears," tears which are an opening up of the heart to the persons or profound circumstances being witnessed (Braud, 2001).

Here's an example of another woman's reaction to hearing her own words read to her (this woman is in her 70's):

Woman: Yes. I'm surprised and kind of shocked.
Anne: Why?
Woman: It doesn't sound like me!
Anne: Why doesn't it sound like you?
Woman: Well, maybe I just don't listen to me! (Laughs.)
Anne: Is it deeper than you thought or what?
Woman: Yes. Much deeper than I thought. Deeper than I thought, yes.

Notice that the woman says, "Maybe I just don't listen to me." Once again a participant doesn't recognize her own words, doesn't realize that she has, within an hour's session with other women, tapped into a source of knowledge.

A third woman remarked, "And sometimes when I first read the material, I would think 'I can't do this. It doesn't make any sense to me.' But …then things would kind of pop out of me and make more sense. I think the group was crucial. And also the way it was set up. And I really liked the fact that no one could interrupt you no matter what you said. Yes, I liked that a lot. Because it meant that I didn't have to feel as if I'd have to defend what I was saying – I could just talk. And that was very important to me. Normally, I don't like talking in groups, I'm really shy."

The women were given permission to speak from the viscera, from the gut, regardless of what "popped out." Notice I usually use the word "viscera" where some people might use the word "heart" to picture all deep feeling emanating from that part of the body. One very intellectual and philosophical woman in the group realized her viscera were in her head – that is where she reacted on a primal level. Contrary to contemporary conditioning of screening one's comments, these women allowed their viscera to speak for them. They moved to a different space of consciousness, one which they pierced open through a group energy. They realized that they themselves were Ordinary Mystics. Regardless of whether they understood some of Origen's concepts on an intellectual level, his ideas echoed in varying degrees within them.

A fourth participant commented, "Linear time and truth doesn't exist. And I resonated with what Origen said about that. I don't understand it however. I really don't understand it. But I think in my heart of hearts, I believe it's true. That all things are happening at once and there really isn't a past or a future."

Regardless of whether or not the women agreed with Origen, throughout the SVD sessions every one of the women declared an understanding of their own spirituality, not a church's, not Origen's, not the researcher's.

A woman who found Origen "boring reading" said; "I know (when something) is right – my soul tells me it's right. I don't mean my brain tells me it's right. I mean what feels right to me, therefore it was a message from the Holy Spirit. And it comes from the Holy Spirit. So that's when I say the soul tells me." But in another session this same woman realized that tapping into her own truth was not always easily accessible in the hubbub of our daily lives: "Another thought occurred to me about wisdom is – that while we continue to learn new things, we think they're new, like cures or treatment for medical illnesses or scientific discoveries. They've always been there. God's always had them there. It's just that we hadn't discovered them yet. So maybe discovery is something that we're supposed to be doing. It can give you a headache."

By reacting with the gut, in a safe and structured environment, the women in the SVD group began to understand recondite writings from a long-past century. They dropped the conventional excuses and barriers of lack of education. They argued, debated and sometimes agreed with him, but never shrank with intimidation from this man. The sessions never went past an hour and a half and usually were just over an hour. This is an extremely short time to connect, share and tap into a state which I call "Ordinary Mysticism." Yet it was accomplished – and sometimes the women didn't even recognize the fact until later. The Structured Visceral Dialogue sessions gave these women permission to tap into a source of knowledge. It gave them permission to be brilliant – and they were. It gave them permission to be mystics – and they were.

NOTES

1. For clarification purposes in this document when referring to Origen, except in the biographical and historical portions of his life, I am referring to his writings.
2. Palmer, Barry, Theology and Group Study: Points of Contact. Palmer explains that a member of a group often behaves as though he had been elected to take on a

certain role by the group and leads people being fixed in stereotyped patterns of behaviour.

REFERENCES

Anderson, R. (1998). Intuitive Inquiry: A transpersonal approach. In W. Braud & R. Anderson). *Transpersonal Research Methods for the Social Sciences: Honoring human experience.* (pp.69-94). Thousand Oaks, CA: Sage.

Braud, W. & Anderson, R. (1998). *Transpersonal Research Methods for the Social Sciences: Honoring human experience.* Thousand Oaks, CA: Sage.

Braud, W. (2001). Experiencing tears of wonder-joy: Seeing with the heart's eye. *Journal of Transpersonal Pyschology,* 33(2), 99-111.

Bohm, D. (1996) *On Dialogue,* (p.40). London: Routledge.

Brown, L. editor. (1993). *The New Shorter Oxford English Dictionary on Historical Principles.* Oxford, UK: Clarendon Press.

Denzin, Norman and Lincoln, Yvonna, (2000).*Handbook of Qualitative Research,* Second Edition, Thousand Oaks, CA: Sage.

Hart, Nelson & Puhakka, (2000). *Transpersonal Knowing: Exploring the horizon of consciousness.* Albany, NY: SUNY.

Janesick, V. (2000). The Choreography of Qualitative Research Design, In Denzin, Norman and Lincoln, Yvonna, *Handbook of Qualitative Research,* Second Edition (pp.379-399). Thousand Oaks, CA: Sage.

Moustakas, C. (1990).*Heuristic Research: Design, Methodology and Application,* Newbury Park, CA: Sage.

Nelson, P. (2000). Mystical Experience and Radical Deconstruction: Through the Ontological Looking Glass. In Hart, Nelson & Puhakka, *Transpersonal Knowing: Exploring the horizon of consciousness* (pp.55-84). Albany, NY: SUNY.

Palmer, B, (2000). *Theology and Group Study: Points of Contact,* London: Grubb Institute of Behavioural Studies.

Underhill, E. (1999). *Mysticism: The nature and development of spiritual consciousness.* Oxford, UK: OneWorld.

21. A TRANSPERSONAL PERSPECTIVE IN THE VISUAL ARTS: THE FEMININE PRINCIPLE, SHAMANISM AND SPIRITUALITY

Sue Michaelson

Sue seeks in this chapter to clarify for herself what a transpersonal perspective in the visual arts means. Like Philip Roderick (Chapter 16) and to a lesser extent Elisabeth McCormick (Chapter 19), she tells her story through personal experience, and how she came to see the problem of the lack of balance between masculine and feminine principles in everyday life. She quotes from speakers at the London Conference 2005 and applies some of their thoughts to the issues she has as an artist, attempting to take responsibility for making work that explores and expresses connectedness and interconnectedness. The themes through her life have been art as a tool in the search for meaning, experiments with different therapies as pathways and the search for the inner self or centre. All these within a great love of outward travel as well as the inner sort. She became interested in expressing the feminine principle in art in an authentic way and she describes this and her study of shamanism in terms of her life and career. Making artwork, going on inner journeys and rejoicing in the magic of images informs her research work. Her big sketchbooks become sacred places where thoughts, feelings, dreams, postcards and photographs can be anchored. Also drawings, paintings, photographs and visual themes can unfold as they reveal themselves as she writes her journey as an artist in search of meaning in this chapter, which is one of the more personal in this many-faceted book. Travel with Sue as she learns how working from a transpersonal perspective can help to make art for life's sake rather than art for art's sake – art that is about connectedness in an interconnected world, where life, art and spiritual values are all completely integrated – the art of living and the livingness of art.

Sue Michaelson is a creative artist with a background in transpersonal psychology. She is a lecturer and a counsellor/therapist who runs workshops making bridges in the UK and abroad. At the Royal College of Art her M. Phil was 'A Transpersonal Perspective in Art and Design'. *Her doctoral thesis is on 'The* Importance of the Qualities of the Feminine Principle in Two-Dimensional Image-Making: A Journey through Visual Language'. *She travels extensively doing art work on location, especially in the landscape of Morocco.*

Introduction

This essay describes, very briefly, my attempts to clarify for myself what a transpersonal perspective in the visual arts means, why that is particularly important at this time, and how it might be possible to put these ideas into practice. It is based on work that I did for an M.Phil. at the Royal College of Art between 1993 and 1997, and a Ph.D. that I am still working on at the University in Brighton. Through doing this research, I realised that one of our greatest current problems in the Western world is the lack of balance between the masculine and feminine principles. It affects who we are and the way we work, at a fundamental level. The feminine principle is, above all, about feelings and intuitions, about heart values, connectedness, and the interconnectedness of everything. It expresses itself through the language of the non-rational, the language of imagination and the language of the heart – through images, symbols, dreams, poetry and magic.

We live in a culture in which the feminine principle is still seriously undervalued and neglected compared with the masculine principle and the rational mind. During the EUROTAS conference in August this year, Eva Titus from Belgium said: "We are the universe becoming conscious of itself. The energy of all particles is present in every one of us so it is present in me, which leads to responsibility."

At the same conference Beata Bishop said that we now know that we are made of the same stuff as meteors, and that blood is very similar to seawater, so we are made of seawater and stardust. We are the same as what's "out there", and one of the best ways to experience, express and celebrate the miracle of both our connectedness with each other, and the world around us, and beyond us, is through metaphor, through the language of the arts. My research has shown me ways in which I, as an artist, can take the responsibility for making work that explores and expresses connectedness and interconnectedness.

Parallel Life Themes

Over the past 25 years, there have been a number of important parallel themes in my life. The first of these has been an involvement with the world of the arts, both as a practitioner and a lecturer. I have always produced my own work, and have done many different things: costume, textiles, jewellery, and more recently, drawing, painting and photography. I have had a passion for drawing, for colour, and for image-making, that has been with me ever since I was a very little girl, although I have often lost my way with it over the years. I have also always felt a profound need to search for deeper meanings, a need for life, art and spiritual values to feel connected in some way. I am, and have wanted to be an artist all my life, but have experienced enormous problems with the development of my own work, trying to find a language that felt authentic, real and true, as well as ways of working, and a framework to work within that connected with deeper meanings with which I could identify. I have also experienced great deal of disillusionment with the world of the arts, and art and design education.

A second important theme has been an involvement with different sorts of therapies. I originally became involved in this kind of work because the man I was then married to went through a very difficult personal crisis, and we both went into therapy to try and understand what was happening. Inevitably, I became involved on my own account, and went on to explore different approaches to therapy, including Humanistic Psychology, Bioenergetics, and Rebirthing. Eventually someone else signed me into a Transpersonal Psychology workshop, organised by Ian Gordon-Brown and Barbara Somers in London, and it completely changed my life. It had a breadth and depth that other therapies lacked, and was wonderfully rich and imaginative.

Transpersonal Psychology as I experienced it, had grown out of a mixture of Jung, Assaggioli, and Eastern Mysticism. It was built around the belief that we all have within ourselves an inner SELF or CENTRE that is a central motivating and guiding force within the individual. It acknowledges the fundamental unity underlying the world of separate beings and objects. It gave us practical techniques for going on inner journeys, and exploring inner worlds, including dreamwork, visualisation, active imagination and guided imagery exercises. The inner realm that we visited on these journeys was the same as that part of us that creates imaginative visual work in the context of the arts. The second of the three introductory workshops which was focussed on the masculine and feminine principles within ourselves felt particularly important. I was very at home doing work of this nature, attended a lot of workshops, did a training course, and subsequently became a transpersonal counsellor/therapist, and workshop leader alongside the work I was doing in art and design.

A third important theme in my life has been a great love of travel. One of my worst nightmares is to be stuck, and not able to travel. I have had the very good fortune to be able to spend time in some very special places in India, Fiji, Morocco, the rainforest in Brazil and, more recently, Russia and Siberia. I spent a lot of time exploring inner landscapes in the context of psychology, using techniques like guided imagery and active imagination, and did a lot of artwork on location in the landscape in the world "out there", making drawings and paintings in the context of the Arts.

What happened was that my different worlds, the world of the arts, the world of psychology, and my love of travel, all became increasingly interwoven and interconnected, and grew themselves into a project that I simply had to do. I don't feel that I had any choice about it. Eventually, in 1993, I became a research student and over the next four years did an M.Phil. by project that was about making bridges between Transpersonal Psychology and Image-making. I was not concerned with art therapy, but exploring what it meant to make artwork from a Transpersonal Perspective. The fact that the research was by project meant that I could place a lot of emphasis on the visual work. As it lifted off, the research developed a life of its own, and took me on what turned out to be an absolutely extraordinary multi-dimensional journey, that was at the same time literal, metaphorical, personal/emotional, creative and intellectual. It was like flying on a magic carpet. Landscape played a very important part in this journey, both my own inner landscapes, and landscape in the world "out there". Often the inner and the outer journeys mirrored each other, and were one and the same thing.

By the time I completed the M.Phil., it had become very clear that to make artwork from a transpersonal perspective meant working through the feminine principle – intuition and meditation were crucial. But I still felt dissatisfied. In fact what was missing was a much deeper understanding of what I meant by the feminine principle, why that was so important historically and culturally, and why it was so important in the visual arts generally, a well as in my own creative work.

I also wanted to explore a Shamanic aspect to the making of artwork. I knew that the feminine principle expressed itself very differently from the masculine principle, that it had very different qualities, a different kind of voice, but I wasn't sure how that voice might manifest in the form of imagery. The challenge was to make artwork that expressed the voice of the feminine principle in an authentic way, and to be able to put it out into a world conditioned by masculine principle values, without betraying its true nature.

So I continued my quest in the form of a second research project, this time a Ph.D., the subject of which was, "The Importance of the Qualities of the Feminine Principle in Two-Dimensional Image-Making. A journey through visual language." Once again, the research took me on an extraordinary and mysterious journey, which seemed to have a life of its own. As I worked, I became very aware of the magical and synchronistic aspects of the process – what Gloria Orenstein has called "The methodology of the marvellous", in her book, "The Reflowering of the Goddess". This appeared to be working alongside a more conventional approach to research. In the context of the M.Phil., I explored ways of using some of the techniques I had learned from Transpersonal Psychology as a departure point for making artwork, going on inner journeys and exploring inner threads and themes as they revealed themselves. I also explored what Jung called "The Four Functions of Consciousness", Thinking, Feeling, Sensation and Intuition, as very different ways of approaching visual work.

Working with Images

I discovered that images are very magical. They often appear to have a life of their own, and will take you on a journey if you dare to follow and listen. They can tell you everything you need to know, long before ideas have crystallised in the form of words. Places we respond to strongly in the world "out there" often mirror inner landscapes – perhaps they are one and the same thing. Images have the capacity to flow, transform, and change. Journeying in inner realms can lead us from our inner world, into the world "out there", and that in turn leads back into inner realms once more. We need to value our own inner image-maker, and have the courage to follow the images, allow them to lead the way, and take us where they will.

When I started my research, the project only really came alive when I began working with images in a sketchbook. Some of my own images seemed to carry secret meanings of which I was not aware when I created them, but I didn't realise this until much later on. I also found that working in big sketchbooks was very helpful from both a personal and a research perspective. The sketchbook was like a sacred space in which I could anchor thoughts, feelings, dreams, postcards, photographs and my own images as they emerged and evolved. Perhaps most important of all, I found that as an artist, I loved working in magical places in the landscape. The quality of live experience felt absolutely crucial to making artwork that had any real life energy to it. On one occasion while working in the Jardin Majorelle in Marrakech, I wrote in my sketchbook:

"At four o'clock in the afternoon, the birds all suddenly start to sing: the garden comes alive. Everything shimmers and shakes – the air is alive with little noises, an incredible vibrant aliveness that I want to express in my work. Trying to draw kills it; finding the magic place is crucial – something about 'that view', 'those things' that makes me catch my breath – finding the music in things."

At the same time I was aware of the findings of modern science, which say that observer and observed are one and the same thing, made of the same stuff – we are the same as what's "out there". I was part of my magic landscapes, not separated from them, and in a sense, all my images were self-portraits.

By the time I completed the M.Phil, I had realised that one of the biggest problems that exists for us today in the Western world is a cultural dilemma associated with the lack of balance between the masculine and feminine principles. In his formidable book, *The Passion of the Western Mind*, Richard Tarnas writes:

"The Western intellectual tradition has been produced and canonised, almost entirely by men, and informed mainly by a male perspective … But to do this, the masculine mind has repressed the feminine … The evolution of the Western mind has been founded on the repression of the feminine – on the repression of undifferentiated unitary consciousness, of the participation mystique with nature; a progressive denial of the anima mind; of the soul of the world; of the community of being; of the all pervading, of mystery, of ambiguity, of imagination, emotion, instinct, body, nature, woman – of all that which the masculine has progressively identified as 'other'... But, as Jung prophesied, an epochal shift is taking place in the contemporary psyche, a reconciliation between the two great polarities, a union of opposites: a hieros gamos (sacred marriage) between the dominant, but now alienated masculine, and the long suppressed, but now ascending feminine."

Art and the Feminine Principle

Valuing and understanding the feminine principle was crucial to making artwork from a transpersonal perspective, and also to my own development as a visual artist.

I wasn't concerned with feminism as such, but with the very different qualities, energies, and ways of being in the world that the masculine and feminine principles represented within both men and women. A much more profound understanding of what I meant by the feminine principle was essential, and I went on to look at this in the context of transpersonal psychology, as I had encountered it through the work of Ian Gordon-Brown and Barbara Somers in London, as well as looking at myths and fairy tales, and the Goddess cultures of prehistory. *The Myth of the Goddess. Evolution of an Image* by Anne Baring and Jules Cashford was very important at this stage.

In a beautiful lecture entitled *Sleeping Beauty and the Awakening of Instinct into Consciousness,* Anne Baring describes how Sleeping Beauty, the feminine principle, our soul, our instinctive consciousness, which manifests in the form of intuitions, feelings and the language of the non-rational, has become appallingly neglected and undervalued compared to the rational mind. Head and heart, mind and soul have been separated from each other. We have become unconscious of our soul, and frightened of the non-rational part of ourselves.

She goes on to describe how consciousness makes itself known to us, and makes us known to ourselves, through the language of the non-rational, through myths, symbols, intuition, and the language of the arts. Soul does not yield her secrets to an analytical suitor – the royal road to the soul is through the non-rational. Imagination is crucial.

These perceptions had a very profound effect on me, both in my personal life and in the work I was trying to do as an artist. I realised that a lot of problems that I had thought were personal were not just personal at all, but part of a much bigger picture and collective in origin. My own perceptions of myself, both as a woman and an artist, have been deeply affected and changed by what I learned about the qualities of the feminine principle and its place in cultural and mythological history. I had always loved European Art History, had huge respect for the great heroes of Twentieth Century Art, like Picasso, Matisse, Bonnard, but they were all men, and there was no way that I could do what they did. Now instead of feeling second best, I feel part of a different psychic stream, that has its own special qualities, and that is really a rather wonderful feeling. I went on to try and get a sense of how the feminine principle might express itself visually, how the language of the feminine principle might differ from the language of the masculine principle. I also looked at the way the spiritual manifests itself in the art of other cultures. Obviously there is an enormous amount of literature on all of these subjects, which it is not possible to discuss or describe in this context. A rather unexpected development in all of this work was a growing awareness of Shamanism, and connections between Shamanism, spirituality, and the visual arts.

Between 2001 and 2004, I had the opportunity to attend three seminars/conferences organised by the Institute of Ethnology and Anthropology of the Russian Academy of Science, in Moscow and Siberia. These conferences were partly academic, but also gave us the opportunity to experience Shamanic rituals, first hand, in Abakan, Tuva, and Altai, as well as doing two initiation workshops with Shamans in Moscow. Following these experiences, I have developed a very strong feeling that my visual work as an artist is closely related to Shamanism. I work in very particular places in the landscapes (places of power maybe?). I use rituals to honour the place, the materials, and to shift into right brain mode, and connect with my inner self before I start working. When the work is going well, something happens between me, the subject and "out there" and the work seems to take over and draw or paint itself. I never know if I will ever be able to do it again. The images seem to come through me, through my hands maybe. I also feel that I am in some sort of altered state of consciousness when I am doing creative work.

Shamanism and Cave Paintings

My thoughts on this subject were enhanced when I went to see the prehistoric cave paintings at Pech-Merle in Cabrerets in France this summer. When we look at the extraordinary and spectacular paintings on the walls of the caves at Pech-Merle, we marvel at the images – hands, and horses that seem almost to be flying round the space. It seems clear, however, that what was important to these early artist Shamans was not the images themselves, but the process that they were part of. In its origins it seems likely that art was not art for art's sake, but art for life's sake, that it was concerned with man and woman's capacity for exploring inner realms, their connectedness with everything around them, and their connectedness with the world of spirit. Artists were extraordinary people who either symbolically, or in reality, were able to travel between this world and the other, and who had the capacity to anchor their experiences in very powerful imagery.

Ethnologists have suggested that in Nevada in California, Shamans painted their visions on the rocks the following day, and probably believed that if they didn't, they would fall ill and die. The places they painted became charged with power and facilitated further Shamanic journeys. The larger scale cave paintings probably fulfilled a similar function. The hand at Pech-Merle was important at the moment when it was in contact with the cave wall: the Shaman blew specially prepared pigment over it so that it seemed to disappear into the wall of the cave. The hand thus penetrated the world of spirit hidden behind the veil of the surface of the wall of the cave and this would have had the effect of establishing an intimate relation with the hidden world of spirits. The spirit world would then have manifested itself directly through the drawings created by the hand. Touch and the quality of live experience were central. Shamanism is a world view in which everything is interconnected and animated by spirit. It seems likely that the ancient Goddess-centred cultures of prehistory practised some form of Shamanism and that Shamanism and the origins of the feminine principle are closely related. Visual art had an important and central role to play in these cultures.

In his book, *Images and Symbols. Studies in Religious Symbolism*, Mircea Eliade says,

> "Every human being tends even unconsciously towards the centre, where he can find integral reality – 'sacredness' ", and that "it depends ... on modern man to 'reawaken' the inestimable treasure of images that he bears within him; and to reawaken the images, so as to contemplate them in their pristine purity, and to assimilate their message."

Once when Picasso was asked what makes great works of art so special, he replied that painting is "holy" work, but that's a word you can't use because people would give it the wrong associations. It is very clear though that through the visual arts, it is possible to connect with the sacred in an authentic and contemporary way that is very close to both the origins of the feminine principle, and the ancient tradition of Shamanism.

Rosetta Brooks, in an article about the American artist Nancy Spero, says,

> "The resurrection of the feminine principle in our culture is a re-animation of the mythic that can lead to the re-enchantment of the world ... It is a deliberate regression set against progressive modernism."

Shamanism, inner journeys, and the visual arts, all have a vital role to play in this process. Perhaps, as this happens, the masculine and feminine principles will be able to work together in a new and creative way, and give birth to what is possibly a new sort of human being.

If we use what we can learn from both Shamanism and the feminine principle as a basis for the making of artwork, we can work from a transpersonal perspective, and make art for life's sake rather than art for art's sake – art that is about connectedness, and in which life, art and spiritual values are closely interconnected. Artists can then have a central role in life once more, as Shamans and healers on behalf of the collective, instead of the fringe position they now occupy. Working visually is very different from working with words. Images say what cannot be said any other way. It seems crucially important in our culture at this time, that we learn one again to give real value to the power of our own inner image-maker, the magic of image, and imagination as a way of knowledge.

I haven't completed my Ph.D. yet, but I am trying to put into practice at least some of the things I have learned on the extraordinary journey that has been my research, both in my own artwork, and in the context of workshops for other people.

REFERENCES

Anne Baring, 2001, Sleeping Beauty and the Awakening of Instinct into Consciousness, in David Lorimer (editor), *Thinking Beyond the Brain. A Wider Science of Consciousness*, Floris Books

Anne Baring and Jules Cashford, 1993, *The Myth of the Goddess. Evolution of an Image*, Arkana Penguin Books

Rosetta Brooks, If Walls Could Talk. The Art of Nancy Spero and Kiki Smith, in Jon Bird (editor), 1993, *Otherworlds*, Baltic Reaktion Books

Mircea Eliade, (1991) *Images and Symbols. Studies in Religious Symbolism*, Princeton University Press

Gloria Orenstein, (1990) *The Reflowering of the Goddess*, Pergamon Press

Richard Tarnas, (1996) *The Passion of the Western Mind: understanding the ideas that have shaped our world view*, Pimlico

22. UNDERSTANDING ONESELF AS NON-LOCAL: WHAT EXPERIENCED MEDITATORS SAY

Amy Louise Miller

Western culture predominantly leads us to believe that "I" is a separate (local) individual within the boundary of our skin, with a one-to-one relationship between mind and body. After experiences with Holotropic Breathwork and the study of Advaita Vedanta, Amy changed her views. Using the perspectives of the mystical traditions, transpersonal psychology and ego development psychology, she describes the psychology of a larger self (non-local) which goes beyond that of our ordinary consciousness. At some point in each of these systems the sense of self moves from the local to the non-local.

After describing these approaches, Amy concentrates on her current research which involves working with experienced meditators and looking at the experience of locality of self from the inside — what is called a phenomenological approach. She describes the experiences of a number of these meditators and concludes that when an individual's sense of self as non-local becomes dominant, their view of the world and their place in it changes accordingly. The individuals who have this non-local concept would seem to have a connection with peoples and events in the world, having thoughts, ideas and attitudes which are often shared or interconnected, however distant their physical origin. The world, she concludes, is one big swimming pool and we are all in it together.

Amy Miller *has been a Licensed Psychologist in private practice in Massachusetts, US for many years. The material in her article is drawn from her Ph.D. thesis in which she uses a phenomenological approach to explore non-locality of self in meditators and in individuals with dissociative identity (multiple personality).*

Background

In our post-industrial Western culture, we grow up with the prevailing understanding of the parameters of our individual self. In that system, "I" am a separate individual who exists locally within the boundary of my skin. My thoughts take place in my mind, the wiring for which is in my brain, inside my head. There is an assumed one-to-one relationship between my mind and my body. The reality of self is constructed as being local and unified in all cultures, but, in Western cultures in particular, unity is the sole allowably 'normal' state. Thus, anything other than locality and unity becomes suspect. Though most people have experiences, which contradict this assumption, ordinarily, no attempt is made to adjust one's understanding of the nature and locus of self.

In my graduate studies in developmental psychology, I stayed within this rubric. Years later, I trained in a modality called Holotropic Breathwork as created by Stanislav Grof. This technique combines a musical environment with vigorous breathing to induce an altered state of consciousness without drugs. My observations of my own and other's anomalous experiences during Holotropic Breathwork sessions led to a much expanded understanding of the boundaries of my "self".

Since the early Eighties I have studied Advaita Vedanta, a philosophy derived from ancient Hindu scriptures. These texts outline a psychology of a larger Self which goes beyond that of our ordinary consciousness. As a result of personal experiences with Eastern mystical tradition and expanded/altered states of consciousness, I have gradually come to a new understanding of the nature of reality. I now think of my conscious ego "self" as a phenomenon that, much of the time, appears to be "local," i.e., "attached" to and spatio-temporally bounded by the body, and, simultaneously, one that could, given certain conditions, express itself non-locally, i.e., in ways that appear to transcend commonly accepted properties of time, space, and materiality.

Non-local Aspects of the Self

Evidence is beginning to accumulate which indicates that consciousness may be viewed as having a non-local aspect. Stanislav Grof's schema of expanded dimensions of consciousness was groundbreaking in this regard. Grof has both witnessed the occurrences and examined the protocols of more than thirty-five thousand "voyages" into altered states of consciousness both by psychiatric inpatients given LSD and by participants in the experiential modality of Holotropic Breathwork. In "The Transpersonal Vision", Grof notes:

"In studying transpersonal phenomena, we are forced to revise the concept that human beings are essentially Newtonian objects. A completely new formula… describes humans as paradoxical beings with two complementary aspects: they can show properties of Newtonian objects, and also those of infinite fields of consciousness…Materialistic science holds that any memory requires a material substrate… However, it is impossible to imagine any material medium for the information conveyed in various forms of transpersonal experiences. This information… seems to exist independently of matter, and to be contained in the field of consciousness itself or in some other types of fields undetectable by scientific instruments."

Combine the word "self" with the concept "non-local," and several large areas of discourse immediately demand attention. I will present non-local views of "self" from three important perspectives: the mystical traditions, transpersonal psychology, and ego development theory in psychology. Each of these perspectives has considered the developmental dimension in which the self is described as moving through a series of stages. At some point in each system, the sense of self moves from local to non-local.

In observing the mystical traditions, Huxley coined the term "perennial philosophy" which purports to summarize that understanding of the nature of self which all mystics eventually discover. Happold's outline of the perennial philosophy states,

" … The phenomenal world of matter and individual consciousness is only a partial reality … The nature of man is not a single but a dual one. He has not one but two selves, the phenomenal ego, of which he is chiefly conscious, and which he tends to regard as his true self, and a non-phenomenal, eternal self … the spark of divinity within him which is his true self … he will come to an intuitive knowledge of the Divine Ground and so apprehend Truth as it really is, and not as to our limited human perceptions it appears to be."

The perennial philosophy has been given expression in the mystical branches of every major religion. However, I have chosen to present examples from Advaita Vedanta, an area with which I am familiar to illustrate the application of the perennial philosophy to locality of self.

Vedanta (and many other Eastern mystical philosophies) is grounded in the experiences which emerge during long-term, intense, meditation practices. In the mystical tradition of Advaita Vedanta, one of the best known texts is the Bhagavad-

Gita. A highly respected commentary on this text by Madhusudana Saraswati (16th Century) outlines the 'Sapta Bumica' or seven stages of spiritual development which grow out of a meditation practice. Of the first three he comments, "these ... are forms of discipline...for the world continues to appear as a separate (entity)." [That is the world seems to be made up of objects which are separate from the self.] Then, "the fourth stage ... experience of Reality, consisting in the supersensous realization of the identity of Brahman and the Self." [Since 'Brahman' is infinite and without attributes, the sense of self as local has been deconstructed.] During the fifth through seventh stages, there is an increasing permanence of the state in which, "the subject-object relationship vanishes". At this point, the self is part of everything and everything is part of the self.

Another important idea from Advaita Vedanta is that the true nature of reality is non-dual [the subject-object distinction doesn't exist]. Thus, the individual, in moving from a local to a non-local understanding of self is simply removing her ignorance of what is real, i.e. the self as non-local. While psychology tends to think of progress to a "higher stage" as involving acquisition of additional skills or knowledge, in Advaita the process could be better characterized as a divestment of illusion which allows an opening to what "is."

Non-locality of self was given significant credence by the ancients and is re-emerging as a focus of serious endeavours in several areas of contemporary psychology.

Over the past thirty years, western-trained social scientists with transpersonal orientations have emerged. In their theories we see a mix of these mystical influences with an academic grounding in the social sciences which has resulted in significant contributions to the understanding of the phenomenon of consciousness.

Stanislav Grof, based upon extended observations of altered states of consciousness (see above), has divided the landscape of inner consciousness into realms of experience. The innermost realm is the transpersonal domain. In The Holotropic Mind, he comments that;

"In the transpersonal realm, we experience an expansion or extension of our consciousness far beyond the usual boundaries of both our bodies and our egos, as well as beyond the physical limits of our everyday lives... It is a region in which there appears to be 'an expansion or extension of consciousness beyond the everyday concept of time and space.' "

Reminiscent of the mystical traditions, Grof sees the transpersonal dimension as ever-accessible yet conventionally overlooked in the Western mindset.

Regarding Ken Wilber, another prominent transpersonal theorist, Christian de Quincey notes that he: "provides a post-modern worldview that includes the best of empirical science and rational philosophy and the best of visionary religion and mysticism." Wilber, integrating material from multiple sources, has posited a nine level theory of the evolution of individual consciousness. The sixth level is Vison-logic. As Suzanne Cook-Greuter notes;

> "Wilber ... suggests that during vision logic the previously taken for granted way of meaning making gets deconstructed and its limitations self consciously explored and exposed ... At its most advanced, vision logic opens the door into the spiritual, transpersonal, non-egoic, non representational realm of being."

Wilber himself comments that Vision-logic is, "the highest integrative structure in the personal realm; beyond it lie transpersonal developments." Wilber's next level is the Psychic level of which he remarks that it marks, "... the beginning or opening of transcendental, transpersonal or contemplative developments." We can see the reflection of the mystical traditions in these transpersonal theories.

Developmental Models of the Self

Recently, researchers in the area of ego development theory in psychology have begun to look at additional stages of development of self beyond the conventional. The classic theories of Jean Piaget described human development as a sequence of increasingly complex and integrated stages or coherent systems of meaning making. Piaget's highest stage is that of formal operations which, according to Cook-Greuter, views the world as, "... Newtonian, as scientific and, with positivistic overtones, as a progressive or 'modern' stance.' "

Cook-Greuter explores ego development beyond formal operations, using the labels "post-formal" and "post-conventional," thus challenging Piaget's notion that formal operations is the highest level of integration possible. Her research involves looking at developmental stages in a range of ordinary people using a Sentence Completion format. Cook-Greuter describes postconventional ego development as, "...a stepwise deconstruction of the previously unconsciously constructed permanent object world." including deconstruction of the permanent self-identity. She has developed two postconventional stages which she calls Construct-aware and Unitive.

In the Construct-aware stage individuals become aware of the constructed nature of their maps of reality and their need to create stability by taking these maps to be what is real. In the Unitive stage, she remarks,"... people understand the fundamental instability and the illusion of the permanent object world more deeply." Cook – Greuter found evidence of these two stages in a very small percentage of her research participants.

In contrast to the transpersonal psychologists who focus on the expansion and transformation of the self in non-ordinary experience, ego development theorists focus on the self as a meaning maker and integrator of experience and the gradual deconstruction of self as the machinations of self move from transparency to visibility. One cannot avoid noticing, however, that evidence from altered states of consciousness, meditation, and analysis of ego-constructs, leads to very similar conclusions. In the end, 'the Emperor has no clothes,' that is, the illusion of self as local becomes transparent as our sense of self moves into the area of the non-local.

A great sage, Swami Muktananda Paramahamsa, once said, 'The world is as you see it; change the prescription of your glasses.' In each of the systems discussed, mystical, transpersonal, and ego development, the individual becomes increasingly aware of the way in which her sense of self and of what is 'real' is largely arbitrary, that is, constructed as she intends to construct it. At this point, priorities change as a natural result of one's new vision. Ego-boosting and desire driven activities such as striving to own material objects or to impress others tends to fall away. One tends to see oneself as part of what Rhea White calls the 'All-Self' which can include all humanity, all living beings, the planet, etc. Contributing to the greater good often becomes a priority value, usually accompanied by the humility of realizing what a small part each individual plays. Traits such as dispassion emerge in which strong reactions to self-important events such as praise and criticism or gain and loss are modulated by the awareness that all such events are part of the natural ebb and flow of the larger picture rather than reflections of individual importance.

The Self-Sense and Meditation

My current research project involves looking at the experience of locality of self from the inside, a phenomenological approach. In order to look at how one understands the nature of the locality of one's self, I have chosen to research the self sense of long-time meditators. Members of this group, especially in Western settings, tend to have several traits in common. They have voluntarily sought to follow a practice which looks within by quieting the mind. Therefore, they feel in control of their endeavors. They have a community of others who follow similar practices. If they have non-ordinary experiences in the course of their practice, these are considered expected and part of the norm. Their attitude towards their practice and the changes it may bring in their sense of self is positive and accepting.

The implicit and ineffable nature of the sense of self does not lend itself to direct questioning. Therefore, there are two semi-projective methods which I designed specifically for my research project. The "semi-projective" exercise provides some structure which guides the participant towards the research target area while, at the same time, allowing the participant to "dream into" the target area while completing the exercise in a relatively free-form way.

I have called the first of these methods the Personal Construct Exercise. The inspiration for this Exercise came from George Kelly's Personal Construct Theory. I explore the participant's personal construct of "self" using small individual cards each of which has a single word. The word list contains common words for aspects of life in this world (e.g. people, thoughts, death,) as well as terms derived from discussions of expanded sense of self in the spiritual and psychological literature, (e.g. consciousness, soul). I ask the participant to sort and lay out the word cards in terms of how they are seen to relate to the central card labeled "self." The format is very flexible, allowing the individual to discard or add cards freely. The Personal Construct Exercise (PCE) bypasses verbal expression while still remaining in the comfortable arena of words.

The second semi-projective method combines two similar 'map' drawing techniques: Buzan's "mind-map" and Novak's "concept map". Again, verbal instructions are minimal. The participant is shown two model maps using concepts unrelated to this project. The instructions involve putting the word 'self' in a circle at the starting point with several lines going out from the term "self." These branches are labeled with concepts directly related to 'self.' Additional branches are added as needed. It is emphasized that there is no right or wrong way to do this, it is a creative exercise. For both the Personal Construct Exercise and the Mapping Exercise, an informal conversation that begins with an open-ended question such as, "Tell me about what you've done here" follows the exercise.

Here are some examples of responses to these exercises by research participants (all names are pseudonyms).

Jen: This participant, a professional oil painter in her early-sixties, is a student of Advaita Vedanta (described above) and reported that she now meditates daily for about 20 minutes, but was meditating heavily for about ten years between 1985 and 1995 for about 2 to 3 hours daily.

Jen presented a consistently non-local view of self. Her PCE was divided at the point of the 'knowledge' card which she described as being on a dividing line. [See Appendix #1] To the right of this vertical line were sixteen cards. For one of these cards, Jen replaced the DEATH card with a handwritten card labeled 'transition' indicating her understanding that death was simply a transition not an ending. The participant commented that the right side of her PCE represented mithya, a Sanskrit word, which she translated as, 'that which appears to be real but is impermanent.' On the left side of the line were two 'self' cards flanking the 'reality' card surrounded by four other cards. These were CONSCIOUSNESS, HEART, LOVE, and SPIRIT. This left side of the line was described by Jen as satyam, 'that which is really real' and the 'irreducible.' The KNOWLEDGE card was straddling the line to indicate that it is knowledge that leads to the understanding of what is really real. Jen's two SELF cards surrounding the REALITY card indicated that self was equated with what is real. It is evident that Jen's primary identification of the nature of her self is as expansively non-local, that is equal to all that is real.

Jen's MAP was also consistent with her sense of self as liberated from the strictures of the material dimension which was not represented at all in her MAP. [Appendix #2] In it, 'self' is qualified as synonymous with consciousness, the quiet, the great relief, the only safety, [that which] urges the person towards union, and that which 'permeates all known and unknown.' Her MAP illustrates a primacy of awareness of non-local qualities of self. Her view of her self has clearly shifted in the direction of non-locality.

Sue Ellen: Sue is a 55 year old accountant, part of a Hindu-based spiritual practice, who has been meditating regularly for 30 years, daily for the last 10. Sue Ellen's MAP shows a playful mixture of everyday (e.g. her cat) and esoteric spiritual elements. An example of her description of a spiritual element [pointing to an outline of a cloud-like shape with a tiny spiral in the middle] follows:

"So right here, this sort of was like a central point of Vortex that everything came out of. This was the shape of the expression of that. We'll call it God too, but God is kind of behind it…. Then, I just started to branch out into creation…the Eye of God."

At one point the researcher, in following up on one of Sue Ellen's comments about the mixture of elements in her MAP, asks her, "So, self and universe interplay?" Sue Ellen answers:

"Yeah. Well, I know the difference. It's not like, you know, the same. But the universe is like in me. You know. I think about the universe and everything in me comes from the universe… You asked me about me and I'm everything…everybody is."

This comment reveals a strongly non-local sense of self. She says that she is 'everything' and that everybody is 'everything.' Yet, she lives very adequately in the material world.

Eva: Eva is a 55 year old Nurse Practitioner who has been meditating on her own 5 to 7 times a week for 15 years.

Eva completed her PCE very rapidly and decisively, using just four cards. First, she clarified with the researcher that it was permissible to take whatever meaning of "self" she wished. The SELF card was centered below three cards, UNIVERSE, CONSCIOUSNESS and LOVE. Again, it is clear that, for Eva, in her depiction of the "higher" meaning of the term "self," local dimensions of self are so irrelevant that they are not included.

Jane: Jane is a retired school counselor in her early 60's who recently experienced the transformative effect of caring for a parent through the dying process. She has been meditating daily for ten years and is part of Hindu-based spiritual practice.

Jane's PCE proceeds from left to right and identified what she has been going toward [on the right]. [Appendix #3] When she finds a satisfactory way to use the PCE to represent the culmination of her journey, SELF is paired with LOVE as a "verb" followed by a triad containing GOD, ONENESS and UNIVERSE. In the discussion of her PCE, Jane discusses her understanding of what the concept of CONSCIOUSNESS, which is instrumental in her recently changed understanding of the nature of reality, means to her:

"It's very much like a field. It's like a constant field not in a bad sense, a mind field, but that the connection to whatever one is engaged with. Whether it be natural beauty, or compassion, or mundane tasks that need to be done, but it's the pregnancy of existence. That every moment of existence can be a teacher and a friend if you will. Not looking for that, but being present in that.

So, it's the reality, it's the present moment. I guess the kind of thing that's said by others, but to really embrace that as an experience, it would be that kind of present moment. What would it be? Present moment, wonderful moment, whatever Thich Nhat Hahn said. It's like having Thich Nhat Hahn inside of you. [both laugh] Just kind of walking with that inner awareness."

In a similar manner to the others, Jane demonstrates both in the arrangement of her PCE and in her interview response that she is increasingly realizing the primacy for her of self engaging a constant awareness of something larger than her. Each of these long-time meditators has a sense of self which is defined non-locally in the sense that their primary identification is with non-material dimensions and concepts and is expanded beyond the domain of the individual.

Conclusion

When an individual sense of self as non-local becomes dominant, their view of the world and their place in it changes accordingly. Since this book grew out a conference on Citizenship in an Interconnected World, it seems appropriate to relate non-locality of self to this topic. In other words, how does the individual whose sense of self is predominantly non-local understand their connection to the matters of this world? First, since the boundary between self and All Self has tended to dissolve, the separation between individual minds has less importance. Ideas, attitudes, and concepts may be seen as floating freely in some type of non-local 'field,' such as Jung's collective unconscious, to which all may have access. Following from this emerges the understanding that the individual does not 'own' their 'original' ideas and guard them competitively, but that building the knowledge base of the world is a shared cooperative endeavor. Similarly, an alternative understanding of the way in which events are interconnected develops. One senses a non-local type of 'resonance' so that events which appear to be distant in space can be seen as inter-related synchronicities. Following from this is the understanding that there is no way to be separate or uninvolved when war or famine, for example, occurs in distant parts of the globe. The world is one big swimming pool and we are all in it together.

REFERENCES

Buzan, T. and Buzan, B. (1993). The Mind Map Book. London: BBC Worldwide Ltd.

Cook-Greuter, S. R. (2000). Post-autonomous ego development: A study of its nature and measurement. PhD Thesis. Harvard University, Cambridge, MA.

Dayananda-Saraswati (1994). Three-Month Course on Advaita Vedanta [tape]. Saylorsburg, PA: Arsha Vidya Pitham.

De Quincey, C. (2001).A theory of everything? A critical appreciation of Ken Wilber's collected works. Noetic Sciences Review, # 55 9-15 &38-39.

Flavell, J. H. (1963). The Developmental Psychology of Jean Piaget. New York: Van Norstrand.

Grof, S. (1992). The Holotropic Mind. New York: Harper Collins.

Grof, S. (1998). The Transpersonal Vision: The Healing Potential of Nonordinary States of Consciousness [tape and transcript]. Boulder, CO: Sounds True.

Happold, F. C. (1970) Perennial philosophy [online]. Available from: www.mythosandlogos.com/perennial.html

[Acessed: 21:05:03].

Kelly, G. (1955). The Psychology of Personal Constructs. New York: Norton.

Madhusudana-Saraswati (1998). Bhagavad-Gita with the Annotation Gudhartha Dipika. Calcutta: Advaita Ashrama.

Novak, J. D. and Gowing, D. B. (1984). Learning How to Learn. Cambridge, UK: Cambridge University Press.

White, R. A. (1997).Dissociation, narrative, and exceptional human experiences. In: S. Krippner and S. M. Powers (Ed.) Broken images, broken selves: Dissociative narratives in clinical practice, Philadelphia, PA: Brunner/Mazel, Inc. 88-121.

Wilber, K. (1986).The spectrum of development. In: K. Wilber, J. Engler and D. P. Brown (Ed.) Transformations of Consciousness, Boston: Shambala. 65-105.

APPENDICES

1. PCE-JEN

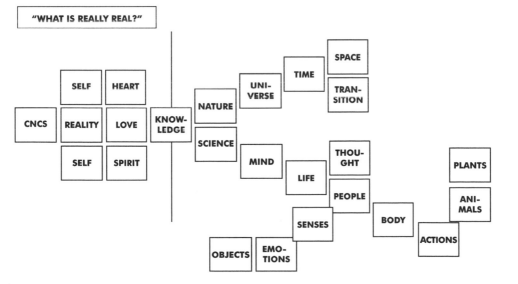

2. MAP-LMP-02-JEN

ALL ART RESIDES

NON EGO BASE – AVAILABLE

THE GIFT – THE OBVIOUS/ HIDDEN TEACH (THIS)

IS CONSCIOUSNESS

PERMEATES ALL KNOWN · UNKNOWN

THE QUIET

SELF

URGES THE PERSON TOWARD UNION WITH THE WORLD/UNIVERSE WHICH (S)HE FINDS AVAILABLE

BRINGS OUT COMPASSION

THE SILENT 'PEBBLE IN THE SHOE' URGING ONE TO AWAKE

THE GREAT RELIEF

ROOT OF ALL PLEASURE

THE ONLY SAFETY

KILLS FEAR

AGAIN AND AGAIN

MIND GIVES OVER

3. PCE-LMG-02-JANE

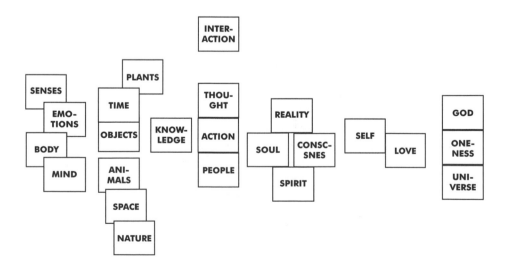

INTER-ACTION

PLANTS

SENSES

THOU-GHT

EMO-TIONS

TIME

REALITY

GOD

OBJECTS

KNOW-LEDGE

ACTION

SOUL

CONSC-SNES

SELF

ONE-NESS

BODY

MIND

ANI-MALS

PEOPLE

SPIRIT

LOVE

UNI-VERSE

SPACE

NATURE

23. FROM AWAKENING TO LIBERATION: SUPPORTING THE DECONSTRUCTION PROCESS OF SELF-REALIZATION

Bonnie Greenwell

Bonnie describes stages of experience in spiritual development, including initiating events, shifts in energy and consciousness, spiritual cul-de-sacs and the de-construction of the personal identity as one moves toward liberation. Supportive interventions for people in this process include setting a context; identifying physical, emotional and spiritual needs; and creating a foundation for remembering one's true nature. Exterior and interior practices are identified that point a person who is in spiritual emergence toward true liberation. Spiritual emergence is an important theme for those involved in transpersonal practices because they can be opened up to a process that will deconstruct their self-identity and lead them to what mystics have termed liberation. When the implications of this process are not understood people often end up in cul-de-sacs, caught in new "spiritual" identities that do not serve their search for self-realization. Transpersonal therapists and healers can greatly serve the collective needs across all cultures by understanding and engaging this process. The optimal outcome of self-realization is that one loses all sense of separation from others, and embodies peace, appreciation for life, compassion and intuitive wisdom.

***Bonnie Greenwell**, is a licensed therapist with a Ph.D. in transpersonal psychology from the Institute of Transpersonal Psychology, where she once served as the director of its counseling center. She currently teaches on the adjunct faculty. She has worked with clients in spiritual emergence, and trained therapists in this field for over 20 years. She is the author of the book* Energies of Transformation: a Guide to the Kundalini Process, *published in five languages, and numerous other publications related to spiritual issues. Recently she edited the book* Emptiness Dancing: A Selection of Dharma talks by Adyashanti, *and* *was given transmission as a teacher in his progressive Zen tradition. She has personally and professionally researched and practiced in depth in the traditions of Ashtanga Yoga, Kundalini Yoga, Advaita Vedanta and Zen Buddhism and is also certified in Process Acupressure and Radiance Breathwork.*

Spiritual "seekers" are people who feel driven by an inner movement that pushes them continuously to understand or experience something they might define as "God", "Truth" "meaning" or "the nature of reality". Of course scientists, scholars, and others may be pursuing these questions as well. What is unique about a spiritual seeker is that they seek this wisdom within their own being, joining countless pilgrims who have pursued the inner passages over thousands of years, in response to this same inner drive.

The awakening that may come forward on such a journey may occur in many forms. It has paradoxically been called both a gradual process, needing years of disciplined practice, and also a sudden event, an act of grace, completely beyond the power of the subject who is seeking it. As a transpersonal therapist and a spiritual teacher who has followed spiritual practices for a lifetime, and also listened to the spiritual journeys of many hundreds of people, I have seen that both of these perspectives are true. Awakening is always a sudden in-this-moment-event. You know you are awake, where before you were not, and you see the same truth whether the revelation lasts a few moments or forever. The root source of your life and all of life is exposed. This realization of Self can occur spontaneously, or following years of practice, or in response to a transmission from a spiritual teacher and for many other reasons. As my spiritual mentor, Adyashanti, who awakened in the Zen Buddhist tradition, likes to say, "God can do this any way it wants."

My observation is that, although the realization is the same, no two people reach the remembrance of their true nature in exactly the same way. Thus it is challenging to create a model that would encompass all the nuances of this life-changing shift in the psyche. Yet, as spiritual guides, therapists, healers or educators, we are the ones called upon to offer pointers and support in this process, because for all its power and potential it is so outside of the paradigm of western culture that few uninitiated people can offer any support at all.

So without claiming that any of this model is the whole truth, and stating categorically that your experience may look entirely different, I put forth the most common patterns and conditions I have both experienced and witnessed in the spiritual search.

The two most common starting places might be labeled with the simplest terms: deliberate or accidental. Those who choose deliberately to follow a spiritual tradition are people who have a sudden urge to answer major questions about the meaning of life and seek out teachers, practices, studies and even long and difficult outer journeys in search of the answer, or the one who can deliver it. Every spiritual tradition has a way of accommodating such people, even through this may be a secret to the majority of believers. Practices for mystics are often hidden from the mainstream. Most of these ways of seeking focus on turning inward, and will probably emphasize either being in deep silence, or working with energy.

Some systems work with visualization, breath, sound or ritual. Others push all activity aside in favor of staring at a wall for weeks on end. Practices like Chi Gong or Yoga are offered in preparatory and advanced forms; shamans do drumming and explore intimacy with nature, and take one on inward journeys; Christians use contemplation; eastern systems may work with heart energy, meditation, or manipulation of energy flows (pranas) in the body to raise kundalini energy, which is basically the life force. There are a myriad of methods for turning attention within in search of the grail of realization.

It appears, however, that the majority of people who follow these practices may experience radical energy shifts, changes in perception, psychological upheavals, and even deep insights or visions, and yet never come to completion with the full realization of Self. Some do, and these few become proof to others that the system must work, but many are left frustrated and feeling they have failed to achieve their spiritual goals, and so they give up the search halfway up the mountain.

At the same time it is clear that some people have unexpected and very deep realizations, who never intended them at all. A beautiful example of this is described by Eckhart Tolle in his popular book, *The Power of Now*. He describes himself falling from a deep depression suddenly into a full awakening, which never left him. Even more common are initiating events which show an individual a vastness beyond their limited mind and body, and throw them into an on-going process they had no idea existed, a process designed to de-construct their identity in the service of Self.

So the model I am offering you takes in two starting points – the one that is chosen, and the one that is thrust upon an unsuspecting subject. An initiating event, whether spontaneous or occurring as a major psychic shift during meditation, or through a relationship with an awakened teacher, usually begins the process that supports Self-realization. For some people, there may only be one event, and it makes such an impression upon the psyche that the life feels forever changed. Richard Bucke, an eminent psychiatrist at the turn of the 20th Century, described such an event in his classic study of spiritual experience, called *Cosmic Consciousness*. An initiating event may be a vision, a sudden activation of energy tearing up through the spine, a psychic opening, a feeling of falling into space and seeing the meaning of things, a heart opening that seems to open the floodgates of love, or many other kinds of experiences.

In my research with dozens of people who have had the initiating event of kundalini awakening, I identified seven categories of phenomena that might subsequently occur. Usually everyone does not experience all of these phenomena, but most will experience some of them over a period of months or years. These are:

1. Pranic Activity or Kriyas: These are intense involuntary body movements, shaking, vibrations, jerking, and the sensation of electricity, tingling, or rushes of energy flooding the body.

2. Yogic Phenomena: Body involuntarily performs yogic postures (asanas) or hand movements (mudras) that the subject has never before seen, and the psyche may produce symbolic images, or the sound of chanting, Sanscrit words, tones or a variety of specific sounds such as bees buzzing, or kettle drums beating. Some people spontaneously create and enter into a ritual.

3. Physiological Problems: Activation of latent illness or pseudo illness, apparent heart problems, gastrointestinal disorders, nervous energy and hyper-activity, eating disorders, dramatic rushes of heat and cold, pains occurring in back, head, stomach, or big toes. These and other difficulties are atypical and usually prove difficult to diagnose and treat because they are not consistent with known illness, and they come and go spontaneously.

4. Psychological and Emotional Upheavals: Intensification of unresolved psychological issues, fear of death or insanity, mood swings, overwhelming waves of anxiety, anger, guilt or depression which may feel unrelated to any personal issues, waves of compassion, unconditional love, and heightened sensitivity to the moods of others.

5. Extrasensory Experiences: This may be visual input (i.e. lights, symbols, images of entities, the reviewing of other lives, visions); auditory input (i.e. hearing sounds, a voice, music or a helpful phrase from scripture); or olfactory input (i.e. smelling sandalwood, perfume or incense).

6. Parapsychological Experiences: Psychic awareness, unusual synchronicities, healing abilities, seeing or feeling auras, channeling, electrical sensitivity, and psychokinesis are the most commonly reported occult phenomena. Sometimes there is dramatically awakened creativity, far beyond what the person ever accomplished before. All of these phenomena can lead to spiritual cul-de-sacs, where one is distracted from realization for a lifetime.

7. Samadhi or Satori Experiences: The absorption of consciousness into mystical states of unity, peace, light or energy, sometimes with a clear perception of existential truths; or a profound sense of "I am that," or "This pure and open consciousness with no identity is what I truly am". There may be less intense trance-like states that bring peace, joy, or waves of bliss. These may occur during or after meditation, or spontaneously at other times. Being lost for years in emptiness or ecstasy is another spiritual cul-de-sac.

Please note that any of these phenomena can occur independent of a kundalini awakening, for various reasons. But if a person has had a dramatic initiating event, and this is followed over time with experiences from several of these categories they are probably in a kundalini process.

I believe the primary reason these phenomena arise, both in spiritual practitioners and those who "accidentally" have an awakening event, is that the subtle body field is being reorganized. The subtle body (the field of mind, emotions and senses) is greatly influenced by the quickening energies of kundalini, and this causes the release of blocked trauma and pain, the arising of repressed memories and emotions, and the opening of the energy field into new experiences which have not been known before, including the opening of brain centers with capacities that are not commonly utilized in ordinary mental states. This is consistent with the teachings of kundalini science, as understood by practitioners in India. Our subtle body is the invisible flow of energies that carries all of our thoughts, feelings, impulses, sensations, and memories – basically every part of us with which we identify that is not in a physical form. All of our conditioning, which has shaped our patterns of thinking and assessing what is happening to us, is woven into the subtle body field. When kundalini arises, either before or after a spiritual realization, this is coming undone. Our structure of identification, how we think of who we are, is falling apart. For some unfortunate people, the outside world, and all the crutches of personal identity, also fall apart. I have heard dramatic stories of spiritual initiations that were followed by exterior losses of jobs, homes, lovers, and friends dropping away, in conjunction with the inward collapse of personal identity during this process. This is one form of the dark-night-of–the-soul consistently referred to in spiritual literature.

Having been involved deeply in Ashtanga yoga, kundalini yoga, Advaita Vedanta, and Zen Buddhist traditions, I have seen two interesting patterns that occur in those who have full awakenings to their true nature. Those who teach the gradual path to awakening, such as the eight-limbed yoga of Patanjali, or kundalini practices, believe that one must be fully prepared, and follow a process in which yoga and meditation practices awaken the latent coiled energy of kundalin, then move it through correct channels until it reaches the crown, where one then experiences the bliss and fullness of samadhi or satori states that reveal the nature of Self. Along the way many chaotic events may occur, but also many openings and positive experiences, so there is a sense of moving forward to a particular completion, especially if a teacher is at hand who knows the territory. A qualified teacher can tell from the reported experience just where the kundalini energy is activated or blocked.

On the direct path, for example in Advaita Vedanta or Zen Buddhism, realization of Truth may occur first, through reading a scripture, hearing the Truth clearly spoken, or being in the presence of a teacher who lives it. (Practically speaking, long silent meditation periods are essential parts of the Zen path.) There is a sudden recognition that might be called "I am that!" a movement of the psyche that cannot adequately be described for the mind, but shifts the identity outside of its narrow boundaries and into a vastness, emptiness, spaciousness and timelessness which shatters any illusion of a separate self. This is awakening. As the Buddha reported simply "I am awake." People who have such awakenings when they have never been on a gradual spiritual path, will find later that the de-construction moves in to support their realization. Thomas Keating, who wrote several books about a meditation process called Centering Prayer as well as Christian contemplation, calls this de-construction the unloading of the unconscious. Other systems have called it purification, or clearing. If a person feels either inflated or dejected by this drama and has no understanding of its function, they can stay stuck in this cul-de-sac of suffering for a long time.

Along with the turmoil of having all the unfinished psychological issues arise, people may remember apparent other lives, activate kundalini energy, open up psychic and healing potentials, feel extremely different inside, as if unfamiliar with how to live their lives, since they now feel unable to follow old interests and drives, and fall into unpredictable emotional states. This can lead to another form of the dark-night-of-the-soul, the sense "I had it and now I've lost it." There is a great distress that something has gone wrong because after such a mind-altering realization they believe they should be healed of everything that ever bothered them.

They are horrified to find themselves caught once again in an old and painful memory or habit. But in time the personal system surrenders and the past moves on. There is a new openness, followed by more clarity in perceiving their underlying nature, and with this, contentment and peace.

So if we look at my model we can see these possibilities:
• Initiating Event that triggers a spiritual opening and search
• Energy Awakening (followed by many phenomena)
• Deconstruction of the identity or unloading of the unconscious
• Dark Night of the Soul
• Clarity, resolution and surrender
• Learning to live in a new way
• Self-Realization (which might also have occurred as the initiating event)

While it is clear that awakening is both sudden (a quantum leap in perspective and sense of who I am), and gradual (the rest of the psyche and body/mind catching up to support the changes), what usually takes a long time is liberation. Self-realization liberates us from certain constraining belief systems and emotional patterns, but true liberation is the embodiment or the living of this realization. When someone really wakes up, they see the entire world as one divine dance, coming out of nothing, ever fresh and new, and it seems as if the old life was nothing but a dream. It is like arriving suddenly on another planet, and knowing nothing of the territory. There can be a lengthy period of orientation. Zen Buddhists have called it being a baby Buddha, and some say it can take as long as 12 years to learn to live from this new place, which is not reliant on the mind.

As this realization becomes embodied, there is also a return to the world as part of the natural flow of things. A few highly introverted types may stay in caves, but the pull, if one stays on the path long enough, is usually to return and be of some service. This is not an injunction or a mental attitude, but more of a leaning, an urging of the heart. If one has to escape from the world in order to be free, one is not really free. If one can only abide and be happy in the emptiness and the spaciousness, they are as stuck as if they could only enjoy what is worldly. Both sides are part of the dance of the whole.

So these are usually the three final steps to liberation:
• Embodiment of the Truth
• Orientation
• Return

But of course nothing is ever final. There can be a continual re-cycling of some of these patterns, gifts, and phenomena. The journey is often described as a spiral, where consciousness keeps returning to collect more of itself into the freedom of awakening. But after realization there is no drive to collect experiences, or to go anywhere beyond where you are.

Transpersonal therapists need to understand these processes, because they can become the source of support for anyone on this journey who does not have the grace to work with an enlightened spiritual teacher. It also needs to be recognized that many of the dramatic processes offered in the transpersonal field, such as breathwork, psychic training, regression and even guided imagery, can trigger an initiating spontaneous event that will set someone on this path.

So there a few guidelines that may help you to support people who are in the process of deconstruction.
- Provide a context to help them understand that what is happening to them is a spiritual process that has been known for thousands of years. It is natural in the context of spirituality, not an abnormal reaction.
- Help them identify physical, emotional and spiritual needs and find ways to create a support system to meet these needs.
- Encourage creative expression through art, writing, music, dance or whatever inclinations they have, so they have an outlet for the inexpressible.
- Help them to be in the presence of whatever is arising without self-judgment or the need to do anything. To simply meet themselves with compassionate awareness and benign indifference.
- Help them to find their own rhythm for what feels right to them. Sometimes more openness of body, or mind, or heart is needed; sometimes relaxation and ordinary daily living. Using the will to push through things does not help this process. Listening to the inner guidance, and developing flexibility is more useful. There is a natural timing, which varies from one person to another.
- A consistent meditation practice can help to deepen the process and understanding. The best form is one that is not directed by the egoic mind, but rather just sitting in silence, being the silence, perhaps with the questions of self-inquiry, "What is this?" or "Who Am I?" as suggested by the great Advaitic sage, Ramana Maharshi. The answers are not in the mind. And yet the answer is known and can be found within everyone.

The movement from Initiation to Awakening to Liberation is an extraordinary opportunity in a lifetime, one that allows a return to a foundation of peace and happiness that is our birthright. Although there can be many vivid experiences along the way, one finally becomes uninterested in seeking any experience, and is able to enjoy simple pleasures as completely as any other more dramatic event. There is no more pressure to acquire anything, and no more wandering into past stories or future fears. There is just what is, here and now, and a freedom to respond to it without conditions. The impact of liberation is that individuals lose their sense of separation from others, and are free to live with appreciation, compassion, and joy, even under trying circumstances. It does not create a perfect life, but allows a greater relaxation within the life you have.

Where therapy focuses on improving the personality and the egoic structure, awakening is about seeing through these as only impermanent and illusory, and remembering the root or source of the vitality and presence that is actually behind the scenes living our lives. When this source remembers itself and lives freely it then uses the flavor of the personality, but no one is there to claim any special benefits or credit for it. Life simply is as it is.

BIBLIOGRAPHY

Adyashanti, (2004) *Emptiness Dancing: Selected dharma talks By Adyashanti*, Open Gate Publishing: Los Gatos, CA

Adyashanti, (2002) *The Impact of Awakening*, Open Gate Publishing: Los Gatos, CA

Bucke, R. (1969) *Cosmic Consciousness*, E.P. Dutton: NY

Greenwell, B. (1995) *Energies of Transformation: A guide to the kundalini process*, Shakti River Press: Saratoga, CA.

Hari Das, B. (1981) *Ashtanga Yoga Primer*, Sri Ram: Santa Cruz, CA.

Harrigan, J. (1996) *Kundalini Vidya: The science of spiritual transformation*, Patanjali Kundalini Yoga Care: Knoxville, TN.

Keating, T. (2004) *Intimacy with God* Crossroads Publishing: NY

Maharshi, R (Trans: Natarajan), A (1994) *Ramana Gita*, Ramana Maharshi Center for Learning: Bangalore

Tolle, Eckhart (1999) *The Power of Now: A guide to spiritual enlightenment*, New World Library: Novato, CA.

CONSCIOUSNESS AND HEALING: THERAPEUTIC APPLICATIONS

24. SPIRITUALITY AND THE NATIONAL HEALTH SERVICE

Tony Turvey

Tony describes the National Health Service (NHS) in the United Kingdom and in particular its developing spiritual perspective citing the example of Tayside in Scotland and his own interest in Spiritual Emergence (see David Lukoff's comprehensive article in Chapter 10).

While many will see holistic and spiritual approaches as separate from the NHS, Tony shows how there are a wide range of initiatives which involve a more interconnected approach to public health. He gives examples of transpersonal therapies, some comments on the creative arts and the increasing demand for complementary therapies within the NHS. Mindfulness and meditation is also developing because it can be explored in a secular context grounded in scientific research, as are developments in psycho-neuro-immunology (see Beata Bishop in Chapter 1.) While this work is embryonic in the NHS, compassion in caring, looking after ourselves and others are part of a successful healthcare service and part of wider social systems which include interfaith and spiritual issues. The article shows that the NHS is a living landscape and is developing connections to a wider society through a number of creative responses.

Tony Turvey *is in the final stages of completing his Transpersonal Psychology Scotland psychotherapy training (seeking UKCP accreditation). He has worked as a clinical psychologist in the NHS for 24 years since qualifying. His current post is in primary care adult mental health services.*

I work as an NHS clinical psychologist in primary care in Scotland. This year I was fortunate to be part of a group that organised a three day conference on Mental Health, Well-being & Spirituality. The conference bought together 180 professionals (clinicians, service managers and development workers), service users, carers, and independent health practitioners from diverse backgrounds across the UK and abroad. The conference themes included spiritual emergency & psychosis; interfaith & multicultural dialogue, clinical applications of meditation & mindfulness; complementary therapies, creative arts & psychological therapies; looking after others & ourselves as carers and compassion in caring.

The British National Health Service (NHS)

Growing out of the aftermath of World War II, the 1946 NHS Act established a system to provide equitable healthcare for all, free at the point of delivery. As I was enthusiastically carrying out my clinical psychology training in 1979 to take up an NHS post this healthcare system was being described by one author as '*bankrupt*', '*on the brink of collapse*' '*a vast and ruined city of dilapidated buildings whose echoing corridors are walked by the exhausted wraiths of underpaid doctors and nurses . . . haunted by . . . spectres of departed patients who after years in queues and waiting lists have passively given up the ghost*'. From its inception, the structural problem that '*We will never have all we need. Expectation will always exceed capacity*' was recognised. For politicians of almost all persuasions the NHS is always 'safe in our hands' because it has a special place as a cornerstone of British society, carrying a powerful collective archetypal expression of care and compassion. Alongside this, it carries equally deep frustrations about continuing limits in the NHS's ability to provide services and projections onto it as representing a 'nanny state,' robbing people of their responsibility and choices. Against this backdrop NHS staff do their humane best to help people facing death, illness and suffering through these often imperfect services although by 1966 it was being described as '*the unique spectacle of an undertaking that is run down by everyone engaged in it*'.

(all quotations in italics from Garner, 1979 p1).

Since then 'The NHS' survives, grows and thrives, providing 83% of healthcare in the UK at a cost of £66.8 billion in 2002 (ONS). It is the largest single healthcare organisation in Europe, currently employing 1.3 million people and delivering treatment and care in hospitals and communities through over 630 different professional groups. From its 'bankrupt' state of 1979 it has gone through a range of metamorphic changes: dividing itself into discrete services that further split into an internal market of multiple service providers. Radical changes in its role have kept it in the focus of public attention and political controversy (e.g. choices in the long term care of some of the most vulnerable groups in society: older persons, mental illness services and people with learning disabilities).

Over the last few years it has been rebuilding itself back into one unified NHS with increasing focus again on providing healthcare in a social context equitably and trying to shift from treating illness to increased promotion of health and disease prevention. Yet with this expanding staffing and a budget now representing 6.3% of the UK's gross national product problems of waiting lists, complaints and political debate over the best way to provide health care continue and may overshadow the positive developments in treatment, care and understanding that are occurring.

A Spiritual Perspective

It is from within this context that 'spirituality' in healthcare has become increasingly present in some parts of the NHS. The NHS has always contained pastoral, hospital chaplaincy services. Traditionally the NHS provides treatment in a secular, biopsychosocial framework but something else is emerging. Professional groups such as The British Psychological Society established a Transpersonal Psychology Section with academic and healthcare members in 1997. The Royal College of Psychiatrists established a Spirituality Interest Group in 1999 that now has over 800 members.

This increasingly explicit exploration of a spiritual/transpersonal dimension in healthcare can be seen in many professions e.g. Occupational Therapy (Styles & Morrison 2004). For other professions, such as nursing, concepts of compassion in caring are central to their core role. The British Medical Association has accepted articles on 'spiritual intelligence' (e.g. McMullen 2003). Topics that may be seen as 'spiritual care' are being reviewed as part of evidence based healthcare practice, (e.g. Roberts, Ahmed & Hall 2004). The NHS in Scotland carried out a major review and extension of its chaplaincy services leading to it implementing a model of 'spiritual care', where every health board will establish a Department of Spiritual Care as part of national policy (Scottish Executive 2002). A similar project on spirituality and mental health is being considered in England and Wales (NIMHE 2002).

All of these independent developments reflect a deeper shift that may be emerging to maintain the balance of technological treatment advances with human responses to illness, trauma and suffering.

One Example – NHS Tayside

What may be happening? Using NHS Tayside, where I work, as an example there has been for many years been a small, but officially recognised 'spiritual care interest group' – a multi-disciplinary group bringing together like-minded people for lunchtime training events. Triggered by serendipitous chance (a patient complaint about the need for spiritual emergency to be recognized), the active support of NHS senior managers in response to this, the development of the Department of Spiritual Care and the presence of pioneering groups nearby (e.g. 'Spirited Scotland') and new staff arriving created a momentum to enable this small group to organise a conference (NHS Tayside 2004).

This conference brought together many of the themes that seem to draw people towards 'spirituality' in its broadest sense as having a role in healthcare alongside other models of treatment and care. Does this reflect spiritual care in the NHS in 2004? Anyone in our organising group might give a different explanation of why this particular pattern of content developed. For me there is an elusiveness about what exactly 'spiritual care' is that is reflected through the diversity of these conference themes and I discuss this here with some examples from my clinical practice.

Spiritual Emergence

Prior to beginning my transpersonal psychotherapy training I was working in primary care: a routine clinical psychology service in a general practice. One routine referral was of a woman, in her late fifties, troubled by panic attacks for a few months. Treatment was based on the clinical evidence base – cognitive behavioural therapy Roth & Fonagy (1996). Within a few sessions her panic improved and therapy ended. Three months later she was re-referred: unfortunately the panic attacks had returned.

The trigger for the new panic attacks had been her walking out of her house where she had lived for years. She had twice seen the face of Jesus on the wall of the house opposite her own. What was breaking through the wall? Suddenly nothing was routine and the therapy went off into other directions, exploring her life of protecting and caring for her children through trauma and poverty and now finding herself at a transition point where this sacrificial role of caring for others whatever pain it cost her was no longer needed. At that time I had not heard of spiritual emergency but had some interest in Jungian therapy that helped in working therapeutically with this lady (e.g. Edinger, 1972).

Such explicit presentations of overt spiritual experiences have been rare in my NHS primary care work. Lukoff and colleagues (Lukoff 2003) have successfully promoted a wider understanding of spiritual experiences alongside mental health issues. In the UK Clark (2001) and others have been developing this work within the NHS. Generous bursary funding by the Scottish Executive enabled many service users to attend the conference and these workshops were the setting for many delegates to speak of their experiences and process of understanding and recovery.

Transpersonal Psychotherapy

Transpersonal therapies (Rowan 1993, Wellings & McCormick 2000) are a group of approaches that explicitly acknowledge the value of experiences that take us beyond our usual sense of self, sometimes to glimpses of other ways of being. Much of this therapy has developed outside the context of public health services. A short segment of a transpersonal psychotherapy approach shows how this can be relevant in a routine NHS service.

My client, Fred, had recently retired through work-related stress. At our first session he described how he had first broken down when his son developed anorexia at university dropping from 13 to 6 stones, and he had had to carry his son home. Therapy covered a wide range of issues over 47 sessions. As a young child he had experienced painful relationships and escaped into a world of nature, culture and learning. Early in therapy he spoke of his time as a teacher, losing the enjoyment of teaching as he took on the role of disciplinarian in a tough school: he described himself as the 'gauleiter'[1] His images of the SS reminded him of seeing photographs of concentration camp victims and also connected to anger he felt towards fundamentalist Islamic treatment of women, and man's inhumanity generally. We returned to this theme in session 23. Scanning his body he connected with feelings in his stomach. He saw the image of a man:

> "Vivid, not speaking, giving out the feeling of aggression, violence, black eyes, beard, unloving, an alien warrior".

As he held this image I encouraged him to dialogue actively with this man:

247

Therapist	Fred	Shadow figure
Can you ask him his name?		'Ba Akbar'
Will he tell you about his life?		
	Why doesn't he speak? He sees me as a threat. I'm alien. I feel he despises me.	
Why?		
	I'm the enemy I'm wrong They have power of organised thought — Cold reason Not human	
[a pause]		
	The organised power prevents him from answering. Islam	
What can we do together?	He can't speak	Shake hands
	I want to It's the bridge Then I can shake your wife's hand – That's the other side of the coin	He says no
[a pause]		
	It's all in his face — a symbol. A tiny step of human contact	
	We shake hands	
	His face softens. I'm not so frightened - more equal. I feel his smile I see a skin of wool & paper Intermingled, Golden, medieval, spheres of gold, the movement of the stars. Working in harmony.	
	Purple as the image breaks up	

The immediate meaning of this for Fred was 'friendship puts the fear away'. At our next session he told me he that the next day, walking his dogs, he had met a tall bearded Indian, and for the first time they stopped to talk. They walked together for a while and before parting they shook hands. A few weeks later the events of 11th September 2001 occurred. Fred felt the sessions helped him work through his response to those events:

> 'working on the unconscious has helped me understand that everyone has the Taliban inside.'
>
> (from a brief case report and discussion, Turvey 2003).

Complementary and Creative Art Therapies

Space does not permit more than a brief acknowledgement that creative arts are offered by an increasing number of therapists in the NHS as a vehicle for treatment, personal exploration and recovery (BAAT 2004). As well as being meaningful creative activity and a medium for psychological therapy, they can also be seen as routes for individuation, connecting people to archetypal images of spirituality that have collectively been expressed through religious and other symbolism (Jung 1968).

The demand for complementary therapies outside the NHS has contributed to an increasing provision of these therapies within the NHS, (e.g. therapeutic touch, Hallett 2004). Conference workshops looked at underlying theories of therapies, research evidence of their outcomes and considered how they may be developed in NHS settings. The roots of many of these therapies in Eastern models of mind-body-spirit naturally suggest them to be part of 'holistic care' integrating traditional western arts and psychological therapies with eastern spiritual care practices. (e.g. Judith 1996).

These therapies may be seen as paths of healing and ways of transforming the meaning of experiences that may complement well established cognitive, behavioural and other psychotherapies particularly because they offer other ways to help people work with somatic and emotional experiences.

Mindfulness & Meditation

Studies of relaxation (Benson 1975) and meditation as stress management treatments have been well established (Lehrer & Woolfolk (1993). The work of Kabat-Zinn and colleagues using a mindfulness approach has recently been gaining increasing interest in NHS services (Kabat-Zinn 1990).

Why is this? Firstly because a specific treatment training programme has been presented for which there is a clinical evidence base that is readily accessible that presents encouraging results of effectiveness. These studies contribute to evidence based practice and use well-known psychological research outcome measures and study designs so they can be readily understood, assessed and compared to existing treatments.

Secondly, key researchers and clinicians in the UK have shown how 'mindfulness' can be theoretically understood in the context of well established psychological concepts (Teasdale 1999, Baer 2003). This has been seen as an extension of existing good practice within mainstream cognitive-behavioural therapies rather than as something completely different (Segal et al 2002).

Finally, focusing on a major priority health issue (e.g. depression) and considering how this service development might best be implemented knowing that very limited NHS resources (therapists) will be available (Hawks 1981) translates knowledge about the usefulness of mindfulness meditation into a practical format that health service planners and managers can develop onto existing therapeutic services.

Teasdale has suggested that one of the most important shifts that occurs in the course of therapy is a decentring of personal identity with thoughts and feelings to a different awareness of these mental events. In the area of mindfulness meditation there is a meeting of many therapeutic approaches. Mindfulness practice may be a common meeting ground where many different therapies and practices can paradoxically find a common language through the experience of sitting silently together.

So the paradox is: what traditionally has been a mainly spiritual practice may be developing because it can be explored by all in a secular context, grounded in scientific experimental outcome research. And yet the mystery that lies just behind the ordinary that most spiritual and religious traditions point towards (Fontana 2003) can be present in this practice. The central role of a commitment to a personal practice means that, through this silent sitting together, a bridge of connectedness between therapist and client can be built that doesn't have to be labeled as secular or spiritual, scientific or mystical.

I live on one side of the River Tay and after work watch the sun setting over the river. At my clinic the next day my client struggles with her despair from a lifetime of neglect, abandonment and abuse, she still hears the voices of her children crying out as the house fire engulfed them. In our sessions her confusion overwhelms the time and space but a small, fleeting moment happens where she talks about the relief she finds from that confusion when for a few moments she can watch the sun setting over the river. Catching this entrance into a small refuge is a way of being in the moment of that session that we have gradually been building to help create a space outside of her problems.

Mind-Body-Spirit

One major problem for the lady in this example above was her range of illnesses as well as her emotional distress and poverty. Though reunited as a service, the NHS sometimes still subtly reflects a broad western mind-body split.[2] Working with this lady her treatment and care was divided between her GP, acute medical services and myself for various problems. Models of 'holistic' care reflect concerns that the physical/biological world cannot be separated from a psychological one. Developments in the area of psychoneuroimmunology (Azar 2001), for example, extend the understanding of a biopsychosocial model.

Adding a spiritual dimension may further emphasise ideas of an underlying connectedness e.g. Braud (1990) demonstrated non-local effects of mind on biological processes. Historically the Sanskrit word 'namarupa' meant bodymind as one unity so perhaps the subtle divisions that are slipped into 'mind-body-spirit' are holding back a fuller understanding of an underlying unity. While Dossey (1999) sees this as a potential new era in 'reinventing medicine' his vision may not yet be accepted as having a substantial enough evidence base for UK healthcare. However, Pearmain (2001) has summarized how some of these subtle processes can have a significant effect in any personal relationship demonstrating transpersonal processes may be relevant in many healthcare contexts.

Compassion in Caring

The third group of conference themes compassion in caring, looking after others and ourselves, and interfaith addressed some wider dimensions in healthcare. Conference workshops on spirituality in children, valuing older people, supporting creativity in people with complex needs, valuing cultural diversity and carer's needs reflected how successful healthcare services are part of wider social systems, all of which can impinge of people's lives positively or negatively. Fontana (2003) pointed how frequently people have positive, meaningful spiritual experiences and Griffiths shows how it is possible to train staff to feel confident in exploring these areas with clients (Griffiths & Griffiths 2003). While the mindfulness programme of Kabat-Zinn (1990) does not explicitly describe itself as being based on Buddhist ideas and practices this is quite apparent in the text. Some services and forms of therapy have explicitly adopted a spiritual model (e.g. Karuna Institute) as the basis for their practice. Of course, in most societies, healthcare has long historical links within religious beliefs and practices of care and compassion. Frank (1961) described parallels between traditional and modern practices.

Working in a public health service quickly presents you with a wide range of people whose problems are multi-faceted, often having a chronic history and background of social deprivation. So while many people have successful treatment for their problems there can be a significant group who appear to gain little or no benefit and life appears to be one long struggle of frustration & survival. Gilbert (1989) considered suffering as part of human nature. Underlying healthcare, beliefs of whether suffering has to be endured, treated, transcended or removed are themes that have long been considered within spiritual models (Edinger 1972, Wellings 2000).

Are there sometimes aspects of life that are a challenging wall, not to be broken through but calling for a way of accepting, living with, or creatively responding to? (de Beausobre 1984).

Conclusion: The Place of Healing is Embodied in the World

Carl Jung often suggested wholeness is symbolically represented by a quarternity. If so, 'mind-body-spirit' lacks a fourth component to be truly whole. When I originally trained in clinical psychology one dominant theme was behaviour modification. This emphasised the external determinants of human behavior and avoided consideration of any inner world of imagination or feeling. This may conflict with more usual ideas about 'spirituality' and yet perhaps it also points to an important point - that we do not live apart from the world around us. 'The Healing Environment' (King's Fund 2001) is an NHS initiative contributing to improving NHS workplaces. Creating therapeutic 'spiritual care' may involve connecting fully to this world. Whatever aspirations people may have, this world is the ground of our experience.

Our social world can affect us deeply. Gilbert (1992) has shown how social powerlessness contributes to depression which points to caring needing to include and go beyond individual therapy.

Hay & Heald (1987) found a sizeable proportion of the UK population reported mystical experiences (cited in Fontana 2003, p108) with 16% describing awareness of 'a sacred presence in nature'. Darch (2003) and Dunn (2004) explore the importance of the nature world and our relationship to it further. So healing environments may not just be a man made, psychological or social world: they can also be found in nature.

There may also be a mythical dimension to practical services. Garner (1979) presented an image of the NHS as a 'wasteland'. The Grail legend represents a quest for a meaningful life and restoration of the wasteland to harmony (Jung & von Franz 1970). In John Boorman's film Excalibur (1981) the answer to the quest - 'the king and the land are one' - highlights an intimate link between the ruling principle (king) for a person / organisation / society that will be reflected all its constituent body parts (land).

'The NHS' is a living landscape, and the quest is to find creative responses that break through the wall of tensions around public healthcare: transforming people's aspirations into practical realities in this interconnected world.

> *I am the red thread*
> *Between Nothingness*
> *And Eternity*
>
> Sri Chinmoy (1972)

Acknowledgement

'The NHS Tayside conference, Mental Health, Wellbeing & Spirituality' was funded by The Lawrence Bequest, NHS Tayside Primary Care Division, Endowments Committee. Service user places were funded by The Scottish Executive, National Programme for Improving Mental Health & Well-being. Additional sponsorship was provided by University of Dundee Departments of Psychiatry and Nursing and Ottakar's bookshop. The conference was organised by a multi-disciplinary group: Georgia Adams, Cate McMillan, Helen Fulford, Stephanie Gooding, Brian Kidd, Gillian Munro, Barbara James, Hugh MacMillan, Jane Beresford-Smith, John Rutherford, Bernadette Templeton, Callum Cockburn Lindsey Kidd and myself. We are grateful for the contributions of all our presenters and other helpers.

My transpersonal psychotherapy training is supported by a clinical psychology bursary from NHS Education Scotland. It would not have been possible to carry out this training or be involved in the conference without the study leave allowance and support of my Head of Department, Professor Kevin Power. Thanks.

NOTES

1 Gauleiter — a Gestapo officer controlling a district.

2 NHS Tayside, for example divides into an 'acute' division of mainly hospital medical and surgical services and a 'primary care' division caring for the elderly, mental health and community services.

REFERENCES

Azar B (2001) A new take on psychoneuroimmunology. Monitor on Psychology 32 (11) www.apa.org/monitor/dec01/anewtake.html

BAAT (2004) British Association of Arts Therapists. website www.baat.org contains links to a wide range of references on creative arts.

Baer R.A. (2003) Mindfulness training as a clinical intervention: a conceptual and empirical review. *Clinical Psychology: Science and Practice*. 10 (2).

Benson H. (1975) *The Relaxation Response*. Morrow, New York.

Boorman John (1981). 'Excalibur'. Film.

Braud W. (1990) Distal Mental influence of rate of haemolysis of Human Red Blood Cells. *J. Amer. Soc. Psychical Res*. 84 1-24.

British Psychological Society, Transpersonal Psychology Section www.transpersonalpsychology.org.uk

Chinmoy, Sri (1972), excerpt from poem 'My Flute' in sleeve notes of LP 'Between Nothingness & Eternity', The Mahavishnu Orchestra, 1973.

Clarke I. (2001) *Psychosis and Spirituality: exploring the new frontier*. Whurr, London.

Darch P. (2003) *Being Alive to Nature*. Paper presented at West Midlands Institute of Psychotherapy. UK.

de Beausobre I. (1940) *Creative Suffering*. SLG Press. Oxford.

Dossey L. (1999) *Reinventing Medicine. Beyond mind-body to a new era of healing*. Harper Collins, San Francisco.

Dunn M. (2004) website www.cavespirit.net

Edinger E.F. (1972) *Ego and Archetype. Individuation and the religious function of the Psyche*. Shambhala. Boston.

Frank J.D. (1961) *Persuasion and Healing*. Schocken. New York.

Fontana D. (2003) *Psychology, Religion and Spirituality*. BPS Blackwell. Oxford.

Garner L. (1979) *The NHS: Your Money or Your Life*. Penguin, Harmondsworth. UK.

Griffiths J.L. & Griffiths M.E. (2003) *Encountering the Sacred in Psychotherapy*. Guilford. New York.

Hallett A (2004) Narratives of therapeutic touch. *Nursing Standard*, 19 (1) p33-37.

Hawks D. (1981) The Dilemma of Clinical Practice – surviving as a Clinical Psychologist. In McPherson I & Sutton A. (eds) *Reconstructing Psychological Practice*. Croom Helm. London.

Judith A. (1996) *Eastern Body, Western Mind. Psychology and the Chakra system as a path to the Self*. Celestial Arts, Berkeley.

Jung C.G. (1968) *The Archetypes and the Collective Unconscious*, Collected Works 2nd Ed. Routledge, London.

Jung E. & von Franz M.L. (1970) *The Grail Legend*. Princeton University Press.

Kabat-Zinn J. (1990) *Full Catastrophe Living*. Piatkus, London.

King's Fund (2001) The Healing Environment. www.patientexperience.nhsestates.gov.uk/healing_environemnt/he_content/home

Karuna Institute. Core process psychotherapy www.karuna-institute.co.uk

Lehrer P.M. & Woolfolk R.L. (eds) (1993) *Principles and Practice of Stress Management*. Guilford Press. New York.

Lukoff D. (2003) *The Spiritual Journey in Recovery*. www.centrechange.org/ejournal/article.asp?id=106

McMullen B (2003) *Spiritual Intelligence. British Medical Journal* 326 (7385): 51S.

NHS Tayside (2004). Mental Health, Wellbeing & Spirituality Conference, Dundee Scotland. www.mentalhealth-wellbeing-spirituality-conference.info

NIMHE (2002). National Project Programme Proposal: recognising the importance of spirituality in a whole person approach to mental health. *NIMHE project report No 10.*

ONS Office National Statistics online, Total Health Expenditure, 16th Dec 2003. www.statistics.gov.uk/cci/nugget.asp?id=669

Pearmain R. (2001) *The Heart of Listening.* Continuum. London.

Roberts L Ahmed I & Hall (2004) Intercessory prayer for the alleviation of ill health. (Cochrane Review). In *The Cochrane Library*, issue 3, 2004. John Wiley, Chichester. UK.

Roth A. & Fonagy P. (1996) *What Works for Whom? A critical review of psychotherapy research.* Guilford. New York.

Rowan J. (1993) *The Transpersonal: Psychotherapy & Counselling.* Routledge. London.

Segal Z.V. Williams J.M.G. Teasdale J.D. (2002) *Mindfulness-based Cognitive Therapy for Depression. A new approach to preventing relapse.* Guilford. New York.

Scottish Executive (2002). Guidelines on Chaplaincy and Spiritual Care in the NHS in Scotland. NHS HDL (2002) 76. Health Dept. Edinburgh.

Scottish Executive National Programme for Improving Mental Health & Well-Being. www.show.scot.nhs.uk/sehd/mentalwellbeing

Spirited Scotland, 12 Buccleuch Place Edinburgh EH8 9LW. Funded by the Scottish Executive Health Quality Division. www.spiritedscotland.org

Styles K. & Morrison S. (2004) Spirituality within Occupational Therapy Services. thesis, Dept of Occupational Therapy, The Robert Gordon University, Aberdeen.

Teasdale J.D. (1999) Emotional processing, three modes of mind and the prevention of relapse in depression. *Behav. Res & Ther.* 37 553-577.

The Royal College of Psychiatrists Spirituality and Psychiatry Special Interest Group. www.rcpsych.ac.uk/college/sig/spirit

Turvey T. (2003) Bursary: Training in Transpersonal Psychotherapy. Poster presentation at NHS Education for Scotland Psychology Conference 2003. www.nes.scot.uk/psychology/documents/tonyturveyposter.doc

Wellings N. & McCormick E.W. (2000) *Transpersonal Psychotherapy.* Continuum. London.

Wellings N. (2000) *Naked Presence.* In Wellings & McCormick.

25. PRESENCE AND ABSENCE: A CASE STUDY IN ADDICTION FROM A TRANSPERSONAL PERSPECTIVE

Jason Wright

Jason has chosen to write a case study about an addict who ended his use of heroin and became free from addiction. He is able to describe the work of the Core Trust in this field and the contribution of the Centre for Transpersonal Psychology to the work.

The Core Trust's model is based on experience, enquiry and responsibility. The model adopted by CTP through latterly the work of Elizabeth Wilde McCormick and Nigel Wellings highlights a number of issues, and Jason seeks to give a flavour of the work of both organisations in describing his work with Leo.

Jason is very open about his own failings and learning along the way, and this article will be of interest not only to the practitioner but also to the general reader who might be asking how the transpersonal approach works in the everyday life of the therapist who is dealing with difficult cases on a daily basis.

That so much could be achieved working with a young heroin addict in such a relatively short period of time, Jason argues is down to a combination of body therapies and the transpersonal spiritual framework.

Jason Wright *is the Chief Executive and clinical director for CORE. He is also Chair of The Centre for Transpersonal Psychology and outgoing Chair for the Psychoanalytic and Psychodynamic section of the UKCP.*

In this paper I will describe the path a client from the CORE trust took through ending his use of heroin and becoming free from addiction. I have chosen this client because of his conscious commitment to transpersonal ideas and his continued devotion to his spiritual self-development. I shall describe his treatment and highlight the issues that this case raises for transpersonal psychology using the model adopted by the Centre for Transpersonal Psychology (CTP), most lately articulated by Nigel Wellings and Elizabeth Wilde McCormick (2000). My aim is to offer a flavour of the work at CORE and CTP.

The CORE trust is a voluntary sector organisation working with addicted people. It is housed in a row of working men's cottages near Marylebone Station in central London, providing a homely space. We treat people for one year and use a combination of complementary therapies and psychotherapy in individual and group settings.

We offer a programme which comprises three groups daily, one ear acupuncture and two psychological groups. We expect everyone to attend every day for the group work, but to return to their homes in the evening. On top of this each client receives psychotherapy, body acupuncture and one of a range of complementary therapies weekly.

We see the unifying element to this wide plurality of therapies, both psychological and physical, as a transpersonal or spiritual intent. Although this view is non-denominational and secular in approach the perspectives that have best informed the project are mindfulness based. The principal theoretical influences that have informed the project are Jungian Analytic in nature and have been since its inception, and the work of Hillman has been particularly influential. However, other psychological metaphors fit comfortably within the project.

CORE casts a very broad philosophical and theoretical net. Such a diversity of theories and practices offers considerable opportunity for confusion and conflict. We have found that a synthetic model held in a pluralistic context offers a means of both sustaining philosophical authenticity within practice and dialogue between therapists and therapies. This accords with CTP's vision of a transpersonal psychotherapy, which does not limit itself to one model, be that humanistic, psychoanalytic or behavioural; rather the transpersonal work is contextual to the practice of the therapy.

CORE's model is based in experience, enquiry and responsibility. Here we are taking the lead from Jungian ideas of embodiment and incarnation. Personal experience of the members of the community and the way we can take responsibility for these are the foundation of the work. What is happening, how can I think about it, what am I responsible for?

CORE believes the different models we use to understand our experiences and to engage with them fit together as a community of therapies, similar to the way the members of the community come together around a common theme: in this case the letting go of addiction. This places an emphasis upon the relationship treatments and their philosophies. The polycentric archetypal model for the structure of the psyche that Hillman (1989, 1976, 1971) emphasises, orientated toward "particularisation and complexity" (Samuels1985) offers a vision of wholeness that accords well with this sort of communal living. Hillman's intention to deepen what is there into itself offers a practical frame for understanding the community of therapies as well as the individuals' and the individual self. This then becomes a method: to deepen and explore experience, describe its actions, both internal and external, to define responsibility in this context and observe relationship.

This grounding of intervention and understanding in material experience offers the opportunity to explore the meaning generated by the client for these experiences and to challenge those meanings. This is the key to understanding the interactions within the project and in what context interventions may be made. Here again Hillman is useful. To follow through and elaborate the images thrown up by individual's experiences offers practical engagement with their psychic processes and the psychic processes of the community. This is met in a context of wonder, unknowing and responsibility: to listen to what is there, and to take responsibility for what we find, not what we imagine.

In this first vignette showing Leo's progress through CORE I shall describe the beginnings of my work with him and its foundations in traditional psychotherapeutic practice. This is the period of ego building.

He presented with a heroin problem of some years. During the initial three months at CORE he attended regularly and worked hard in the sessions. This represented a good start. He was articulate and made good use of my interventions and those of others in the project. He had been in therapy before and had a good understanding of how therapy might be. Generally, the most useful interventions at this point are cognitive. The clients are usually disoriented by having just finished using drugs and find it difficult to ground themselves in day-to-day experience: concrete interventions such as 'don't go into the pub' and 'don't hang out with your 'using mates' work best. This is a period of boundary setting and the foundation of containing daily structures: for instance regularly sleeping, eating and establishing a daily routine; there is no overestimating the importance of these factors. They begin to break habits that trigger using behaviour and clients begin to recognise their normal feelings. Leo was much the same as most in this regard and equally resistant to appearing to be told what to do. The central theme to his story was a description of abandonment and isolation, with an absent father and busy mother.

Toward the end of this period he described a time when he was in a relationship that started perfectly, that was 'everything that he had ever wanted' and that turned to utter and prolonged hatred and 'horrific break-up'. The way he spoke of this described an experience of merger with his then partner and his falling apart as it failed. I asked him if he could describe how this felt now in the session, he was unable to articulate this clearly and described feeling numb. Like before he used. He said that his head could think about it, but he was not able to feel it. His head was judging this and was taking him away from the experience.

Here I turned to using something of Gendlin's focussing technique (1978). I find it useful with clients who are particularly schizoid and show a marked psyche soma, head body split. I asked him to place the feeling in his body, where was it, he described it as all over, but mostly central to his abdomen. I asked if he could describe now what that felt like and he reported it to feel empty: 'terrifyingly empty'. I asked him if he could describe this feeling. It made him tearful, but he was able to and he was able to describe further that the feeling was apocalyptic and with a voice of silent screaming. We spent some time in this place, an experience of despair filling the room. After 20 minutes or so I wondered aloud if these feelings arose before his using and he agreed that they did or at least what he considered the precursors to them arose before he used. He found these experiences almost unbearable.

I asked if he had been left as a child. He laughed as if it were a predictable question perhaps posed in his earlier therapy making me feel belittled, cliché and inadequate as a therapist. He went on to say that his parents had said that he used to scream when left as a child, eventually they would come to him he would stop so they would go away: he would start screaming again. He believed himself to be left for long periods.

The course of the next three sessions took a similar vein deepening his experience of abandonment and despair. He returned repeatedly to the oceanic feelings that filled his life. We stayed with them for long periods in the sessions, until he was able to describe them. He also came to recognise a persecuting superego figure that defended him against this despair through destructive self-criticism.

I use a principally psychoanalytic model to think about this sort of symptomology. I see it to be indicative of a narcissistic wound founded upon a lack of maternal mirroring. Under these circumstances there would need to be a considerable amount of mirroring in the transference. (Kohut, 1971, 1977; Jakoby, 1990; Schwartz Salant, 1983)

I asked him to describe how he had come to be a user. He talked of gaining an identity at school as the kid who smoked dope and the one who could get drugs. He did not develop his drug using then, but drank a lot at university and then entered a series of jobs, which involved a great deal of crisis management. This enabled him to experience situations of stress, anxiety and rage which one might imagine mirrored his inner world. The difficult often violent crisis situations that he put himself in offered him a brief outlet for these omnipotent feelings.

He had the difficult relationship briefly outlined earlier, at the end of which he vowed never to be open like this again. He enrolled on an enlightenment intensive course, which involved a period of meditation, during which one would expect to have an epiphanal experience. Leo had such an experience, feeling that he had found his true essence in love. Six weeks after his return from this course he took up the use of heroin. Some months later he tried to clean up and returned to this enlightenment intensive training and again had an epiphanal experience after which he returned to heroin use on a fairly constant basis.

I understood Leo's need to be for a sense of self and holding through merger with others, in relationship, in meditation practice or via heroin use. Unable to tolerate any destructive feelings, ambivalence, envy or aggression, because of the 'too loose hold' of mothering in his early life he had to seek an external means of containing, repressing and expressing these feelings. His destructiveness was acted out through his using heroin, which beautifully mimics the merged state he had sought through relationship or meditation, but expresses the hatred of self and violence in the life that is led.

His ambivalent dependence upon the project and his dependence upon me brought these feelings into the safety of the therapeutic vessel. He was able after a few more sessions to begin to get nearer to expressing genuine feelings of anger and frustration towards me. At about this time I had had difficulty travelling to a session and was twenty five minutes late. He was accepting of my apologies, but his anger showed. We discussed the difficulties in his relationship with his wife, how she made not unreasonable, but to him unmeetable demands and that he could not bear this. He felt like using and giving up, he felt as if he disappeared into the emptiness inside of himself. I understood this as a transference comment about my demands upon him and his inability to bear them: I saw this as hopeful. His ability to hold his aggressive feelings and bring them into the session was a step nearer to him being able to martial them for himself. I made no explicit interpretation at the time, but waited until the next session.

It was clear that in a Winnicottian sense I had failed him (1963) and that the anxieties and difficulties that he was experiencing although denied were present in the room. His idealised need for me to be mirror to him was being challenged and coming to the surface.

The following session he was twenty-five minutes late and opened the session commenting that this was not retaliation for my previous lateness, but he had just been held up. He described that he had been able to become angry with his mother and realised that she might have changed. She was accepting of some of the things that he had to say, also his wife was being easier with him and able to accept more the struggle he was facing. However he felt he was stuck between fear of moving forward and taking responsibility for his feelings and actions and falling back into potential annihilation in his feelings of despair. He was afraid that his destructive feelings would destroy him and everything around him, but that if he did not act he would be destroyed by collapse into his inner emptiness.

I interpreted this to him at the time, both the retaliatory attack of being late and his attempts at reparation. I framed it in terms of a change in Leo from needing to idealise me or CORE, to feeling that he had just enough inside of himself to withstand my failure as a mirror. He was able to understand and think about this and to recognise his expression of anxiety about his annihilating and omnipotent destructive feelings, showing him poised to move forward and step away from his narcissistic ego defences.

He was challenged in group by another member of the community to join in more and had not felt comfortable doing so. When asked by me in the session about how this felt and where it felt in his body he reported the sensation emanating from his legs as if they were immovable. He felt that this was a paralysis brought about through his fear of contact with the others in the community. He asked if it was legitimate to ask that the others in the community should address working at this depth in groups. I encouraged him to bring this to the group. He did and received more support than he expected. Now for him other people existed outside of him as separate and related beings rather than objects of his psyche, which he needs omnipotently to control. Concomitantly he existed inside and could relate from this existing place to real others. He could now step toward others from a position of strength as he began to lose his narcissistic anxieties of inner emptiness.

I have used this description of our early work together to cover some the practical psychotheraputic actions we might use with this narcissistically wounded young man.

I would argue that the primary reason that so much can be achieved psychologically in a short time is the input of the body therapies toward stable foundation of the psyche in the body. All clients receive body acupuncture, as did Leo. He also practiced Qi Gong and received other body therapies. CORE is founded upon the twin interventions of psychotherapy and acupuncture; this offers a mental physical and spiritual framework within which to progress toward a deeper sense of his wholeness and health. The Qi Gong offered both a philosophical and physical framework in which to contain the up rush of some of his more powerful psychic experiences.

Now I will describe the end of this clients' time at CORE and the shift that separating from the project offered him from Wellwoods (1977) perspective of horizontal and vertical shifts. By the time Leo came to leave the project some 18 months after starting he had managed to give up some of his defensive ego structures leaving him open to an up rush of psychic energy. He became very excited by these experiences. I became anxious that so near the end of our time together we had generated a transition that he would be unable to contain and would regress catastrophically. His philosophical interests offered him support to contain the excitement without being overwhelmed by his manic feelings. He was able to use the energy constructively by consciously "surrendering to it".

This vignette is a description of a horizontal felt shift: a translation from one psychic experience to another. During the session Leo described the return of a feeling of anger, which we have linked to his infantile feeling about his mother's absence. He was frustrated. I asked him to describe where the feeling was physically. He located it in his lower abdomen. We moved imaginatively closer to the physical experience and he described his feelings. He mentioned that there were two angers, so I suggested he give images to both. The first was of a small angry child the second surprised him. As he drew himself closer to it he experienced not hate, which he was expecting, but 'compassion' creativity framed in angry terms.

The first image we thought about as his ego defence against the pain of his mother's absence and of how it offered him a means of imaginatively engaging with this injured part of himself. However the new second image was we felt connected to the feelings he had that were concealed under the defensive structure formed in infancy; these were compassion, and a lust for life, felt with anger. To him this was the more moving component to his experience and it was the most difficult for him to remain close to. Attached to it was a great deal of energy and something of an archetypal quality.

It is perhaps useful to notice the context in which this experience took place. We met at a 9:15 am in my room in central London. It is situated in a peaceful south-facing courtyard, which catches the sun. This meeting was on a bright early April morning, full of springtime energy, resonant of the experience my client was describing. The experience he described was of being conscious of spring evoking the springtime injuries of his early life and enabling him to feel how then he had managed them and that now he was able to bear the memory of those experiences sufficiently that he could experience something different within himself. I would imagine this as a re-orientation internally toward this archetypal life affirming energy without the frustration of his history. A felt shift. It is also worth noting that this shift was felt in the area of the body which in Qi Gong terms is the seat of the confluence of the energies from heaven and earth.

I would identify this as a horizontal felt shift as described by Wellwood, borne out of interpreting a meaning for the event through description of the experience and remaining true to it. Thereby allowing it to develop in the way Hillman argues we develop an image, he experienced a spring day, echoing the spring of his life and the frustration therein. In these feelings of now and then; in the tension between an imagined self, which is constructed, has a narrative and meaning, and the simple experience of spring with the energies this evokes, he changed his relationship to his defensive meanings for this experience. Entering into the experience in an inquisitive manner let some shift happen, that both changed the meaning frame he had created to contain his experiences and enabled him to experience more fully this archetypal creative energy within himself. As this was a translation of experience, all be it as a deepening, I would see it as a horizontal felt shift as described by Wellwood.

The second experience I will describe was during a group. This particular group was significant to him in that it was the last meeting of the whole community he would attend. He was aware of his narcissistic feelings toward this meeting wanting the whole event to be about his leaving. He saw this with some irony and wit, whilst neither denying nor resisting these feelings. As a matter of coincidence I was to facilitate this group. When it came to the meeting we were surprised that he did not need the kind of validation that he was expecting and that he was able to be in the room with the group of people that he had been close to for some time without the need to make demands upon them or himself.

During the meeting he was able to talk about these feelings and then shift to a place where he was simply able to be with his experience of the group and me. He described this as similar to experiences he had had whilst practicing meditation. However he felt that it had no meaning per se and no action required to sustain. It was simply there. One could chose an interpretation that describes this as a transferential experience of the mothering he had longed for on a personal or an archetypal level and indeed these might be component experiences that constellate around the kernel of this moment. This would though frame it as a pre egoic regression. However I would say, because of Leo's consciousness of the experience it falls within the frame of Wellwood's vertical shift. In some way it felt to both of us that it was the completion of a journey that this client had embarked upon at the beginning of his heroin use, containing all the components within it, but transcending them and their intrinsic meaning. Wellings would describe this as a moment of unintentioned presence. (2000. p200-1)

It has to be said that this particular client came to us with a sophisticated sense of his own path and a fairly stable ego structure, especially compared to the general population of the project. He was particularly orientated toward the transpersonal components of the project and used us to develop this aspect of his life. This is not usually the case the focus normally would be upon the psychodynamic or cognitive aspects of the work.

Notwithstanding this caveat this client in many ways shows the possibilities for the project and continues to develop in this direction. I continue to see him we meet currently in my private practice. He continues his practice both of meditation and Qi Gong our work has changed, as has he. He now has a successful career in IT, and his family has grown. His journey will continue and ours together for a while yet.

REFERENCES

Hillman, J. (1971) *Psychology: Monotheistic or Polytheistic?* Spring Dallas Texas.

Hillman, J. (1977) *Revisioning Psychology* London New York Harper Collins. Harper Perenial (1992)

Hillman, J (1989) *A Blue Fire*. London Routledge.

Jakoby, M. (1990) *Individuation and Narcissism: the psychology of self in Jung and Kohut*. Routledge

Kohut, H. (1971) *The Analysis of the Self,* New York International University Press.

Kohut, H. (1977) *The Restoration of the Self*. New York International University Press.

Samuels, A. (1985), *Jung and the Post-Jungians*, London RKP.

Schwartz-Salant (1982) *Narcissism and Character Transformation*. Toronto Inner City Books.

Gendlin, E. T. (1978). *Focusing*. New York: Bantam Books.

Winnicott, D.W. (1963) *Dependence in Infant Care, In Child Care and in the Psycho-Analytic Setting: The maturational process and the facilitating environment* London Karnac.

Washburn, M (1994) *Transpersonal Psychology in Psychoanalytic Perspective*. New York SUNY press.

Wellings, N. Wilde McCormick, E. (2000) *Tranpersonal Psychology: theory and practice*. London, New York: Continuum.

Wellwood, J. (1977) Meditation and the unconscious: A new perspective 1977 *Journal of Transpersonal Psychology*.

26. WORKING WITH THE HEART

Serge Beddington-Behrens

Serge believes that the core of who we are is to be found in matters of the heart, which have been much neglected in recent Western culture. Scientific materialism cannot explain things mystical, spiritual, feminine and loving. In his practice he explores with his clients the state of their hearts – how can feelings of ease, healthy relationships, happiness and meaning come back into our lives? What is required to grow a heart life is first of all to want to change. A healthy, balanced diet might include all or some of meditation, music, prayer, being in the presence of nature – all leading to a deeper awareness of the sacred world inside us. This can lead to a natural awareness of being part of a wider plan in an interconnected world. Talking about aspects of an expanded heart is one thing, but living the journey is another. We may need to learn about the shadowy sources of our past conditioning and to work through this sacred challenge to develop a happier personal life and contribute to a healthier world. It is one of the most important activities that any of us can be involved in at this time.

This contribution is so simple and so obvious that its significance could be lost in our busy material world. Serge is not afraid to say how working on the heart can bring us health and wealth in special and different ways, and his own experience comes through in this profound but heartfelt message.

Serge Beddington-Behrens, *M.A. (Oxon.), Ph.D., K.S.M.L. is a transpersonal psychotherapist, writer and spiritual educator. He gives lectures and teaches seminars and retreats in England, Europe, Russia and America. Co-founder of the Institute for the Study* *of Conscious Evolution in San Francisco and, more recently, of Inward Bound Training, he is a trustee of the Wrekin Trust, which is dedicated to advancing spiritual education in the U.K. He is the author of* Entering the Mystery, *a series of CDs chronicling different aspects and challenges of the Spiritual path, and of* The Politics of Heartwork, *to be published in 2005. He has a private psychotherapy practice in Gloucestershire and London. For information on his heart-oriented workshops and retreats please contact him on 01451 860726 or at serge@hampnettglos.fsnet.co.uk*

Our hearts are the core of who we are, and within their deeper essence are to be found all those many qualities that make us feel fully alive and connect us to our profounder humanity. Despite this, the life of the inner heart tends, sadly, to be much neglected in our Western culture.

This negation of the subtler life of the heart is not new. It is connected to the whole rise of our scientific materialism, where only what can be seen, touched, and measured is given value and where things that cannot be explained rationally – things mystical and feminine and loving and sacred – are deemed unimportant. At school, for example, I never learned anything about my heart. Our motto was 'A healthy mind in a healthy body'! Similarly at university. There I was taught to know about all sorts of things but never to look into my heart, which is actually the true source of our wisdom and power.

We pay an enormous price for this exclusion of the domain of heart. Indeed, I would suggest that many of our major world problems reflect this omission. At one level, I see our planet being out of balance and polluted and riven by conflict, essentially because we, as a species, have not tapped into the laws of harmony or touched into the qualities of reverence, kindness, compassion, wisdom, love, conciliation and forgiveness that can only be accessed in the deeper layers of the heart.

When clients come to see me for psychotherapy, I always look closely at how healthy their hearts are. I believe that many of their problems – especially their inability to feel happy, at ease, enjoy healthy relationships, or find meaning – can be traced back to a dysfunctional heart life or, in many instances, to a virtually non-existent one. The problem is that without a healthy heart life, our capacity to handle life's inevitable vicissitudes is diminished and even if we are wealthy outwardly, we may still tend to experience a sense of inner impoverishment. In fact, our hearts allow us to live meaningful lives and to respond appropriately to different situations. One of the main reasons that so many people today seek their ecstasies through drugs or alcohol is that they are bereft of the experience of natural joy that would come out of a properly lived heart life.

When a person's deeper heart life begins emerging, it is signalled by the presence of awe and gratitude, a greater ease of being and ability to appreciate the beauty and blessedness of life together with an enhanced capacity to accept life the way it is. As someone in one of my 'Heart Aerobics' workshops said recently, 'I can only begin to be me and to feel a full human being and approach the wonderful mystery of God through this awakening of my heart. How important it is to work at this awakening!'

So surely, then, what our world needs if it is to function better – indeed, if it is to avoid disaster – is the emergence of more awakened or deeper-hearted human beings. My experience of such people is that they are not afraid to take courageous stands on behalf of a healthier world and to confront the darker sides of life.

So let us now ask ourselves: what is required for this to take place? How may we begin to 'grow' our heart life?

First, we must want to do so. We must be aware of the price we pay for our small-heartedness and the benefits to be gained from becoming larger-hearted. It is helpful to seek out the often-inspirational presence of those who already are in that state. I always feel valued in their company. I never feel put down or that I have to be anything that I am not, and this in turn, reminds me to value myself. And when I value myself, I am reminded of how important it is to make time to love and respect myself, which implies that I must take good care of my heart and feed it well!

The Heart Diet

And what most feeds our heart is our choosing to live a life where, instead of always letting ourselves be led by externals – doing what society or 'others' think we should do – we choose to 'follow our bliss.' We give up compromising ourselves and instead honour what we discover to be our inner truth at any time. For where our truth lies, so too does our real self. To help us come into this new space, I would recommend the following heart diet.

First on the menu is Meditation. This is a very important heart food. As the restless mind is gradually quietened, the heart can gently begin to open. Music is also significant. Certain sublime pieces cause the heart to resonate in harmonious patterns and in doing so, it can begin gently to blossom, as if it were falling in love. In a similar way, prayer can be very powerful as is having someone or some thing or some cause to be passionate about. Our hearts love feeding on the beautiful – sacred art, soulful literature, etc, and, most important, they can be protected by our avoiding things and people that 'uglify' our lives.

Being in the presence of nature is also very important; its pure essence can activate the remembrance of our own pure heart essence. It is similar to sitting with an enlightened spiritual master. This is because their beautiful open heartedness and purity of being can cause our often blocked and sticky little hearts to vibrate quicker. As this occurs, we can begin releasing some of the dense energies or toxicities that may have accumulated in our hearts over the years.

As our hearts expand more and more and begin revealing their hitherto hidden treasures, we realise that we have a new and inherently sacred world available inside ourselves. We can use this not only to heal ourselves more – to bring a greater quality and value into our personal lives – but also to add new dimensions to our relationships. Here, we realise that so long as we are fixated in our small (clenched)-heartedness, we can never see the world through our lover's eyes; we can never appreciate them properly, love them unconditionally, deal with them wisely, forgive them effectively, or stay open-hearted when the going gets tough.

When deeper heart begins to flower, however, it becomes completely natural and easy to accomplish all of the above. Many people also report that they realise that the purpose of their lives is to serve the great divine plan, to work to help create a new 'culture of love' (as the spiritual teacher Peter Deunov saw it) on the planet. In this state, many people come to see that they are not and never have been, separate from their world. Not only are they in the world but they also are the world, and while they may have their own personal families to look after, their heart will have become big enough to include the entire human family, regardless of race, religion, class or colour. The bigger our hearts, then, the wider the sphere of our responsibilities.

However, talking about expanded heart spaces and actually living 'out of' those places are two very different things. The journey from small heart into deep heart is a gradual one and there are many stages that the heart pilgrim goes through and many obstacles to be circumvented along the way. For essentially what hearts contain is light – spiritual light – and what spiritual light does, among other things, is that it illumines our darkness for us, shows us where our hearts may also be wounded, that is, numb, cold and clenched.

We may need to understand that our heart wounds can come from many different shadowy sources. They may be the result of unresolved and still-haunting memories of traumas spilling over from past lives. We may even be carrying wounds belonging to our ancestors that have never been effectively resolved. We may also be suffering from traumas relating to a difficult birth or even have our inner heart 'invaded' by some unwanted form of 'spirit attachment'.

Similarly, if we will have been raised by soulless and small-hearted parents, or caregivers, who never knew how to enjoy or celebrate us, but who instead, pumped us full of their anxieties and resentments, our hearts may still lie small and dormant, never sparked off properly. Until we take steps to heal ourselves, we may remain insecure, emotionally damaged and deeply fearful and suspicious of life's joys for which we also secretly yearn. This emotional abuse can be just as toxic for the heart as sexual abuse, and many who have suffered in this way, may grow up to associate love and intimacy with pain and rejection.

Furthermore, if we are someone who has – figuratively speaking, 'given their hearts away' to someone and not known how to reclaim them afterwards, we may well be left with half or even a quarter of a heart! Our hearts can become further damaged from working all our lives in a 'cold, bottom line' corporate culture which can require us continually to split off from what is most warm, loving and tender about ourselves.

If we truly wish to live with greater open-heartedness, it has to be a conscious decision on our part to do so. In certain instances, it may require a radical re-alignment of our entire lives. Since our hearts cannot begin opening until they feel more healed and secure, often a lot of work may be involved, at many different levels. For the person who is willing to undertake this eminently sacred challenge, and to surrender more and more to the tutelage or guidance of their hearts, there are many blessings to be gained as the higher realms of heart are very sublime and peaceful. If we wish for a happier personal life and a healthier world, I see heart work as being one of the most important things that any of us can do at this time.

27. THE INFLUENCE OF FAMILY CONSTELLATIONS ON FEELING AT HOME IN HOLLAND

Anja Brasser

Anja Brasser found Hellinger's technique of Family Constellations very helpful in gaining a deeper sense of her own identity by resolving unfinished business. She illustrates the value of this approach with the stories of three people living in Holland but who have foreign roots. They are helped to feel more at ease with themselves and happy about living in Holland. The resulting grounding helps people feel at home wherever they are.

Anja Brasser *(b. 1946) obtained a degree in Social Pedagogy at the University of Amsterdam (1987). She has worked for the Transpersonal Association in Poland, Hungary and Russia. She is internationally oriented and is interested in intercultural citizenship. Her work with Family, Career, and Organisation constellations is known for its deep reach and meeting with the soul. She is a member of the Dutch board of Family and Organisation constellations, called SONT. She is responsible for programming in the board of Dutch Female Consultants: NVOA.*

Introduction

In spite of being born and growing up in Holland it took a long time to feel at home in my home country. During a long period of personal growth I found out several things about this. I felt more at home working for EUROTAS in other European countries. Working with what I sense as the greater soul of the Eastern European people gave me more ground in Holland. My soul received nourishment, which helped to heal the loneliness I experienced. The reason for this, besides many past life experiences in Eastern

European countries, was that my soul was much connected with family members who died at an early age. Because of these events, which were traumatic for my parents, I identified with them. My parents could not mourn them. The pain was too much.

Through several family constellations I learned that I was identified with this little sister who died after four days of life and with the first husband of my mother who died after three months of marriage. By resolving this identification I became more grounded in Holland. As a child, schoolmate,s because of the communist background of my parents, cheated me. In several negative circumstances I experienced what it was like not to be a member of Dutch society.

I realized that this position and experiences in my home country were a big obstacle in feeling at home in Holland. It was even too difficult to do a constellation about it in Holland. So I decided to go to Germany. In this great constellation, political issues were included, as well as my Dutch compatriots and my parents and their comrades who died in the war, and my little sister.

This took place two years ago and slowly I feel and experience that I am a real Dutch woman with a large soul (it's still great to work in other European countries) and I am becoming successful in my work. This was due to the public honouring of my father and his underground work during the war which was of great influence to open myself for success in my home country.

Interview 1

Nina (1970) came to Holland because of love. She married a Dutch man in 1998. She said: "I don't feel myself Dutch, more Slovakian plus something extra. I feel more European. Having friends make me feel at home. Before Holland I also lived in England and Germany. For the last year she feels at home in the Netherlands."

"The family constellation was an important addition to my life. It gave more clarity to parts about the puzzle of my life. A part my life journey was clarified by it. Especially because it gave me an understanding of why I am as I am and how important my Slovakian background is. Through this I can find my place in the Netherlands more easily. Because of the growth of my self-awareness about my roots I feel more powerful. I can have more courage to be myself. To say what I think and to express my opinion."

The last constellation was especially important. In this (one to one) constellation Nina worked with her place in the family. Growing up without her (biological) father has given her the feeling of: "I am worth nothing and have no right to exist". During the constellation we worked with the family and her place in it. Especially the words of her mother: "You are one of us. You belong to us. You are my daughter" were important.

After the family constellations I am more proud of my country and the town I come from. I wish I had done family constellations earlier.

Nina did 5 family constellations in two years about the following subjects:
1. About career and her wish to be a photographer.
2. How to deal with a violent (ex) husband
3. What about finding a home?
4. When I visit my family there are a lot of arguments. How to handle this?
5. About self-respect. What is the barrier and how do I get it?

Interview 2

Ora. (b. 1958) I married with a Dutch man out of love.

In 1989 I came to Holland. My family emigrated from Iraq to Israel in 1950. Because of my marriage I got struck in Israel. I had the idea and the wish to become freer and to develop more my being an individual. Especially also in my work as a choreographer. Now I feel that with hard work that I get what I dreamed for.

I feel that 'international citizen' is the right term for me. I call myself an earthling. I am a child of the earth. I feel like that. Then I am Israeli from an Iraqi background, and then Jewish. Yes I feel at home at the Netherlands. I feel at home especially after the individual constellation we did with my female ancestors. Now after five years I have the courage to say I am Jewish. The great influence was the programming coming from an Islamic back round (Iraq). It was hard work to free myself from it.

The family constellation gave me deep insights into underlying patterns of my ancestors. I learned to accept their importance. I learned to know and cultivate my own landscape. The most important was the programming of being weak as a woman. After my divorce I felt I was nobody. I felt very fearful. That was the reason I wanted at first to go back to Israel. During the individual sessions I realized that I am a product of my background. I carried a lot of their sorrow. Now I am free to enjoy and be powerful. And I have the power to stay in the Netherlands as a single woman. During the last month I feel I am a woman. During the last constellation we worked with my violence against men. During the constellation we found out that it had to do with my father. He has to be more as a man because he was not been in the army. Because of this subject, being in Israel and being Jewish, Ora felt as a victim. (The other side of being a victim is being a perpetrator - AB). During the constellation we also set up the Palestinians and the Israelis. Ora always had the feeling that she wanted to do something big to resolve this terrible violence between them. We also set up Israeli and Palestinians. Looking to each other there came peace. It freed Ora from her responsibility of doing something about it. Now she does not feel guilty again that as an Israeli she is living abroad. She said: "I can leave it there and feel peace inside. I am happy in the Netherlands. I am free to choose where I want to live. I belong here. To come into contact with the unseen reality gave me tools to ground myself in reality."

All together Ora did nine constellations, four in a group and five individual based, during the last 3 years. Items were:
1. About her female ancestors to develop her female side.
2. Her career. She after it developed her own course with dance and power animals.
   Title: energetic gateways.
3. Her relationship with men.
4. Her relationship with men focused on her father

Interview 3.

Aster: It was mainly my mother who wanted to leave Indonesia; she was fearful because of the political situation. Both my mother and father are of Dutch-Indonesian background. We came to Holland in 1957. Born in 1955, I was almost three years old. For myself I'd say I'm Indo-European. When I am in Indonesia I'm European, and when I am in Holland I feel Asian.

Nowadays I do feel at home in Holland. I feel I'm very Dutch in my mentality, rather rational and with Calvinistic work ethic. I have often had a hard time expressing my more sensitive and intuitive aspects, qualities I associate with my Indonesian origin. I'm still trying to give these qualities full play and also to apply them within my work. It's hard to say exactly what makes me feel at home in Holland now.

The first constellation (Aster did two constellations in 2003) was about intimate relationships.

The inner images about relationships had to do with the family-background of my mother. We set up the father and brother of my mother, along with the boy who I realized then was the first one she fell in love with. The Indonesians killed them in 1945.

Being Dutch-Indian subjects, they were held in a camp by Indonesians (Indonesia is a former Dutch colony, which in 1945 declared its independence and was internationally recognized as an independent republic in 1948. Before that time Indonesia was called Dutch-India) I can still see the images of the constellation. It certainly made an impression.

Later (after the second constellation) about my work, I went to Indonesia for a month, together with my two sisters. This time being in Indonesia I felt very European (it's different every time).The first time I went back I recognized the sounds, fragrances and the atmosphere. Maybe because I was so young when we left Indonesia. During our holiday my sisters and I visited the grave of my grandfather, the brother of my mother and my mother's first love. After that we also went to the Java Sea, because my other grandfather and the eldest brother of my father had perished there in the Second World War. The grief of my father about this has always been even further away from our family life than the loss my mother experienced (of this you can hear her loyalty to her father - AB). The first time I visited the grave of my mother's father was the first time I felt he was my grandfather. Before that, he only was the father of my mother. During the second constellation, about my work, I was irritated when my Indonesian background surfaced once again.

The manager was then set up in the constellation. He didn't see much perspective for me in the firm, and has lost his job in the meantime because of malfunctioning. After this constellation I discussed my Indonesian origin at work, and now (also with a support of a coach) I see more possibilities of integrating and applying all my qualities.

It's hard to say what made me feeling at home in Holland. Since the last time I returned to Indonesia, for the first time together with my sisters, old family patterns emerged strongly. Now the three of us are having therapy for this.

Between my eldest sister and me, my mother had a miscarriage. I didn't use to feel at home in our family. (Note of the interviewer: maybe the dynamic of perpetrator-victim relationship still plays a role within the family and also the miscarriage of her mother). I did decide, however, after I returned from Indonesia this last time, to enjoy all my sources of power and inspiration. I can write the scenario of my life myself.

Family and Career constellations are an important and powerful method to free the soul from unaware identification. The being of the soul as present in the here and now gives the person more possibility of being grounded. Grounding gives the possibility to feel at home, wherever you are.

28. THE PSYCHOTHERAPEUTIC TIME MACHINE

Vladimir Maikov

Vladimir believes that psychotherapy can be assimilated in to a sort of time travel. This idea is clearly present in many pioneer works of transpersonal psychologists, especially works by Stanislav Grof. Psychotherapy also can be considered as informational-energetic interactions in expanded states of consciousness. Both psychological and healing time-machines have the same nature: their main engine is the holistic state of consciousness, entering into which we can travel in time, genuinely connect to traumatic events, and integrate them in the present. The metaphor we introduced of the psychotherapeutic time-machine allows us to understand better many elements of the psychotherapeutic experience.

In his mature works, Carl Gustav Jung assimilated the process of psychotherapy to the "great work" of medieval alchemists, who managed to explore secret mental transmutation under the mask of transforming base metals into the noble ones. Borrowing a metaphor from Marcel Proust, it is possible to characterize psychotherapy "as a search for lost time," absorbed in the world of our experiences, but not incorporated into our daily presence. The language of this alchemical work is still dark, holds much back, and is mostly unspoken. It is a lived language of experience, not just the language of speaking and naming. Here the following rule entirely works: we must have an experience first – understanding will come later and can never substitute for an experience.

Vladimir Maikov is a practitioner and author who has made a significant contribution to the development of transpersonal psychology in Russia. He teaches and lectures in Russia and internationally and has written and edited a number of books in this field as well as developing training programmes. He is a senior research associate of the Institute of Philosophy at the Russian Academy of Sciences and a Board Member of EUROTAS.

Consciousness and Ritual

Everything in the world is subject to change. Even rocks eventually are erased; climate ceaselessly varies. Living systems, while they are alive, maintain relative stability due to an openness to the world instead of monadic isolation. Human beings support a relative constancy of consciousness, and the continuity of "I," exchanging information, eating food, establishing identifiable personality structures, "habits," and finally, creating diverse social orders and institutions. A human being is alive while she "breathes" in flows of dialogue/energy with the world, herself, and other beings.

A feature of living systems is that they develop by leaps when rather uniform, more or less predictable movement, reaches a point of bifurcation. The ways in which the system will develop depend both on itself and from surrounding energy and information flows. If a cell is affected in a moment at bifurcation, then instead of remaining healthy, it can develop along a cancerous pathway of bifurcation. The chemical reaction will proceed in other ways if – at a certain moment – a catalyst is added. The universe will develop differently if in some critical situation a handful of electrons is lacking. In the physics experiment with two slits, an electron will pass through one or the other slit depending on some unpredictable conditions, perhaps depending on the state of the whole universe. Also, a thunder will burst, if traveling in a thought psychological time-machine, the past is thoughtlessly reshuffled, casually having crushed seeds of the viable future and thereby crystallizing an adverse or fatal script of development. Truly, for those who are blind – a tangle of times is like a tangle of snakes: trying to untangle it – one will be bitten.

Psychotherapy and other practices of healing, self-knowledge, and transformation can also be considered as informational-energetic interactions in expanded states of consciousness – when our tacit, wounded experiences, breaking through protection, through barriers of space and time, are capable of tunneling in through the past to reunite with our presence in the present moment. And at times, through mere touching, we can restore a lost connection with a caress, which did not suffice in childhood, or we heal a drama of love, recollecting the broken "fabric of consciousness."

We shall note one more feature of living systems, which according to a modern science is that they are specific "amplifiers" of primary chaos. At a quantum-mechanical level, individual events are spontaneous. At the level of the everyday world, determinism appears to reign. The thrown stone falls downwards, rivers flow to the sea, the polarity of the magnetic field of the earth remains relatively stable. Changing weather situations have their beginning, development, and mechanisms.

"Mechanisms" of a similar sort work in our mental life. The machines of desire "work" in us forcing us to do something again and again, to keep searching for something, or obsessively to scroll by stuck ideas. And these cycles are supported at a level of the body, at a level of muscle knots, at a level of self-perpetrating emotional and mental circles, at a level of repetitive images. Machines of emotions, machines of perception, corporeal machines, characteristic gestures and reactions...

So there is a connection between the degree of freedom of living systems and primary quantum spontaneity at a fundamental level of the world. As Terence McKenna (1988) says, living systems, in the process of their evolution, generate more and more freedom. The plant is more free than a single cell; an animal already moves on dry land. A human being is even more free and, having consciousness, can not only change the external environment but also move in the world of imagination, travel in psychological space and time.

On such travels, consciousness also passes critical points and rites of passage that are reflected in structures of myths and processes of initiation. The pioneer of this theme in European ethnology, A. van Gennep, in his book Rites of Passage (1961), remarked that in traditional societies the initiation into the new order and steady rhythms of life was always carried out through rituals of death, painful experiences, and personal and social chaos.

When society is plunged into chaos, history becomes a nightmare, interfering with everyone's life. The world of neurotics or psychotics, too, is a nightmare, in which feelings, ideas, and acts which are inadequate for the present and are connected by a spatial-temporary tunnel with traumatic events are obsessively repeated. The force of chaos becomes a nightmare, protective mechanisms are destroyed, but inside, it is possible to find salvation if one can find hope and overcome fear and open oneself to change and freedom.

In expanded states of consciousness we are able to enter into resonance with all events of life. Here, it's as though our rigid structure "melts" and we have an opportunity for much wider choice. It is possible not to choose something concrete, but to leave open the opportunity of choice; it does not make sense to program experiences; it is better to drop all expectations and prescriptions, allowing everything to be as it is and to support it as such. Such support corresponds to a new type of ritual – an evolutionary one, and replaces an old type of ritual saving human beings from chaos by means of the law and repetitions. In this respect, rituals are simply situational forms and ways of assembly, support, and the rest of developing consciousness assists people not to be lost in groundless freedom.

Languages of Experience

Before introducing the concept of a psychotherapeutic time-machine as a key metaphor of the process of soul-healing, it is necessary to present one more theme. Since the time of C. G. Jung and M. Merleau-Ponty, modern psychology has made a distinction between the languages of diverse psychotherapeutic schools and the languages of experience. The languages of experience are more primordial, in the sense of being fresh, not edited perceptions of the world. Examples of such languages could be the: (1) "language of dharmas" of Buddhist psychology; (2) languages of the Tao, Way, in Taoism; (3) languages of mytho-drama, where the levels of cosmological, historical, and personal mythology are woven together; (4) languages of holons or gestalts of experiences; and (5) languages of psycho-semantical topology. These languages have many dimensions, from the corporeal to the spiritual. So the corporeal dimensions, for example, consist of our corporeal reactions, stereotypes of behaviour, corporeal knots, illnesses, and ecstasies which are manifested in the time of psychotherapeutic sessions and daily situations. There are also emotional dimensions, with their topology of emotions, topology of psycho-semantical landscapes, and so on.

But each of the dimensions of the body, emotions, languages, thoughts, and vision is not torn off from the others. These dimensions are interconnected. And the corporeal dimension, the corporeal block, having reached its peak and having resolved into a new landscape, can pass through the specific sorts of conditions, through the tunnel, say, even to completely different visionary or emotional landscapes. And having dived into a well, having climbed up a mountain, having performed some physical feat, we can experience a condition of flight or birth revealed in multidimensional landscapes of experiences.

The topology of experience, or the topology of a Path, has a history in the sense that within each of us is manifested a path that is relentlessly and progressively enfolding and unfolding. Everything that is a part of our Path enters into us and forms various nuclei, layers, landscapes, an interlacing of our soul and body. Our gift of language is advanced during these interactions. Our ability to govern situations and to supervise them is a consequence of the Path through which we have passed, a consequence of whether or not we were conscious in critical situations of a trauma, ecstasy, choice.

"Path" is a key metaphor of what we are. It is an enfoldment of what we are in interaction with other people and with circumstances. There is an old story about this: In a valley there lived a mother with her small son. The mother told the son about a wonderful man, his father, whom by all means he would meet someday when the son would grow up. Once when the right constellations were formed and the signs appeared, the mother and son set off on a trip to meet the father. They departed in the early morning, crossed a valley, climbed mountains, wandered on paths, had a rest in caves, passed groves, and, at last, by the end of the day, close to sunset, came into a valley…to their own house, entering it through the opposite side. The boy saw an unusual being, tall, shining, smiling, coming towards him. He realized it was his father, who now embraced him. The search was over. The meaning of this story is that there are no children without adults, and that adults want to be a child again and the child, an adult, and so this is their way to freedom, which they achieve simultaneously.

One can ask isn't it easier simply to open the door on the other side of the house and to show the boy his father? Our life is arranged such way that we understand and we esteem something only after passing through a journey, only after having overcome some barrier. Only then can we comprehend something, having pieced it together along the way, having formed new landscapes of experience and "bodies of consciousness," with the help of which we can now apprehend and esteem this world in a new fashion.

These laws of consciousness are fixed in the structures of myths, in the structures of processes of initiations in all human cultures. The journey contains critical points of transition. A. van Gennep, in his book Rites of Passage, writes that in ancient communities there were always rituals of initiation, situations of painful experiences, confrontations with death. For example, when teenagers were initiated into adulthood they spent some days in darkness, which symbolized a cosmic womb of space, mother darkness. They experienced the process of death themselves as teenagers and heard from elders the story about the creation of the world, about the origin of the tribe. Here again the language of landscapes of experience is close to the language of myths.

There are two basic mythological cycles. In one – the cosmological-cycle of myths – it is related about how the First Man came about and how the universe, gods, and the tribe were created. This experience is in some sense present in our mentality and according to modern research, surfaces in consciousness during re-experiencing one's own conception and birth.

The other cycle is one of heroic (historical) myths; here the hero's journey is related, about his birth, youth, and calling. Each hero hears the call and journeys in pursuit of it. He finds the teacher, and magic abilities, confronts death, passes tests and temptations. The hero must win out over creatures and passions that symbolize ignorance and fears which are rooted in the unconscious and that symbolize lack of wholeness and lack of connectivity with other people, ones self and the world as a whole. Only after passing all these tests, each of which can be fatally dangerous, does the hero become king, find integrity, and come back home, establishing a new order.

These two cycles are experienced by people in concrete forms, individually, for which the term "personal mythology" has been coined (Feinstein & Krippner, 1988) to account for the uniqueness of each individual case.

According to modern linguistics, our knowledge is constrained by different languages. The language of experience, in its development, continues to gain more and more freedom from verbal forms. There are also languages of visual thinking and languages of virtual realities. And, finally, languages of direct communication seem to be possible. For example, in a number of ayahuasca shamanic rituals in the Amazon River region, language becomes a three-dimensional dynamic formation. And what the participants of a ritual speak of becomes visible for all other participants. It is true telepathy—not the reading of ideas but vision of all levels of landscapes of experiences. In this direct communication with others there is no distance between the people involved. The fatal duality between me and others, between me and torn-off, alienated parts of myself, is overcome. But this clarity and directness, describing such experience, is nothing other than the expression of the fundamental ontological property of holistic consciousness – the effects of all-connectivity.

In all the deepest philosophical and religious-mystical systems and schools there is no distance in consciousness between one point and another. Consciousness is unitary and devoid of qualifications. And consequently, all-connectivity means that there is no difference between me now and me somewhere in another period of life. There is no difference in speed and completeness of communications between face-to-face dialogue of people and dialogue over distances of tens of thousand of kilometers. This means that what occurs in psychotherapy as time-travel is in some sense also a realization of this fundamental quality of consciousness.

All-Connectivity and Communication

Let's think more about how this property of all-connectivity is realized in modern psychotherapy and communication technologies. Some tens of thousands of years ago language arose from primal cries and gestures as a means of direct influence of one human being upon another. According to Julian Jaynes (1976), even during the time of the ancient Greeks, human beings had the so-called "divided brain." That is, the left and right hemispheres were connected to one another rather poorly. The voice of another person and one's own voice both were perceived equally as one's own voice. And the voice of another person had the same demanding action as one's own voice. When language, as the external organ of consciousness, began to come back into consciousness, to be enfolded in it, then there appeared the first distinction between me and another. Somewhere around five thousand years B.C. writing arose. With the help of writing it began possible to fix events and to transfer them into another epoch. When this experience came into consciousness, there appeared the distinction between a symbol and reality, map and territory. There was an expansion of horizon, knowledge of other tribes and epochs. Writing became the first prototype of the time-machine. Reading became a certain kind of travel in space and time.

The next stage of the communication revolution is connected to the rise of the polis – city-state. The ancient Greeks thus invented a unique "organ of consciousness" – "agora." Agora was the marketplace in the ancient Greek city and it was also an assembly of the free citizens, where all questions could be publicly discussed. Everybody's voice was audible by everyone else. It was the experience of collective discussion, when everything could be clarified in the presence of every citizen. When this experience came into consciousness it became the experience of democracy and law. And that which we have now as examples of democracy differs very little from Greek-Roman law. Thus, democracy is characterized by freedom of public manifestation. There are public laws which guarantee freedom of public manifestations, and legal guaranties are created to ensure that I shall not be killed for those manifestations: that I have an opportunity to discuss all problems; that I have autonomy and freedom; that I can complete some ideas without the fear that it will be interfered with by others. Civilization and democracy create some guarantees that make it possible to think. Greek philosophy appeared only then—when there were these opportunities of freedom. And, in thinking, we can travel into deeper layers of dynamic landscapes of consciousness in other worlds and times. We can collect and condense them into certain compact formations which we refer to as concepts. That is how we are given the opportunity to reflect about the world.

The next level of the communication revolution was the invention of book printing, which took place in the epoch of Magellanian discoveries. Unique, hand-written books became accessible to a wide circle of people. And, suddenly, after this revolution, came the epoch of the Renaissance – an unheard-of blooming of culture, freedom, and the arts. Book printing, as the experience of the development of new flows of information, gave human beings an experience of connectivity of a new order. Spatial-temporal borders became even more extended. The Renaissance was a revival of Greek-Roman civilization in Europe which had come through the Arabian world. With the help of such a "cultural time-machine" it became possible to expand the horizons of the world even further and to establish communication with more remote epochs.

The present stage of the informational-communicative revolution is an epoch of mass communications – telephone, radio, TV, computer. Thus, my friend in New Zealand and I are no longer kept apart by a the period of days or weeks it takes to deliver a letter. There is no distance – all-connectivity of consciousness. The informational-communicative revolution is embodied to the greatest degree in computers, as they already can now transfer huge flows information. What will happen when the huge computing abilities of the computer will enter into consciousness? It is possible that with the help of new informational-communicative technology, which has a peak now in multimedia and virtual reality, that humankind can open to new speeds of communication, real telepathy, that is, to direct dialogue between minds, to three-dimensional visual language, to inclusion in the communication of all landscapes of consciousness.

Alpha, beta, and theta rhythms of the hemispheres of the brain usually have a little different frequency for each human. And after noticing that in the meditation of Zen monks there is a synchronization of alpha rhythms, scientists have made simple devices which catch the individual frequency of alpha rhythms of the subject and trained synchronization of hemispheres (Hutchison, 1994). Thus, communication between the two hemispheres improved. The mechanism of a resonance began to work when both hemispheres entered into one rhythm, and what earlier did not cooperate, became connected, the distance disappeared: all-connectivity of unconsciousness.

Irrespective of the concrete brain mechanisms of all-connectivity of consciousness at the moment of instant realization, problems arise. The body, in which traumas are sealed and wounds of previous life are stored, cannot maintain such experience. All conflicts are soaked up, as though by a huge vacuum cleaner, in madness. To be able to maintain such a condition of consciousness, it is necessary to pass through steps of radical psycho-spiritual transformation. And then the transformed body itself will support a holistic state of consciousness.

Some Mechanisms of Healing

In psychotherapy we deal with achieving wholeness – both psychosomatical and psychological. A series of important experiments that could be applied in this area was made by Braud (1991), one of which experiments was carried out with feedback thorough time. The data of the random numbers generator were recorded by a computer, and were shown to various operators later. According to probability theory, in the case of the random numbers generator, we should expect half zeroes and half ones. But when this device was influenced by the subject – not a psychic – it was often found, say, that the number of zeroes exceed by far the number of ones: the probability of that event being random is very low. In a more complex series of experiments there was no prior influence on a computer. Here skeptics, who do not believe in such outcomes, served as subjects. In this situation an identical number of zeroes and ones was obtained, that is, the probability was no different than the case of no influence. In still other experiments, the device was shown to people who had differing degrees of expectation about whether the displacement of probability is possible or not. For the people who believed that the influence of probability is possible, the influence of probability really occurred. For the people who were the skeptics, the influence of probability did not occur. What phenomenon do we have here? It is feedback in time: Somehow the flow of events registered by the random numbers generator already "knew" about the future event that will take place at the moment of registration. In other words, there was some influence from the future, backward causality.

If we connect this idea of feedback through another person as spatial-temporal communication which occurs at the moment of healing with the idea of in time-travel, the following conclusion can be reached: in the process of healing there are not only current events always present, but also causes of these events located in the remote past. And healing occurs not only at the moment of encounter between doctor and patient, healer and healed one, but also in some sense it occurs before. The image of these temporal resonances leads to one of the ideas of the psychotherapeutic time-machine. Seemingly trivial events – the encounter of doctor and patient – appear to be by mutual travels. And to correct something in the present, it is necessary to travel mutually in time to the sources of illness. Perhaps, we are not so far from the practice of shamanism and folk healing: a medicine man speaks, "A spell was put on you, someone jinxed you, and so it is necessary to remove the spell" – which happened somewhere else in time.

According to Tibetan medicine, each illness has a karmic reason, that is, something went awry in the realm of all-connectivity of consciousness. For example, if a person has acted egoistically or has offended someone or has killed someone, since consciousness is all-connected, in killing another, for example, you kill a part of yourself and thereby sever communication with your own death. And by breaking off this communication you lose the opportunity to pass through the ritual of death and rebirth, that is, opening yourself to new freedom through this ritual. Such, is the course of illnesses according to the ancient view of Tibetan medicine.

In this respect, both psychological and healing time-machines have the same nature: their main engine is the holistic state of consciousness, entering into which we can travel in time, genuinely connect to traumatic events, and integrate them in the present. From this angle, it is possible to understand the concept of synchronicity of C. G. Jung that psychological events related to psychological trauma are not connected as reason and consequence but arise simultaneously from a deeper level.

Psychological Time

So we introduced some key themes which are elements, aspects of the psychotherapeutic time-machine. We recall the theme of critical points of transition and informational-energetic surges. We also recall the theme of a direction of evolution of humankind towards realization of a fundamental property of consciousness – all-connectivity, that is, recollections of all landscapes of consciousness, all landscapes of experience, establishment of communication between them both within the individual psyche as well as between people, and transition to new languages of communications. The various stages of evolution of such languages were in some sense steps in the development of the ability of time-travel, breaking through spatial and temporary distances with the help of new language and new faculties. And we can recall the theme of virtual reality and mechanisms of healing, including spatial-temporary feedback connections. We can recall, as well, that the function of a psychotherapeutic time-machine is aided by various technologies, both communicative and psychological ones. And now we can proceed to understanding what time is and how the psychotherapeutic time-machine functions.

From the psychological literature it is known that time can be stretched or compressed, that in a moment, we can go through events in life normally taking hours, weeks, years; or, sometimes, one might feel that hours, years, or all of one's life has passed by in a flash. Some researchers define psychological time as the number of events registered per unit of time. To be in communication, in contact with these events, to be able to register more of these events, means that we are in such a state of consciousness characterized as more pronounced all-connectivity. And as we noted, the realization of this opportunity forms one of the main vectors of development of humankind.

Philosophy provides many answers to a fundamental question on the structure of time. "Time is a child playing with multicolored balls on a coast of Eternity," says Heraclitus. In his Confessions Augustine says that perhaps I know what time is, but "simply do not know how to express what I know." Physics describes time as some coordinate in a fourth-dimensional spatial-temporal continuum, as a special geometrical frame of reference of events occurring in the world. According to Terence McKenna (1996), perhaps the deepest insights into the nature of time were provided by Chinese mystics, who, meditating in lonely caves, recognized that the flow of time has some pulsating nature: time consists of elements like the periodic table by Mendeleev. The world consists of elements, and similarly time consists of elements. And what we perceive as time is really an unfoldment of these temporal elements in our world and in our experience.

At a formal level, the ancient Chinese described these elements as the 64 hexagrams in the Book of Changes. And we know that in conformity with divination practice, the Book of Changes has several levels of interpretation and is one of most interesting predictive tools of ancient times. The practice of throwing reed sticks down for obtaining hexagrams and having a question constantly in mind, being receptive to a flow of events and tuned to a level of experiences (which Jung named psychoid, where mind and matter are an inseparable unity), allows one to have an opportunity from mechanically arriving at the hexagrams to receive information about some historical, psychological events, because one was at a deeper level of the common origin of events, and thus the seemingly random manifestation of certain hexagrams would really be a display of pulsations of the cosmic flow of time.

Jung, reflecting upon the nature of the psyche and the essence of psychotherapy, introduced the concept of synchronicity. This is one of the key concepts of his depth psychology. He discovered that the major events connected with healing happen simultaneously. Synchronism implies noncausal connection. One separate event is not the reason for another; both events arise simultaneously from a more fundamental level. But the fact of their simultaneity and semantic correspondence, speaks of some interaction on a most basic level of experience; on the level of primordial language, time, and causality; and that leads us to a level of quantum spontaneity, leaving behind the framework of mechanical causality. Here we are really capable of becoming amplifiers of quantum instability, which is modulated, in turn, by this flow of time, and expresses this flow.

The visual interpretation of such elements of time was discovered by the modern visionary and philosopher Terence McKenna. This interpretation has been developed in his theory of the time and of the time-machine – Time Wave Zero, based on the ancient arrangement of hexagrams in the Book of Changes and in the corresponding computer program. Thus he based his conclusions on the assumption that time consists of elements and that these elements can be represented as a fractal curve. Fractals in modern mathematics denote objects which are endless: that is, zooming into them we see the same patterns again and again.

With the help of the computer, time, as such, can be stretched to any interval, and the curve exhibits more and more details. We can see on the screen a range of some billions of years in ten minutes or so, due to the power of McKenna-like computer programs. The specifics of this curve are that it is corresponds with the level of organisation or level of entropy or with a level of novelty: the higher it is on the axis, the more entropy, the less novelty and creativity in the world.

A characteristic of this curve is that at a certain moment it reaches zero, at which point any disorder disappears. Disorder, as we know, is a lack of connectivity of all the elements. And the order – all-connectivity – is a fundamental ontological quality of consciousness.

Experimenting with this curve, McKenna found that if we position the curve crossing zero (maximum creativity, zero entropy, zero disorder) at the moment of December 21, 2012, all major events of human history coincide with the kinks of the curve, that is, with those places where the tendency for increasing novelty and order changes to the tendency for the increasing of chaos, and vice versa. Due to fractal properties, this curve has one surprising feature: it shows that similar trains of events take place during very different intervals of time. The events taking place say, within 40,000 years, in a range from 47,000 years BC up to 7,000 years BC, have exactly the same form of a curve of time as in a range of 625 years from AD 1181 until 1806. There is some kind of a temporal resonance. The elements of time have the same dynamics and, if we were to look in the future, the next resonance will appear after a certain number of years, and this interval will occupy not 40,000 years, not 625 years, but, say, 9 years, 9 months and 5 days, from 1999 until 2009, with the same temporal dynamics. And the same temporal dynamics in times close to 2012 will occupy an interval of some minutes, and in times even closer to 2012 the curve of the same temporary dynamics will occupy several seconds, and then – fractions of a second.

Such is the nature of time according to McKenna. Time is composed of enclosed cycles that are in resonance with all other cycles. If we were to use this curve for forecasting, it will be necessary to take that interval of time which interests us in the present or future, and to determine what temporary resonances and time periods corresponded to it in the past, what kind of historical events took place during these past times. This means that time is not linear, as it is described by modern physics, nor cyclic, as described in many ancient doctrines and philosophies. These models, it is fair to say, hold only partially.

Another comment McKenna makes is that it is not just a simple spiral of time consisting of cycles having the identical period. Time is cyclic, but its cycles have different periods from the standpoint of physical time. This understanding corresponds better to our intuition of psychological time, when one moment can be an eternity. The presence of a temporal resonance is essential for understanding how time is involved in a psychotherapeutic time-machine. In holistic states of consciousness we get into a temporal resonance with various events of our life. That is why it is not meaningful to preprogram a psychotherapeutic session; it is better simply to release all sets and to allow anything to happen, just supporting it. Like therapeutic time-travel, being in a holistic state of consciousness soaks up, like a huge vacuum cleaner, all problems which resonate with our present condition.

Steps from a Psychotherapeutic Time-Space Machine to a Metaphysical One

We have discussed all the major components of a psychotherapeutic time-machine. And now, let's ask what the world must be like to make possible such phenomena as the holistic state of consciousness, time-travel, the phenomenon of healing, backward causality, and finally, the end of time according to the theory of time by McKenna? Take, for example, the last issue of what is the end of time? We know that "the end of time" means the end of entropy, maximum creativity, complete all-connectivity. And the realization of these qualities leads to the unity of all-consciousness, the full command of all organs of consciousness created in the course of computer evolution; direct perception, real telepathy.

We can follow the explanation offered by McKenna. Let's imagine, that at the very moment when time comes to an end, a time-machine is finally created. One can suppose that the time-machine cannot travel to the past before it was invented, since then we would have another order of things. But it can travel to the future. And since it can travel to the future, the very moment when it is created and the first travels to the future have begun, in this very moment of 2012, travelers in time from all future times appear, bringing with them all knowledge and technologies of their civilizations. That is, it's as if linear time, as we know it, becomes transparent, replaced by the "absence of time," or eternity. All the world, which was submissive in an earlier era to time and could be developed only as a sequence of temporal events, can now arise, to be present, to be experienced simultaneously.

This is the state of "all-oneness," technological "all-mightiness," all-connectivity, which can be described as the ultimate aim of mystical searches and the evolution of humankind. In other words, the state can be described as complete exteriorization of psyche and interiorization of body and external world. We can imagine still more. If everything that was created by the informational-communicative revolution comes back into consciousness, telepathy arises. Furthermore, if what is corporeal really comes back to consciousness, that is, if our body becomes conscious, we receive complete power over our body. Our body becomes truly spiritualized. These possibilities are discussed in modern transpersonal research, for example, in Michael Murphy's book The Future of the Body (1992), which is a modern encyclopedia of unusual, extreme, or supernatural manifestations of corporeal abilities.

Furthermore, we can imagine that not only the body will return to consciousness, but also all the material world. What in this case will take place? We shall approach a level of "laws of nature" or, it would be better to say, "habits of nature". Because that which we call the laws of nature are just means of maintaining relative stability. Modern science states that the laws of nature and constants of the world evolve, and moreover, laws are just "habits of nature" – that is, once a mechanism starts to work, it will keep a certain rhythm, but it does not mean that this rhythm and this order are absolute. Thus, the world, corresponding to experience revealed by some psychotherapies, is the world where spirit and matter are not subordinated to each other but are two aspects of a dynamic unity. It is a world where all landscapes of experience at all levels – corporeal, emotional, verbal, cognitive, visionary – are infinitely-dimensional virtual realities.

The muddle connected with the time-machine in modern science fiction and in works analyzing paradoxes of time-travel is that the time-machine is supposed to move in time – whereas the time-machine really changes time so drastically that the machine itself becomes time. The time-machine is created during normal time, but once in existence, it becomes time itself. Time-travel changes time, and that change removes all paradoxes – which are derived from our attachment to the usual understanding of time, which is only an expression of our attachment to certain sorts of characteristics, laws, and habits of nature. The time-machine is not a kind of mechanism one can drive like a car, allowing one to travel from one landscape to another. The essence of the concept developed here is that the engine of the time-machine is the cumulative consciousness of humankind; it is basic freedom, which is actualized through modern technology. Thus, the metaphor we introduced of the psychotherapeutic time-machine allows us to understand better many elements of the psychotherapeutic experience.

REFERENCES

Braud, W. G., & Schlitz, M. J. (1991). Consciousness interaction with remote biological systems: Anomalous intentionality effects. *Subtle Energies*, 2(1), 1-46.

Feinstein, D., & Krippner, S. (1988). *Personal Mythology: The Psychology of your Evolving Self*. Los Angeles: Tarcher.

Gennep, A.. van (1961). *Rites of Passage*. Chicago: University of Chicago Press.

Grof, S. (1985) *Beyond the Brain: Birth, death, and transcendence in psychotherapy*. Albany, NY: State University of New York Press.

Grof, S. (1998). *The Cosmic Game: Explorations of the frontiers of human consciousness*. Albany, NY: State University of New York Press.

Hutchison M.(1994). *Mega Brain Power: Transform your life with mind machines and brain nutrients*. Hyperion.

Jaynes, J. (1976). *The Origins of Consciousness in the Breakdown of the Bicameral Mind*. Boston: Houghton Mifflin.

McKenna, T. (1988). *A Magical Journey*. Thinking Allowed Productions – videotape.

McKenna, T. (1992). *The Archaic Revival: Speculations on psychedelic mushrooms, the Amazon, virtual reality, UFOs, evolution, shamanism, the rebirth of the goddess, and the end of history*. San Francisco: HarperSanFrancisco.

Murphy, M. (1992). *The Future of the Body: Explorations into the further evolutionof human nature*. Los Angeles: Tarcher.

29. THE HEART OF BEING: OUR INNER CONNECTION

Sarajane Aris

Sarajane asks you to reflect on your personal journey and your sense of "being." This chapter looks at "being" and consciousness in relation to you both as an individual and in an interconnected world. It asks you to consider mental health and well-being and how this can be applied to our everyday personal and professional lives as well as to society.

It is a self-help chapter full of lovely quotations from a wide range of special sources. It contrasts, as do a number of chapters of this book, with those from teachers, leaders in their research fields and academics enabling the future of transpersonal psychology. It contrasts also with the contributions of the faith traditions. Sarajane and Tony Turvey (Chapter 24) and others are contributing to transpersonal work in the mental health field. The heart of "being" cultivated through stillness, meditation, mindfulness and reflective imagery is considered in the light of her experience. There is growing research evidence which suggests that those in touch with their own spirituality have a better chance of staying mentally healthy and recovering when they are ill.

Sarajane brings together her clinical, research and personal experience from her heart and asks the readers to connect with their own hearts. How do we sustain our connection to the heart of being? She asks us to reflect on this as do Serge Beddington Behrens (Chapter 26) and Sue Michaelson (Chapter 21) and a number of other contributors. They stop us in our tracks and ask the fundamental questions which the researchers and academics, the practitioners and the philosophers, ask in different ways. We must honour each of these approaches as we seek to find our little paths along the way of an interconnected world. Some of Sara's bullet points may pass you by, maybe one or two will stop you in your tracks. The purpose of this book is to help you think or feel, and perhaps change one or two things in your life – that is very important

Sarajane suggests that "being" is the essence of all faith and other traditions. Another set of reflections is followed by exercises and then a view of the relevance in therapeutic work and NHS activities of our connections with one another and with the wider world. Patients in touch with a sense of being are more likely to improve mentally or to recover if they are ill. Seen in the context of a fast changing and developing National Health Service in the UK these thoughts and reflections take on a more pivotal role. Part of being a citizen might be to discover these forces. As a result of 9/11 the National Institute for Mental Health in England, (part of the modernisation Agency within the NHS) set up a steering group to look at spirituality within Mental Health. We need to develop methods of applying these concepts in our daily lives (also described in the Muslim tradition by Azim Nanji in Chapter 17).

Sarajane finishes with an exercise and questions for reflection. She points out that we can tackle challenges easier if we access the "heart of our Being" to enable the evolution of consciousness. You will find the quotations at the end relevant and thought provoking if you are not looking for an academic article but a fertile ground for ideas, thoughts and feelings and their development for you in a wider interconnected world.

Sarajane Aris *is a Chartered Clinical Psychologist and transpersonal psychotherapist. She has worked in the National Health Service for a Mental Health Trust for over 20 years and holds the first specialist post to be created for transpersonal psychotherapy within the NHS. She has founded the Transpersonal Network for Clinical, Counselling psychologists and therapists, which meets quarterly. She is also involved in organisational development for the mental health trust, and governance work for the Commission for Health Improvement. She seeks to 'bridge', bringing a transpersonal note and sense of being to this work and her moment to moment awareness in her life in general. Her work and life is informed by a spiritual search located in transpersonal psychology and the mystical traditions.*

---

*"**Just like every true spiritual teacher, just like the ancient sutras, the thoughts within this chapter don't say, 'Look at me', but 'Look beyond me'. Because the thoughts came out of stillness, they have power – the power to take you back into the same stillness from which they arose. That stillness is also inner peace, and that stillness and peace is the essence of your Being. It is inner stillness that will save and transform the world.**"*

From 'Stillness Speaks' by Eckhart Tolle.

Before you start reading this chapter, just go inside yourself and see what resonates within you from reading the quote on the previous page...

Before embarking on the main text of this chapter the author invites you to become aware of the quality of your Being as you both read and engage in the words and exercises in this chapter. You may want to make some notes for yourself as you go along, so that it becomes your own personal journey.

Chapter Summary

This chapter will focus on Being and the consciousness of being in relation to the individual, and collective perspectives. It will also consider the relationship to mental health and well-being and how this can be applied to our everyday life, therapeutic work and issues in society.

This chapter does not attempt to provide an in-depth or comprehensive account of the subject. Rather, it is a brief introduction and exploration of the theme. It aims to be interactive.

'Being' is at the heart of esoteric psychology, the eastern traditions and is at the core of many maps of human and spiritual consciousness. It is the heart of the mandala and goes by many names depending on the tradition concerned, for example, Atman, the Self, Buddha, Nature. This chapter will also offer exercises for the reader to explore what 'Being' means for them and how our understanding and experience of this important subject relates to therapeutic work, our connections with each other and the theme of citizenship.

As the book is focused on citizenship, this chapter poses a number of questions.

- How does the 'heart of Being' impact on being a citizen in the world?
- 'The heart of Being' is an important ground from which we relate as citizens. What does it really mean for each one of us to be a citizen of the world, and for us politically?
- How does that fit in with discovering and actualising the core of our inner nature, the heart of our Being?
- And how do we integrate all this into our daily living and moment to moment awareness.

The chapter will explore some of these questions.

Introduction

'Being' has been spoken about/referred to in the ancient and mystery traditions throughout the ages. When we explore the nature of Being we find stillness and peace as the essence of Being. Stillness is also a place from which we can access our Inner Being.

We need to learn how to relate from the heart of our Being in all we do personally, in our work, therapeutically and as a fully functioning citizen in this world. However this is a challenge for all of us in this fast paced world where we are expected to 'do' and perform rather than 'be'. The pulls are often away from our inner connection. We need to learn simple and practical ways to bridge and re-connect ourselves to the heart of being and to a sense of stillness. Learning meditation, mindfulness, reflective and imagery practices, coupled with cultivating 'reminder' objects/practices are some ways to do this. If we learn to listen to our inner connection, then our health and well being is both sustained and enhanced. This is especially relevant in our therapeutic work with clients Studies and clinical examples from Mental Health in the National Health Service particularly, cited in this chapter, demonstrate that people who are in touch with their own spirituality have a better chance of staying mentally healthy and of recovering if they become ill.

If we learn to relate from the 'heart of our Being' this will have a powerful transformative effect at all levels of our consciousness, both seen and unseen. It will have an impact on changing the way we relate as citizens, and have a crucial role in facilitating change and deepening trust, awareness and understanding within the world.

This chapter will offer an introductory exploration of this theme. It must be emphasised that what is written here is from the standpoint of a fellow journey person exploring the route and the territory, not from an 'expert' position. Its aim is to help you in your own exploration, not to be a seminal text.

Background to the 'heart of Being'

'There is a place where
words are born of silence,
A place where the whispers
Of the heart arise'.
Rumi.

As you read this, go inside yourself and reflect on the quote. See what it touches inside you.

What do we mean when we talk of the 'Heart of Being'?

'Presence' is another word for being. Is presence a 'doing' thing or 'is-ness'? The 'heart of being' is what we are. 'Being' can be a noun and/or a verb 'be-ing'. Being as a noun as distinct from the verb 'to be'... When Being is a noun- we are just being, until we get caught up in the verb- trying to be (Be-ing)

There is a quality of being part of our real nature, before we want to Be someone, be enlightened, be successful, be centred. So the point being made here is the distinction between the active verb,' to be, get on with things, be active' and the calm/inner state of 'being', of accessing the very essence and nature of who we truly are. Being, however, is not easily located to any one place.

What is the quality of this?

It has qualities of expansiveness and spaciousness, stillness, timelessness, no separateness. It is an essence beyond the personal that we can locate as persons. It is different to a sense of connection; it is something larger, where individual consciousness is wiped out/no longer there.

What would be some of the experiences we might recognise?
• Where we find a sense of stillness and peace, and create a sense of spaciousness.
• Where we feel connected to everything – a sense of non-duality
• Where we feel a deep sense of being, and we recognise, however fleetingly what we really/truly are.

How do we sustain our connection to the 'Heart of Being'?

Being present, as a way to keep/sustain and deepen our connection. There is a point where there is presence itself, whether the personality does anything. It is being present to that – getting out of the way. It is in those moments where silence sits-just there-whether we recognise it or not. In meditation: 'look out of the corner of your eye', to recognise what is always there.

In order for real transformation to occur, we need to connect with the heart of Being.

The Heart is the centre of being. This is symbolised by the sun as the centre of life, radiating energy.

What are your personal experiences of Being? You may want to stop and record these before you proceed with the rest of this chapter.

Useful Notes on The Heart of Being

Below are some bullet points and quotes to help you reflect on the nature of Being and your experiences of this.

- The heart of Being is a realisation of Oneness; the root of a universal love for all beings.
- In the presence of a master or teacher, or when we create a sacred space for ourselves, we are enabled to sink more deeply into the state of being, the place of stillness and silence within. When we touch upon it we know there is something greater and more real beyond the/our normal doubts and anxieties of living. When our intelligence is one with our bodies – that means one with the intelligence that keeps our hearts beating – we are in the state of being. We are behind the senses and behind the restless mind. This being is the god within us. It is absolutely still, silent and potent. It refreshes and nourishes our lives. In practical terms this means the circumstances of our lives are gradually made easier and there is an increasing sense of purpose and freedom. Finally, a profound harmony and merging of being is not only realised but experienced. This is the state of grace available to us all who are willing to start putting love and truth first in our lives. The greatest help to this is being with ourselves by creating a sacred space, meditation or being with a master, and sharing this consciousness.
- 'When you are able to stay in being, your fears disappear. When you die you go into being. The purpose of living is to be able to connect consciously with being, this wonderful nourishing place inside you, while you are alive and awake. Being emotional and thoughtful people we can be fearful people. We are afraid- of what we are not sure. But when we are able to connect with this being, stay in it and actually be it, our fears disappear. Our emotions lose control over our lives. And we live from this space of being'. (Barry Long).
- Only going beyond the structures of egoic existence can there be an opening into the greater Being and transformation of nature and the structure of psychic life.
- 'Every life problem contains within it a sense of a new direction, if only we can let it unfold' (Gendlin). When a problem's hold on us dissolves, we get a grounded sense of presence and aliveness. It is as if we are 'finding our seat', settling into our selves and

the immediacy of being. It often allows a new awareness of verticality – or depth of being to emerge – a 'Vertical Shift – wherein we move from the realm of personality to pure Being. Here we discover a quality of being that is already complete, intrinsically full, settled in itself. The symbol in Tibetan Buddhism for breakthrough of this larger nature is the GARUDA – a mythical bird, born fully grown, which begins to soar as soon as it hatches from the egg. This pure beingness is implicit in all our felt experience. We usually fail to recognise that this ultimate open-heartedness is at the core of all our experiences- 'boddhichitta', the heart-mind enlightenment. (Welwood)

• Being is empty, not because it lacks anything, but because it cannot comprehend in terms of any reference point outside itself. Being is precisely that which can never be grasped or contained in any physical boundary. Nishitani – 'Being is only being if it is one with emptiness'. In that sense, emptiness might be called the field of 'be-ification'. (Welwood.)

• Consciousness derives from Latin, 'con scire', meaning 'to know with', referring to insights shared with others. Later used when talking about knowledge that was to some degree secret. Still later used to create two words. 'Conscious' referred to private thoughts and emotions; 'conscience' used for private knowledge deliberately withheld from others and likely to make one feel guilty. Consciousness can be divided up into three states: waking, dreaming and sleep.

• Consciousness is that in which all else appears. It is there when there appears to be nothing. It can be thought of as the silence between thoughts or as the screen, upon which the movie of life is projected, unaffected by all, yet without which there would be nothing. In the same way as we see a cloud in the sky and miss the sky, we see thought arising in Consciousness and know nothing about Consciousness itself.

• The only way to see consciousness is to turn our attention towards the source of our thoughts, feelings and perceptions, giving up the desire to comprehend it within the boundaries of time.

• The Mahavakayas from the Upanishads; Consciousness is Brahman. Consciousness equates to Brahman, which is the one reality, all that there is.

• The open space of Being continually breaks through into consciousness in unexpected flashes and glimpses; for example when we encounter unfathomable mystery in ourselves or those we love. This simple awakening also happens in meditation when some burdensome mind-state suddenly falls away.

• The spectacles for which we are looking have been on our forehead all the time.

Background of 'Being' in the Traditions

As discussed earlier, 'Being' is at the core or essence of all Traditions. Below are some bullet points for the reader's consideration, regarding Being in some of the Traditions;

- All paths point in the same direction; purpose of all Traditions is therefore the same- to connect one back to truth – variously called Being, God, Self, Absolute. This truth can never be expressed in any objective sense; it is something that must be realised for oneself.
- Being is sometimes referred to as 'The Great Chain of Being'; we have at least five major levels of being; matter, body, mind, soul and spirit.
- 'Leap into Being'- expressed in Buddhist language as seeing 'the insubstantiality of the self on the way to no-self or Buddha mind'.
- In the Tantric tradition, open space of Being as secret because it cannot be located or defined by mind. It's so unfathomable to conceptual mind; the only way to portray it is symbolically through Mandala. At the Centre of the Mandala is wisdom of open space, which is centreless and all-pervasive. Mandala as the portrait of the vast space of wisdom-mind, the creative openness and potentiality of Being, in which the play of consciousness unfolds, without being tied to any central reference point of the self. Qualitatively represents spirit, quantitatively it is existence. (Hindu Temples built as a Mandala, symbolising the universe.)
- In the practise of Mahamudra/Dzogchen-(the supreme mudra, the ultimate seeing that 'lets beings be as the beings which they are)', meditators discover non-dual awareness, resting in open presence. (F.M.Woolf – 'consciousness-without-an-object') This non-dual presence is described in qualities of depth, luminosity or spaciousness. One rests in the clarity of wide open, wakeful awareness, without any attempt to alter one's experience. This is direct self-knowing and recognition of one's own nature as pure Being without self. The ungraspable quality of experience is 'emptiness'; being and emptiness are inseparable. Pure presence is the realisation of being-as emptiness; being without being something. Being is that which can never be grasped or contained in any physical boundary or conceptual designation.
- In the Upanishads (meaning secret and sacred knowledge); there is only One Self, Atman or Brahman. Being Infinite, it cannot be comprehended by anyone completely. Described as 'Sat, Chit and Ananda' in it's essential nature. This manifests in various ways. The innermost Self is one with the divine. The realisation of Oneness is the root of a universal love for all beings. Reached by the practise of contemplative disciplines; e.g. Yoga. 'He who knows Brahman becomes Brahman'.
- In other Sanskrit traditions, such as the Vedas, Being is 'the breath of the supreme'; the Veda is the body of Sanskrit poetry.
- In Esoteric Christianity, Being is referred to as 'Absolute Beingness', the Christ Logos.

Exercise; Journey into the Heart of your own Being

Below is an exercise to help you deepen your connection to your own heart of being.

- Take a moment to see what the heart of being means for you; just notice whatever quality or texture is there…
- As you do this, notice if there is an image for this; getting a sense of its quality, energy, colour.
- Notice how it touches you – perhaps the feeling/energy quality it brings
- Where do you sense this in your body?
- Just take a moment to reflect on your current life and your journey/ your present journey through life….see if the heart of Being has anything to offer… and notice what arises… and where it wants to take you… see if that part of you throws any light on your current situation.
- Rest with this for a few moments and see what unfolds.

As your consciousness returns to the room, take a few moments to draw or make some notes for yourself. If you can, you may find it helpful to share/explore your experience with someone.

Relevance to Therapeutic and NHS work, our connections with each other and Citizenship

Some Questions;
- How does this relate to our clinical/therapeutic work, particularly in the NHS, our connections with each other?
- How does the 'heart of Being' impact on being a citizen of the world?
- What does it really mean for each one of us to be a citizen of the world?
- How does that fit in with discovering and actualising the core of our inner nature, the heart of our Being?
- How can we touch into the heart of our Being on a moment to moment basis for ourselves, in our relationships and as a citizen of this world and sustain it?

How is Being related to our selves, our connections with each other our work and our citizenship? You may want to make some notes for yourself as you reflect on these questions before you proceed.

Within every one of us, Being is the same thread or essence that connects us all; it's just manifest and expressed differently. We'd be in a wise centred place, if we were able at key times and when making decisions, or under stress, to evoke that sense of the Heart of Being within ourselves. What stops that? Often our fears, insecurities and lack of trust, amongst other things, can prevent this connection. We can at stressful times, forget to 'plug in' so to speak, especially when we become distracted.

How can we continually 'be' with 'the heart of Being'? We need to re-cognise on a moment to moment basis that's what we really are and everyone else is. The Upanishads refer to our Being as the 'sun within the sun'.

As a therapist or helper, working within Mental Health for the National Health Service, and a range of other settings and organisations, when we hold the intention of working from the heart of being, we are evoking 'something else' in our clients and others we work with.

Clients begin to appreciate the 'open space of their being', and regard it as friendly. (Welwood), when they are, through the therapeutic relationship, with a particular kind of listening, enabled to connect with their Being.

When we pay attention to spaciousness, both within and outside a person, it brings a potency into the room. That presence is already there. We do not need to speak of this, unless it feels facilitative to do so. The same applies to us in our role as citizens of this world.

It's important to remember that it is not us that does the work – it's the 'something' that calls us – the energy that we are all part of.

Brant Cortwright says, 'Accessing the transformative power of Being is the key to full resolution of psychological difficulties which perplex and confound human existence'.

Research shows that clients who are in touch with a sense of Being are more resilient. They have a better chance of staying mentally healthy and or recovering if they become ill. (Macmin and Foskett – The Somerset Spirituality Project; work published by the National Schizophrenia Fellowship, 2001)

Many psychological models and approaches to therapy used within the NHS are now recognising the importance of working with Being and including tools to facilitate the process, such as with Dialectic Behaviour Therapy, (Linehan) and Mindfulness Training(Kabat-Zin, Teasdale). Mindfulness, in particular has become a powerful tool in enabling change for clients with a variety of difficulties. There is a body of outcome research developing that validates its effectiveness. Reflective practice (Johns) is another tool that facilitates practitioners 'Being', in both health and education. This form of practice also enables a connection to Being, by creating space for a special kind of reflection.

Part of being a citizen might be to discover the larger force which is endlessly there and that joins us all. We'd become alert to connecting with this force within ourselves on a moment to moment basis in our interactions as a citizen. We would as citizens, make wiser decisions and act with integrity. We'd relate heart to heart with openness, creating meaningful dialogues in our communities; we would deal with conflict in a different, more creative and loving way.

So what might be some implications of this for us personally, in our relationships with each other, as a therapist and as a citizen?

Some implications may be to;-
• Create more meaningful and fulfilling relationships with ourselves and others;
• Take responsibility to impact upon the political, social and economic agendas;
• Listen to ourselves and every person we meet from a different perspective, setting up new forms of dialogue and exchange.

It is of significance that, following September 11th terrorist attacks on the USA, a number of people within the National Institute for Mental Health in England and Wales, (NIMHE) part of the Modernisation Agency within the NHS, set up a steering group for Spirituality within Mental Health. This is one example of many that are developing as our consciousness evolves.

Tools to helping us apply, integrate and connect with the heart of Being in daily life/on a daily basis.

One of the challenges we all face is in applying and integrating what we know in our hearts on a daily basis. Below are a few practical suggestions to help us sustain our connection to the heart of being, in both our personal and professional lives, as follows;

• Whenever there is some silence around you – listen to it. That means just notice it. Pay attention to it. Listening to silence awakens the dimension of stillness within yourself, because it is only through stillness that you can be aware of silence.
• Spend some time meditating on the nature of Absolute Beingness…as we do this we become aware that we have within us Power, Wisdom and Love, that Absolute Beingness is continuously there, there is no moment when we are not within Absolute Beingness.
• Look at a tree, a flower, a plant. Let your awareness rest upon it. How still they are, how deeply rooted in Being. Allow nature to teach you stillness.
• When you look at a tree and perceive its stillness, you become still yourself. You

connect with it at a very deep level. You feel a oneness with whatever you perceive in and through stillness. Feeling the oneness of yourself with all things is true love.

- Become aware of awareness – this enables the arising of inner stillness.
- Use noise as a way of connecting with your Being, by allowing it to be as it is. Whenever you deeply accept this moment as it is – no matter what form it takes – you are still, you are connected to your Being, you are at peace.
- Pay attention to the gap – the gap between two thoughts, the brief, silent space between words in a conversation, between the in-breath and out-breath, between the notes of a musical instrument like a piano. When you pay attention to those gaps, awareness of 'something' becomes – just awareness. The formless dimension of pure consciousness arises from within you and replaces identification with form.
- If you want to find out who you are, open directly to yourself right now, enter into the mode of being where you are what you are, and settle into your own nature.
- Simply being the witness to all that arises you are eventually taken back to the ultimate observer-your true Self-Being.
- Invoking a 'Being' consciousness.

(Some exerts taken from 'Stillness Speaks', by Eckhart Tolle, 2003.)

- Use of 'Reminder Objects'. Carrying around a small 'reminder object' in your pocket or bag, for example a stone, piece of jewellery – whatever is meaningful for you, can be a powerful way of remaining connected to your 'Being', and act as a 'reminder' when you are feeling disconnected.
- Practising Meditation and Mindfulness.
- Touching into particular qualities of Being.
- Creating Sacred Space.

Exercise and Ending Question for Reflection;

As we close the chapter, just take a moment to go inside yourself, to that place that connects you with your own 'heart of being' and ask:

'What for you might be a reminder or connect you to your own 'heart of Being', particularly in challenging moments, in your relationship to yourself, with others and as a citizen of this world?'

Just rest in that space. See if an image, word or phrase, or sense of something, emerges in that inner space. When you return to your consciousness here in the room, if you want to, draw or make some notes as a reminder for yourself.

Just invite the image that came up for you into consciousness one more time – it doesn't matter if it has changed a little, just notice – and allow it to be fully felt in your body, notice where that image and it's energy touches you in a bodily way... pause and allow yourself time to be with that...now just allow that energy and quality of the image to reach out to those areas of your life that may need nourishing, may need to be open to that quality of Being. (Aim of the exercise: to allow the essence you have touched upon and sensed as you have read this chapter to be brought into embodied being.)

Conclusion;

In learning to access, connect with and come from the 'heart of our Being', which is always present, we are able to tackle challenges we face more effectively, personally and professionally. The heart of Being is often accessed through cultivating stillness. When we are in touch with our Being, we can bring about a transformation both personally, in our work, particularly as a therapist and as a citizen in the world. In this way, we enable the evolution of consciousness.

REFERENCES

Cairnes, M; 'Approaching the Corporate Heart', 2000. Simon and Schuster

Cortwright, B. Psychotherapy and Spirit. 1997. Suny.

Kabat-Zin, J. Full Catastrophe Living. 1996. Piatkus.

Kornfield, J. 'A Path with Heart'.1993. Bantham Books.

Linehan, M. Skills Training Manual for Treating Borderline Personality Disorder. 1993. Guildford Press.

Merrell-Wolff, F. 'Experience and Philosophy'. 1994. Suny.

NIMHE National Project Programme Proposal; 'Recognising the Importance of Spirituality in a Whole Person approach to Mental Health. 2002. see Newsletter 10 'NIMHE Project Report'.

Atteshlis, S. The Esoteric Teachings. Imprinta Ltd, Cyprus.

Tolle.E. 'Stillness Speaks'. 2003. Hodder Mobius

The Mental Health Foundation; Taken Seriously; The Somerset Spirituality Project. 2002. www.mentalhealth.org.uk

Welwood, J. Towards a Psychology of Awakening'.2000. Shambala.

APPENDIX: QUOTES FOR REFLECTION

'Spirituality is a state of connectedness to life;
It is an experience of being, belonging and caring.
It is sensitivity and compassion, joy and hope.
It is the harmony between the innermost life
And the outer life, or the life of the world and the life universal.
It is the supreme comprehension of life in time and space, the tuning of the inner person with the great mysteries and secrets that are around us.
It is the belief in the goodness of life and the possibility for each person to contribute goodness to it.
It is the belief in life as part of the eternal stream of time, that each of us came from somewhere and is destined somewhere, that without such belief there could be no prayer, no meditation, no peace and no happiness.' (U. Thant. Secretary General of the UN, 1961-1971)

'Just like every true spiritual teacher, just like the ancient sutras, the thoughts within this chapter don't say, 'Look at me', but 'Look beyond me'. Because the thoughts came out of stillness, they have power – the power to take you back into the same stillness from which they arose. That stillness is also inner peace, and that stillness and peace is the essence of your Being. It is inner stillness that will save and transform the world'. (Taken from, 'Stillness Speaks' by Eckhart Tolle.)

'The best and most beautiful things in the world cannot be seen or even touched. They must be felt with the heart'. (Helen Keller.)

'Being is presence. To recognise this is wisdom and freedom'. (H.L. Poonja.)

'Pure presence is the realisation of being- as emptiness; being without being something' (John Welwood.)

'It is in suffering that we discover the strength of our being. It is through wounds that we test the boundaries of who we are. It is in coming to terms with our own weakness that we grow strongest.' (Margot Cairnes.)

'Infinite nature, which is boundless, spirit, unutterable, not intelligible, outside of all imagination, beyond all essence, unnamable, known only to the heart' (Robert Flood.)

'We must close our eyes
And invoke a new manner of seeing,
A wakefulness that is the birthright of us,
Although few put it to use'. (Plotinus, 1964.)

'Our Eyes provide a doorway into the space of Being'. (John Welwood.)

'Two things are infinite; the universe and human stupidity; and I'm not sure about the universe.' (Albert Einstein.)

'It is difficult to find happiness in oneself but it is impossible to find it anywhere else'. (Schopenhauer.)

'All genuine love is based on the possibility the beloved offers to the lover for a fuller unfolding of his own being by being-in-the-world with her' (Medard Boss.)

Our Being/the Self is neither born nor dies. It did not come from anything, nor has anything come from it. It is birthless, eternal, and constant. It is not destroyed when the body is destroyed'. (The Katha Upanishad [II.18])

'As an individual, with your death there will be an end of you. But your individuality is not your true and final being, indeed it is rather the mere expression of it; it is not the thing-in-itself, but only the phenomenon presented in the form of time, and accordingly has both a beginning and an end. Your being in itself, on the contrary, knows neither time, nor beginning, nor end, nor the limits of a given individuality; hence no individuality can be without it, but it is there in each and all. So that, in the first sense, after death you become nothing; in the second, you are and remain everything…here we have undoubtedly another contradiction; this is because your life is in time and your immortality in eternity.' (Arthur Schopenhauer, from 'The Indestructibility of Our True Being by Death.')

True Consciousness, the real Self, is compared with the sun, which is always shining, whether or not covered by clouds and irrespective of the rotation of the earth. (Ramana Maharshi.)

'What is now wanted is a combination of the greatest heart with the highest intellectuality, of infinite love with infinite knowledge…existence without knowledge and love cannot be. 'Knowledge without love and love without knowledge cannot be.' (Swami Vivekananda.)

'There is only Consciousness; Consciousness is all there is'. (Ramesh Balsekar.)

The little boy was drawing when his mother noticed and asked; 'what are you drawing Jimmy?' The little boy, without looking up, answered, 'A picture of God.'
'But Jimmy,' his mother replied, 'nobody knows what God looks like.'
'They will once I'm finished.' (From 'Doing Nothing', by Steve Harrison.)